The Shape of Reason

The Shape of Reason
Argumentative Writing in College

FOURTH EDITION

John T. Gage

University of Oregon

Contributing Editors:

Carolyn Bergquist
Matthew Buonincontro
Stephanie Callan
Denise Krane
Kevin Maier
Nicole Malkin
Arwen Spicer

PEARSON
Longman

New York San Francisco Boston
London Toronto Sydney Tokyo Singapore Madrid
Mexico City Munich Paris Cape Town Hong Kong Montreal

Publisher: Joseph Opiela
Senior Supplements Editor: Donna Campion
Senior Marketing Manager: Alexandra Rivas-Smith
Production Manager: Eric Jorgensen
Project Coordination, Text Design, and Electronic Page Makeup: Electronic
    Publishing Services Inc., NYC
Cover Designer/Manager: Nancy Danahy
Cover Image: Hoffman, Hans (1880–1966) © ARS, NY. "Pompeii." 1959. Oil on
    canvas, 214.0 x 132.7 cm. Tate Gallery, London, Great Britain. Photo Credit:
    Tate Gallery, London/Art Resource, NY.
Photo Research: Vivette Porges
Manufacturing Manager: Mary Fischer

For permission to use copyrighted material, grateful acknowledgment is made to
the copyright holders on p. 186, which is hereby made part of this copyright
page.

Library of Congress Cataloging-in-Publication Data

Gage, John T., 1947–
    The shape of reason : argumentative writing in college / John T. Gage.— 4th ed.
        p. cm.
    Includes index.
    ISBN 0-321-32077-8
    1. English language—Rhetoric. 2. Persuasion (Rhetoric) 3. Report writing.
        I. Title.

PE1431.G34 2006
808′ .042—dc22   2004027590

Visit us at http://www.ablongman.com.

ISBN 0-321-32077-8

The Fourth Edition of
The Shape of Reason
is dedicated to the memory of
Richard A. Filloy
extraordinary friend, teacher, practitioner.

Vale, Rick

CONTENTS

APPENDIX

Essays by Student Writers   **155**

Argumentative writing is writing that reasons its way to a conclusion. It addresses ideas that the writer takes seriously enough to want to explore and support with good reasons. This book is about this process: writing as reasoned inquiry.

You are invited to engage in this process by responding critically to the ideas of others and by writing about your own ideas in such a way that you try to earn the understanding and assent of your audience. In this way, you are invited to use writing to enter an intellectual dialog that should be a central part of your experience in college. This approach has consequences in the way I have written this book.

First, I have tried to challenge you to think about ideas and about writing. I want you to make up your own mind about everything in this book.

Second, I have treated the writing process as moving from a sense of the whole argument to the discovery of specific parts, rather than building separate skills in isolation from complete writing intentions. This means that you will not be asked to produce writing merely for the sake of practicing some part of a whole composition (such as sentences or paragraphs), although you will be asked to write thesis statements that represent the whole intention of an essay and the line of reasoning that it will develop.

Third, I have considered the form of an essay as something that is *generated* by the writer rather than as something *imposed* on the writer. I want you to generate the structures that give your essays their own unique shape based on your ideas, rather than try to fill up empty forms imposed from outside. Form follows function. Ideas come first.

Fourth, I have placed the process of reasoning through an argument and generating the structure of an essay within the context of critical reading. Critical reading underlies the process of inquiry, which requires some kind of response to others' ideas and some basis of knowledge from which to respond. So, I have treated argumentation here as a matter of inventing and shaping the best possible reasons to earn your reader's understanding and assent, not as a matter of trying to win your case by overpowering the opposition. I have challenged you to think about this process further by including in this book discussions of the deep structure and ethics of argument.

Finally, I have tried to be honest with you about why I think argumentative writing matters. Thinking and writing are not processes that you can ever expect to master. By doing them, you learn the rewards of intellectual accomplishment as well as experience the limits of human understanding. Thinking is an adventure that requires risks. It always balances certainties with uncertainties. By facing both, we learn to live with our own uncertainties and to be more tolerant of others' beliefs.

It is important to remember that no writing class by itself can teach you to write at your best. All writers, even if they seem to write effortlessly, learn to write better each time they take on and complete a new writing challenge. Each new writing task is a challenge of its own, and the best a writing class can do is to create situations that allow you, or invite you, to meet the challenge. If you are thinking about these challenges, you may not always feel your writing is improving when in fact it is. As you improve as a writer, you will naturally take on more challenging writing tasks and find yourself writing about more difficult issues. As you respond to new writing situations, you may feel inadequate, simply because they will require you to go beyond what you already know how to do. A feeling of inadequacy (which all writers share, whether they will admit it or not) is therefore nothing to worry about. It is the way you should feel if you are learning.

Writing, as this book stresses, is a process of finding and structuring reasons. When we face a writing task, and when that task emerges from our attempts to find cooperation in a community of diverse opinions, writing becomes more than an attempt to put the right words in the right order. It becomes a search for reasons. It is in this way that the serious attempt to compose your thoughts in writing will often lead you to the very important discovery of what you think and why you think it.

I urge you to treat this book and the writing that it invites you to do as an adventure in thinking. We are all in this together. The possibilities are endless.

In *The Shape of Reason*, I have presented argumentative writing as a category large enough to contain the kinds of intellectual and compositional skills that students should be practicing in college. Argumentative writing, for me, does not focus on one "mode" of developing ideas to the exclusion of another. The process of coming to conclusions may engage the writer in every possible kind of compositional pattern, depending on the nature of the issue and the writer's situation. I have presented argumentation as a process of inquiry into questions at issue that is best pursued if guided by principles but not governed by rules. Consequently, I have adapted the classical rhetorical concept of the enthymeme as the central basis for the invention and structuring of arguments, an approach that blends classical insights about rhetorical reasoning with contemporary understandings of the composing process as generative and organic, situated within discourse communities. This helps to remove logic from the sometimes rigid realm of disabling rules and formulas by treating reasoning as a natural and informal process.

I have included other features in the book that I hope will make the approach more effective. Extended discussions of important terms such as *inquiry, dialectic, ethics, structure, thesis, enthymeme,* and *style* show how these concepts are flexible and shaped by the purposes to which we, as writers, put them. Each chapter ends with "Questions for Thought, Discussion, and Writing" that call for independent evaluation of the ideas in the chapter.

This fourth edition continues to emphasize the generative and collaborative nature of the enthymeme as an informal guide to reasoning and therefore to deemphasize formal logic. Instructors familiar with the third edition might be interested in the most significant changes I have made in this edition:

1. A new chapter on ethical argument is intended to deepen students' understanding of the relevance of reasoned argument in a culture in which they are constantly exposed to manipulative and unfair modes of persuasion. Much is at stake when we talk about our responsibility to argue ethically in a culture in which argument is generally associated with dominance, aggression, and winning. Although *The Shape of Reason* has always treated argumentative writing as an ethical process, this idea is given much more emphasis in this edition, not by prescribing verbal behaviors or laying down rules but rather by inviting students to think seriously about the ethical dimension of their speech actions.

2. The book no longer contains an anthology of readings. Teachers are given suggestions about readily available readings in the fourth edition of the *Instructor's Manual*. In choosing readings for class discussion and analysis, whether in an anthology or from other sources, teachers might wish to look also at the readings in the third edition. For a database of readings that make up Longman's custom *Mercury Reader*, go to http://www.ablongman.com/ and search for Mercury Reader.

3. A new Appendix contains essays written by students in college composition classes using the principles of this book. (These students had not, of course, read the new ethics chapter, though all of the issues in that chapter can be invoked in discussing their essays.) Teachers can use these examples to make the principles of this book more concrete for students by asking them to point out both the most and the least successful aspects of their reasoning, structure, and writing. The essays also illustrate how the writing that this book encourages is developed in relation to a discourse community, a class of peers who have raised and debated issues among themselves. Insofar as the essays engage substantive issues in response to readings and discussion, they also are intended to encourage student writers to think of themselves as vital contributors to the extensive cultural conversation about these issues.

4. Whereas earlier editions discussed visual and graphic forms of argument, especially in relation to the Internet, this edition gives specific examples and includes a number of visual texts. These are not intended to provide a thorough analysis of the many specific ways in which visual communication and argument take place; that is, this book is not about reading images critically. Rather, these additions are intended to enable students to link the concepts central to *The Shape of Reason* to varieties of visual communication they experience. They provide visual analogs to the principles of argument discussed, as a way to broaden those principles and perhaps make them more accessible to students. I encourage teachers to use a combination of readings and visual texts to raise issues for discussion and argumentative writing and to illustrate principles of argumentation, especially in the domain of ethics. Since our students are visually literate, the critical assessment of such modes of appeal is a vital part of their education. At the same time, our primary responsibility remains the teaching of critical reading and reasoned writing, which perhaps becomes even more important in the context of the increasing influence of visual communication.

5. Finally, I have sought, without in any way reducing the challenge to students that I hope this book presents, to revise the text in those places where it needed to be made more accessible. Everything I say in this book as advice to students applies to my own writing, and that includes always being open to the possibility of making it better, knowing that perfection is probably unattainable.

The approach to writing taken in *The Shape of Reason* will work best if students discuss ideas freely and write essays that respond honestly to the issues and arguments that develop during such a discussion. It invites and enables you to respond to students' ideas and writing as a critical thinker and writing consultant. It is in this way that I hope the book serves to enliven teaching as well as learning. This process is one from which both instructors and students never cease to learn.

I urge you to discuss your discoveries and questions about this approach with your colleagues, and thereby to form a discourse community of your own about your mutual insights and concerns. The *Instructor's Manual* for the book can provide a basis for such discussions as well as specific advice about teaching the book.

The fourth edition of the *Instructor's Manual* has been prepared by Stephanie Callan, Denise Krane, Nicole Malkin, and Arwen Spicer based on Margaret Johnson's revision of the third edition, Kathleen O'Fallon's revisions for the second edition, and my original version. These experienced teachers of the book have provided different perspectives from mine, and our collaborations have led to a more useful guide to teaching argumentative writing than I could have produced on my own.

I hope that teachers (and students) will communicate with me about this book. I am interested in your questions, concerns, observations, and experiences. These may be especially useful for future editions. If you have examples of student writing that might be appropriate to include in a new edition, please send them to me, along with the information necessary to contact the student writers.

Acknowledgments

I have been assisted in preparing this edition of *The Shape of Reason* by a group of contributing editors whose outstanding knowledge of the book and the theory behind it, and whose extraordinary talents as teachers and editors, have been invaluable to me. I consulted this group collectively about changes that would improve the book, and many of the ideas for this edition came out of these discussions.

All of the following contributing editors provided me with advice and consultation in every stage of preparing this new edition, including editing suggestions for the whole text and all of the new material. They gave me many new ideas and challenged me to rethink many of my old ones. Carolyn Bergquist (who also contributed to the third edition) contributed ideas and examples for the discussion of visual arguments. Matthew Buonincontro helped me to conceptualize and write the new ethics chapter, consulting me about its ideas and providing me with an extensive and profound critique of a first draft. He also brought the Mathew Brady material to my attention and helped me to develop it for Chapter 2. Stephanie Callan, along with Kevin Maier, collected student essays, and Stephanie contributed visual examples and took charge of the process of selecting those we would include, editing the essays, and writing the introductory material in the Appendix. Denise Krane provided new examples and questions for each chapter and worked with me to create the sidebars that are a new feature of this edition. Nicole Malkin provided examples of visual text, extensive comments on the text, and many helpful suggestions, and she communicated with the student writers about their essays. Arwen Spicer designed and conducted a survey of teachers of the third edition and compiled the results, which were very helpful in setting priorities for this edition and making changes. Drew Morse similarly helped me to review evaluations of the third edition from teachers around the country. Scott Knickerbocker also participated in discussions of the proposed changes. Together, this group formed an ideal discourse community in which it was a privilege to participate. I hope the changes we have made collaboratively are seen as improvements by those who have taught previous editions. The additions and emendations provided by the contributing editors of the third edition, Brad Hawley, Julia Major, Mary Peters, David Sumner, and Kenneth Wright, continue to be part of the fourth.

Several colleagues at the University of Oregon provided me with help and encouragement. James Crosswhite provided me with a challenging analysis and critique of the first draft of the new ethics chapter. I hope I did justice to some of his ideas; the rest will provide me with much to think about as I pursue the issue of ethical argument to greater depths. Anne Laskaya has been a constant source of inspiration for this text and ways to teach it, and her comments on the first draft of the new Chapter 4 also led me to rethink and rewrite. Brian Whaley served as a dependable source of insight into how the text might be improved and provided moral support when needed. Karen Ford inspired me to keep working on the revision, perhaps without realizing it, by helping me to confront all of the reasons I could have used not to do so. James Boren asked me just the right hard questions about ethics to deepen my understanding of what is at stake in my project. Suzanne Clark has been a source of encouragement in her judicious defense of premises of this book, especially in relation to complexities of contemporary pedagogical theory. Tres Pyle challenged my thinking about the relation between the ethics of rhetoric and aesthetics. Thanks also to Marilyn Reid, Susan Dickens, Michael Stamm, Richard Stevenson, and Warren Ginsberg for many forms of assistance.

Christopher Angotti, Daniel Barr, Dana Baxter, Jennifer Bok, Sarah Kirker, Christopher Perdue, Caroline Suiter, Jeff Suiter, Christopher Vincent, and Jeffrey Williams were undergraduate students in a class on "Ethics and Argument" I taught in the fall of 2003, assisted by Matthew Buonincontro. It is to them that most of the credit goes for the new chapter on ethics. They read and discussed theories of ethical argument by thinkers ranging from Plato, Aristotle, and Cicero to Deborah Tannen and Chaim Perelman. Then they read some of my earlier efforts to write about these issues and pushed me to revise my thinking by raising insightful and challenging objections to my ideas. Not only did these students deeply affect my thinking by confronting me with new perspectives, but they also modeled for me the ideal process I hope to encourage others to strive for in this new chapter, and indeed in this book. We truly danced our disagreements rather than fought them. I am deeply grateful, therefore, to the sponsor of this class, The Oregon Humanities Center, which appointed me as the first Coleman-Guitteau Research and Teaching Professor and thereby enabled me to teach the class and do much of the research for the new chapter. Very special thanks to David B. Stern and Nancy Guitteau, the benefactors of the Coleman-Guitteau professorship, and to Steven Shankman and Julia Heydon, director and assistant director of the Center, and to Ruthann Maguire and Elena Rudy, for making my work in the Center enjoyable and productive.

Our work on this edition was made easier and better by the excellent advice of the following consultants who provided extensive comments on the third edition for Allyn & Bacon: Victoria Aarons, Trinity University; Janet Bland, University of Denver; Heidi Kaufman, University of Oregon; Jeff McCarthy, Westminster College; Ce Rosenow, University of Oregon; and Sundy Watanabe, Weber State University. I'm grateful for the cooperation of all the teachers of the book who filled out questionnaires (most of them anonymously) and to those who submitted student essays for us to consider for this edition, including in addition to those already mentioned Cliff Boyer, Kristy Bryant-Berg, Ann Ciasullo, Teresa Coronado, Craig Franson, Miriam Gershow, Ryan Hediger, Gretchen Langton, Daniel Mackay, Chad May, Carter Soles, Kelly Sultzbach, and Linda Tredennick. Others whose expertise has guided me in previous editions, and whose influence continues to show in this one, include Victoria Aarons, David Bartholomae, Wayne C. Booth, Suzanne Bordelon, Ann Dobyns, Julie Farrar, Martin Jacobi, and Charles Paine. I have been privileged to know many people who have taught this book, discussed it with me, or helped me to think about argumentative writing and ethics; these include (among others also thanked in earlier editions) Ralph Batie, Jamie Blumberg, Grant Boswell, Mark Chilton, Gregory Clark, Georgiana Donavin, Larry Ferguson, Bill Gholson, David Gilcrest, Lawrence D. Green, Jill Kelly, Dennis Lynch, Peter Mack, Joan Mariner, Candace Montoya, Kathleen O'Fallon, Clifford Peterson, Carol Poster, Ellen Quandahl, Bart Queary, Karen Schaup, Katina St. Marie, and Lucette Wood. Most of all, I have derived inspiration from Linda Bensel-Meyers, once my student and now my hero for her unwavering courage, integrity, and intelligence in the battle (yes, sometimes the word applies) to maintain standards of academic excellence.

It has been a privilege to know and work with Eben Ludlow, my editor since the first edition of this book. Now that he is retiring, I want to thank him here for his faith in this book and the firm guidance which has made it better than I otherwise could have done.

As always, Robin and Molly Gage make it all possible and worthwhile.

JOHN T. GAGE

The Shape of Reason

1

Writing and the College Community

Discourse Communities

All of us are individuals, but we coexist with other individuals in communities. We belong to, or interact with, a variety of communities, each of which makes different demands on us, and which we, in turn, affect in different ways. As a member of your generation you are part of one kind of community, as a college student you are part of another, as a family member you belong to another sort of community, and as a person who holds certain political beliefs you are part of another sort of community. Such a list of examples could go on practically indefinitely: different communities for different aspects of our lives. Each of us belongs to a large number of overlapping communities.

Although we share some characteristics with the other members of each community we belong to, as individuals we are also unlike those members in other ways. A community is defined by some characteristic that unites its members, but diversity among people is present in every community. Diversity of opinion may be set aside to one degree or another for the good of the community, or it may become an obstacle to cooperation. Communities are dynamic things in which the members are always seeking cooperation but not at the expense of loss of individuality.

Some communities may be called *discourse communities*. A discourse community is any kind of community in which the members attempt to achieve cooperation and assert their individuality through the use of language. We are all members of a variety of discourse communities, each of which uses language in different ways. Family communities have their own ways of using language, some of which you use only when you are among family members (and some of which you may try to avoid). Political communities have their own ways of using language. Communities of natural scientists use language in some ways unique to them, as do communities of artists, athletes, businesspeople, farmers, and others. Language, because it is adaptable to any purpose, takes on characteristics that help the community to achieve its goals. Communities define themselves to a greater or lesser degree by the way in which they use language.

The uses of language in any discourse community go beyond specialized vocabularies. Yes, certain communities may use jargon—words that members know by virtue of being part of some discourse community and that non-members of that community do not know. But, more importantly, each community differs (more or less) in other ways in its use of language: Different forms of language (such as oral or written, spoken or sung, formal or informal, letters or essays, and so on) may predominate in the discourse of a group; language may be valued differently (language has a different value in the discourse of visual artists, say, than it does in the discourse of newspaper journalists); the purposes of language may vary (such as selling merchandise, persuading voters, praying, reporting information, telling jokes, telling stories, or telling lies). Such differences also overlap from community to community.

As a college student, you are a part of several discourse communities, each of which values language differently and uses it for different purposes. The language used in your biology and math classes differs from the language used in your history and English classes. It differs in vocabulary as well as in style. Short answers, lab reports, and factual questions may be more appropriate to some kinds of disciplines, whereas whole essays, speculative questions, and discussions may be favored in others.

Despite such differences, these discourse communities are also part of a larger discourse community: the college community itself. Like any other community, the scholarly community of the college has goals that in part determine how it uses language.

The purpose of the scholarly community is to inquire and to share with others the products of inquiry—understanding and knowledge. This is the central purpose that unites its members and that motivates them to cooperate with each other despite differences among individuals. *Inquiry,* seen as the active search for answers to questions, suggests certain values and uses that language has in such a community. If language is used to inquire and to share knowledge, it will be used in certain ways, not ways that are necessarily better or worse but that are more suited to these goals. Language is valued in such a community for its ability to aid inquiry and to share understanding and knowledge honestly and precisely.

> *Inquiry* may be generally defined as "looking into," which suggests asking questions. It also involves exploring potential reasons for coming to a conclusion. In this book, inquiry is seen as one kind of argument, as in this definition by Jack W. Meiland: The term *inquiry* may be used to mean "the process of discovering what (if anything) it is rational to believe about a topic."
>
> "Argument as Inquiry and as Persuasion," *Argumenation* 3, 1989: 187.

Diversity of point of view is not only respected in a college community, it is actively sought. A community in which all members think alike on the most important questions is unlikely to inquire into those questions because it contains no alternative points of view. Diversity of opinion is a prerequisite to inquiry and should be valued as such. This is why a scholarly community is one that seeks to open issues of any kind to further questioning by seeking other points of view, rather than to close off questioning by failing to listen to the challenging ideas of others who differ.

As college students, you are invited to join a community of inquiring minds. As learners, you are expected to do more than receive information passively. Like all other members of this discourse community, you are expected to participate actively in the open questioning of that information, listen to all sides, make judgments, and present those judgments to others coherently. The activities you are asked to go through in college—reading, discussion, writing, research, experiments, and so on—have a purpose beyond the acquisition of information in each class. They are meant to help you become better able to cope with the intellectual demands of a complex world, a world in which you will frequently be called upon to make independent decisions among competing ideas in the interest of one or another community to which you belong. Such decisions must be made on the basis of reasoned thought, not by flipping a coin or following the crowd or a charismatic leader. An education prepares you to exercise judgment.

Perhaps it seems strange to you to hear education described in terms of *judgment* at a time when we are said to be experiencing a revolution in our ability to store and rapidly retrieve *information*. The twenty-first century promises to be the so-called information age, and as a student you are often exhorted to prepare yourself for living in a time when the amount of information and speed of accessing it made possible by computers and the Internet will continue to grow. But it is this exponentially rapid increase in the sheer amount of information available to us that will make the quality of judgment even more important to our lives, insofar as we will constantly have to adapt to change, to new information, and to new ways of processing that information. And we will constantly be faced with the necessity to make decisions *about* the information so plentifully available to us. But how does this apply to you as student writers?

Judgment and Writing

Judgment applies to all those occasions when we must decide what to *do* with information. Do we accept it or deny it? How do we measure its significance or value? How should we use it? How does it relate to other information? If people did not exercise judgment, their knowledge would be a useless hodge-podge of unrelated and equally significant bits of information. No educated person can do without the quality of judgment that enables her or him to make sense of all those bits. Yet there are no rules or procedures that can be followed to learn to exercise it. Judgment is learned by experience and practice. It is the act of appraising, discriminating, sorting, adapting, transforming, and applying ideas. Inasmuch as all of these actions require choice, judgment is learned best when one is faced with alternative answers.

Writing argumentative essays in college—a community of inquiring minds—is an opportunity to practice and improve this kind of judgment. If you choose ideas for your essays that are worth writing about, in response to problems that require careful reasoning to solve, you will be challenging yourself on many levels to exercise your best judgment. Writing is not simply an act of finding the right words; it involves looking at issues from different points of view, examining different positions and potential reasons for holding them, and thinking about potential structures and ways of presenting ideas to a reader. In performing such mental acts, you enhance your understanding of the ideas you write about and your ability to reason while you improve as a writer.

Thus, writing is at the very center of what you do as you participate actively in a discourse community of inquirers. Any college student in any class can read, listen, take notes, pass objective tests, and even think deliberately about what it all means. But *writing* about the information with which you are presented in college has an effect that none of these other activities alone can produce. Writing causes you to clarify the information and the problems that come with it, to work out positions for yourself, and to explore reasons for holding those positions. Writing, because it is undertaken to communicate, must be clear. But if writing is also undertaken to influence the discourse community's thinking—that is, to be understood and believed—then it requires more than clarity: It also requires us to find the best reasons we can. Any act of writing that does not stop with the mere assertion of information engages the writer in a search for good reasons, and in that process the writer's judgment, as well as the writer's composing skills, is exercised. Judgment and skills grow together.

This Book and You

The assumptions I have made about the importance of writing in college have led me to approach reason and structure as the main elements of good writing. This book is intended to guide you through a process of thinking and composing that will result in thoughtful, well-structured essays about ideas that matter to you.

The chapters are organized to focus on aspects of this process, but you will find as you compose essays that these aspects are not as separate as the parts of the book suggest. Books about writing must inevitably make distinctions among principles and stages of composing that are arbitrary and artificial in order to spread them out into a sequence of chapters. Ideas and choices that may occur to a writer in any order or all at once must be taken apart and given the appearance of a necessary order. In this book, the order is as follows.

Chapter 1 looks at how our purposes as writers are connected to a community of inquiring minds in college and how our responsibilities as members of such a community affect how we conduct argumentative writing. Chapter 2 helps you to become a more critical reader of others' arguments. Chapter 3 explores ways in which language functions to generate the terms of our thinking. Chapter 4 invites you to consider ethical principles that apply to writing arguments. Chapter 5 gives you advice for finding a meaningful idea to write about in response to questions at issue. Chapter 6 discusses the process of finding adequate support in the form of reasons, and Chapter 7 discusses how to use reasons as a basis for structuring your writing. Chapter 8 gives you guidelines for revising your writing and making stylistic choices. Chapter 9 explores the implications of these discussions for research writing.

Although abstract, this arrangement is meant to represent a process that is intuitively followed by every writer: being confronted with the conflicting ideas of others, responding with ideas of one's own, and developing one's reasons into a form and into language that will enable them to be understood and believed by others. As you give each stage your conscious attention, you can experience a process of thinking from which to draw as you compose, even though your actual acts of composing will never be completely self-conscious or neatly divided into stages.

Ideally, as you use this textbook, you engage in active, open, reasonable discussion with others about the ideas in this book and in any other reading you may be doing for your writing class. Ideally, the members of the class will form a discourse community of inquiring minds, people who engage in an exchange of ideas and who will attempt to offer each other reasonable grounds for changing each others' minds. Ideally, the members of this community, who share your concern about the issues you discuss but who may not share your responses to those issues, will become the audience to whom you write. And you, in turn, will become part of the audience they need to address. In such a class, the activities of thinking, discussing, writing, and judging will not be separate. They will merge and reinforce each other. If you enter the process of reasoning and writing discussed in this book in a willing and thoughtful way, you will write essays that represent your best thinking on issues that are important to you.

Writing classes should be just as concerned with the important issues of a complex world as any other college class. Students who are asked to write about the teacher's favorite idea just to practice writing or who churn out empty-headed compositions on prefabricated topics, such as "My Favorite Movie" or "How to Change a Tire," are doomed to write boring stuff for an already bored teacher. And they are cheated of the opportunity to use writing to learn what they really think and why. It's my intention to enable you to use writing to learn where you stand in the ongoing discussion of ideas that demand serious attention from thinking people. Serious does not mean solemn, though. I also hope you will find the process interesting and fun.

Purpose and Design

As an active participant in the discourse communities of your college and your classroom, you have two main purposes: to find your own way among the ideas of others as you read and listen to them, and to present the result of your inquiry in writing. Finding out what you think is what enables you to know what purpose will guide your writing. In saying this, however, I do not mean that writing comes only after thinking. The search for ideas, the process of inquiry itself, can and should go on *during* the activity of writing. Writing itself can generate ideas and is often the way we find our meanings. Consequently, this book will ask you to write at every stage of your thinking and to rewrite at every stage as well. But before we get to that, we should talk about the idea of purpose and how it is a guide to writing, even though in the process of writing new purposes may be discovered.

The shape that any piece of writing takes on results from the writer's overall sense of purpose. If we think of that shape as the progress from part to part in a composition, it may become easier to see that some sense of a destination, a goal to be reached, is what gives the writer—and the reader—a sense that the parts are held together in meaningful ways. We feel, as we read, that each new part is somehow justified by what went before it and that together the parts are progressing toward some conclusion. You have probably encountered writing that lacked this quality, and your response was to wonder at some point as you slogged through it, "How did I get here?" "Where am I going?" You had this experience because the writer somehow failed to connect the parts in a way that suggested forward progress. Thus, both the reader's sense of progress and the writer's control of this quality come from the same source: a clear sense of an intention that accounts for the necessity of each of the parts and their relations.

That thought reminds me of an episode in *Alice's Adventures in Wonderland*, when Alice encounters the Cheshire Cat sitting goodnaturedly in a tree. She asks the Cat:

"Would you tell me, please, which way I ought to go from here?"

"That depends a good deal on where you want to get to," said the Cat.

"I don't much care where—" said Alice.

"Then it doesn't much matter which way you go," said the Cat.

"—so long as I get *somewhere*," Alice added as an explanation.

"Oh, you're sure to do that," said the Cat, "if you only walk long enough."

Lewis Carroll is having fun here with an idea that is central to an understanding of human actions of all kinds, including writing. That idea may seem self-evident, but it sometimes escapes us: Intention determines choice. When we face a choice of one or another way of acting, it is our intention that guides us. Sometimes, of course, we are not certain whether one or another way will, in fact, serve our intention, but the kind of deliberation we enter into in that case still concerns the relationship of means to ends. Carroll illustrates that if we have no intended *end*, then the *means* we choose hardly matters. In reference to the way in which we shape writing, we might say that if we have no destination to guide us, it hardly matters what parts we choose to put in or leave out. If we have no end in mind to use as a reference point for decisions along the way, any shape will do as well as another.

Whole compositions have unique shapes, or structures, then, because they have unique intentions. Generating the unique structure for your own composition must start with some degree of clarity about your own intentions. The self-evident relation between means and ends in composing gives you three principles to help ensure that the writing you create presents the reader with functionally related parts:

- Try to be as clear as possible about what purpose you want your writing to achieve.

- Use your intended purpose as the test for deciding whether any given part is necessary and whether any additional parts are needed.

- Make your own sense of your purpose clear to the readers too, so they can follow the parts and the transitions between them as they progress through the writing.

The purpose of a composition is its *whole* purpose, the sum of its parts. Its *structure* is the way in which those parts are held together to achieve that purpose. The purpose of a whole piece of writing is best described as an *idea*. Of course, compositions contain more than one idea, but they must all somehow relate to each other because they serve an overall idea of some kind.

Earned Conclusions

The overall or central idea that holds the parts of a composition together is sometimes called a *thesis*. Later, I discuss thesis statements more fully and their role in helping you to generate structure. Now it is enough to say that the purpose of any piece of nonfiction prose writing is to provide the audience with sufficient ideas within its structure to enable them to understand and to accept its main idea.

We can speak of many kinds of actions that ideas perform within a composition, such as *to show, to explain, to illustrate, to develop,* or *to support*. But one kind of action takes in all such particular actions and makes them necessary: That action is *to earn*. Whatever else the ideas in a composition do, they are there in order that the writer can earn the reader's attention or assent. It is one thing to assert an idea; it is another to earn it.

It may sound strange to you to hear the word *earn* applied to a reader's response to your ideas. Why have I chosen it? Consider another situation in which we usually apply this word, other than when we are referring to being paid for work: We sometimes speak, for instance, of earning someone's respect. We apply the term *earning* to human relationships, metaphorically, because we know that another's respect is not automatically given. It cannot be assumed. It is not owed to us. And we also know that whether or not we deserve respect is up to us and depends on how we act toward that person and how those actions are perceived. So, if we want that respect, we need to accept the responsibility to act in such a way that it will be given. Similarly, the sharing of ideas is like building a respected relationship. We cannot assume that we will automatically be listened to or believed. Readers or listeners are not compelled to hear us out, to pay attention, or to accept what we say just because we say it. Whether our ideas are listened to attentively and taken seriously depends on the quality of our communication. Thus, if we wish to be listened to, taken seriously, and believed, we must accept the responsibility of creating earned assent.

The phrase *earned conclusion* suggests that what you write in support of your ideas has an ethical dimension. The term *ethical* suggests fairness and respect toward your readers. When a writer has an idea worth writing about—that is, when she or he wishes to invite others to understand and accept this idea— then that writer feels a sense of responsibility to make the writing do justice to that idea. To do justice to an idea is to try to argue it as reasonably and fairly as possible. (See chapter 4 for a discussion of the ethics of argument in our culture and how ethical considerations can be reflected in how you write.)

A thesis is not just any idea picked out of thin air for no other reason than to have something to write about. A thesis is a special kind of idea, one that you choose because you feel a sense of investment in it and want others to feel that same sense. It is this sense of investment that makes composing seem worth the effort. If you were to compose without caring about the central idea, you would be in Alice's predicament of not knowing which way you ought to turn because you don't much care where it is you go. When you care about an idea, you have a reason to enter the process of searching for other ideas to use to earn that idea.

At one time or another, all writers have the experience of writing like Alice, lost in a confusing wonderland of words, thinking, "If only I write long enough I'm bound to get *somewhere*," In fact, you may have found that writing can lead you into unexpected and interesting discoveries when you let yourself explore ideas freely. I hope that you, like many students, have experimented with freewriting in which you "just wrote" without knowing, or without caring, where you would go in the end. In the process, you may have stumbled onto a new thought that seemed interesting or a purpose that you didn't know you had. If you have had the experience of discovering what you wanted to say *as* you were engaged in writing, you were open to new ideas. But the experience didn't end there. You probably also realized that once you made the discovery you became responsible for doing something with all your freewriting to tie it somehow to that new idea, that new conclusion. Once the new idea was there, new responsibilities came along. Unless you were writing in the form of free association, as in a journal, you realized that the writing you did to stimulate this new idea could not necessarily stand as a composition *about* that idea. This awareness came from a feeling that once you knew just what you wanted to say you somehow accepted the responsibility of making sure that everything else you wrote was relevant to that thought.

Either way, writing is an act of inquiry. Once you know what it is you want to write about—and this decision involves reading and discussion as well as freewriting—inquiry becomes a process of looking into the implications of your idea and potential means of supporting it. It is in this way that having one idea leads to the discovery and testing of other ideas. Having taken responsibility for earning your main idea, you begin to see that there are many, too many, possible things to say *about* it, and you have to begin testing some of those things to see whether they are worth putting into your writing or leaving there. Writing is a process of accepting and rejecting many possible ideas in light of the overall idea they are meant to support. As you decide which ideas to include, you are judging the quality of your own thoughts and considering how to make them accessible to your readers.

Questions for Thought, Discussion, and Writing

1. Think about your own attitudes toward your education and honestly ask yourself whether you generally seek challenges on your own or whether you mostly look for an easy way out of an assignment. Perhaps you can describe situations of each kind. What made the difference?

2. Think about an experience you have had in which you felt that what you already knew was adequate to solve a significant problem. Think about another experience in which your knowledge was not adequate to solve such a problem. Then compare what you learned from these two experiences.

3. Describe an experience in which you came to a clarification of your own thinking through writing.

4. In what discourse communities do you participate? What shared characteristics and values define each? Because of these shared characteristics and values, are there differences in the language you use in each? What areas of overlap or potential intellectual conflict exist between them?

5. Have you ever discovered your own intention in a piece of writing after you had begun to write? What did you do as a result of this discovery?

6. Based on your experience as a reader, how do writers earn your respect? What qualities of writing do not earn your respect?

7. As you read an assigned essay, or in any reading you may be doing for another class, identify the main idea, or thesis, and then identify other ideas that the writer uses to *earn* that thesis. In each case, try to ask yourself how the ideas are structured to make a whole. What makes each part of the essay necessary? Why are they arranged in this order? Having identified what you think are the supporting ideas, try to assess whether they provide you with sufficient grounds for accepting the conclusion. By what means do you judge whether they do?

2

Critical Reading

How We Read

Why is it that we sometimes think ideas are obvious whereas at other times we do not want to believe them? No idea is isolated: We understand ideas in relation to the ideas that surround them in any given piece of writing and we somehow adjust our beliefs to fit what we already know. The act of believing is the result of a decision, and we can decide how *much* belief to give to any idea based on how well it connects to other ideas and to what we know independently. Each time we see a reason, we have to figure out whether it is a good one. So, reading is a process of making our way between the extremes of too much unreasonable belief (when the reasons to believe aren't good enough) and too much unreasonable doubt (when the reasons to *dis*believe are not good enough). Keeping this balance is much easier said than done.

At least two kinds of beliefs are asked of us when we read. We are asked to believe the *information* presented by the writer, and we are asked to believe the *ideas* asserted about that information. In both cases, we read with some awareness that we do not *have* to believe something just because a writer says it. The question is: What kind of mental process do we go through to help us decide whether or not to believe the information and ideas we read?

Whether we are habitual readers, casual readers, or infrequent readers, we are all readers, and a lot of what we know and think has been the result of *how* we have read whatever we happen to have read. *Somebody* must be reading all those ads for fat vanishing cream with hopeful credulity, even if *we* all know not to believe them. And somebody, similarly, must be reading the front page of the *Washington Post* as if it were part of a well-orchestrated foreign conspiracy. We change our reading habits to fit the nature of the reading matter and our reasons for reading it. It would be silly to adopt the same skeptical attitude when reading the Sunday comics that we might adopt when reading the advertisements. But might the comics ever be trying to sell us anything? Are they not sometimes asking for our belief in cer-

What does this comic strip invite you to believe about homework, trust, telling the truth, sisters?

tain ideas? We might change our reading habits to fit the occasion, and we should, but we might not want to give up our ability to think critically about what we read.

Whether rightly or wrongly, we must often rely on reading when we need information. We may not believe everything that we read, but we nevertheless know that if we are to have reliable information, we probably ought to seek it in a reliable written source. Part of becoming educated is learning to distinguish among sources of information. We have all learned that some sources of information are more reliable than others. The *New York Times* is usually going to be more reliable than the *National Enquirer.* I say *usually* because when dealing with questions of belief there are always exceptions. There are probably examples of some fact being reported in the *National Enquirer*, denounced in the pages of the *New York Times* as a lie, and then discovered independently to be correct. There are certainly many examples of facts reported in the *New York Times* that have turned out to be wrong, or even intentionally fraudulent. Most of us have surfed the Web enough to know that the reliability of information varies greatly on the Internet. Because of our easy access to a wide range of websites and the sometimes ephemeral quality of those sites, the integrity and authority of the information we find on the Internet may be more difficult to assess than when we read well-established printed sources.

For example, I found the usual huge number of sites when I typed "Global Climate Change" into an Internet search engine. The three home pages seen on pages 14–15 were among the top five. Based on what you see there, is there any basis for assessing the relative credibility of these three sites as sources of information about the topic? For what different purposes do they seem to be designed? What different audiences do they seem to serve? The answers aren't obvious, but it is nevertheless possible to see by the way in which text and visuals interact that these sites offer a range of information from the most selective for purposes of advocacy to the most extensive for purposes of inquiry.

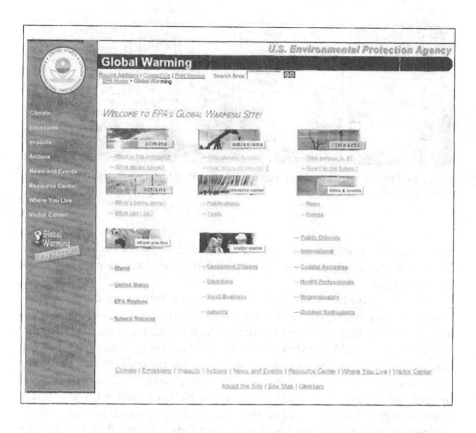

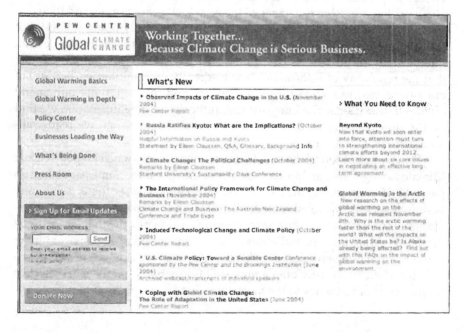

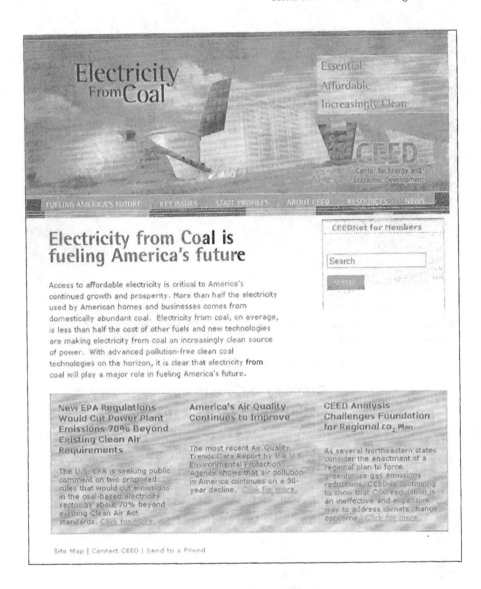

It is important for reading both written and visual information to remember that no written or graphic text can present a complete picture and that it must rely on the reader's understanding of other ideas. Although my emphasis in this book is on written arguments, parallels may be drawn to how we read visual text as well. Let me illustrate these points with two graphic examples.

On the next page is a photograph and a chart that accompanied an article in the *New York Times International* newspaper. The article was headlined "British Worry That Drinking Has Gotten Out of Hand." As you look at them, consider how they add information to the article's claim that England's "growing inability to hold its liquor has taken on the scope of a national crisis."

Revelers in Birmingham on a Saturday night. Sometimes partying goes too far, angering the neighbors.

Drinking to Excess

Ireland and Britain have the highest levels of binge drinking, defined as five or more drinks in one sitting.

*Percentage that
binges at least once*

MEN		
Ireland	48	
Britain	38	
Finland	16	
Italy	11	
Germany	9	
France	8	
Sweden	8	

WOMEN		
Ireland	16	
Britain	12	
Italy	7	
Finland	3	
Germany	2	
France	2	
Sweden	1	

Source: Institute of Alcohol Studies

Each provides us with reasons to believe the claim. In the case of the photograph, we are meant to see visual evidence of the idea that "partying goes too far." How persuasive is that evidence? In the chart, we are provided data to support the belief that "Ireland and Britain have the highest levels of binge drinking." What data are left out? In both cases, the viewer is assumed to hold certain beliefs already, to trust the reliability of the photo and the data, and to lean toward a certain kind of response. The information provided in both the photo and the graph does more than support the claim factually; it calls for an emotional response consistent with the charged language of the headline. How?

The reliability of a source may depend on the type of information we are seeking. If we want to learn about the possible benefits of nuclear power, for instance, we may seek information from the nuclear power industry rather than from an envronmental group, but if we want to learn about the possible dangers of nuclear energy, we will go first to the environmental group instead. Yet this convenience in finding appropriate information is also a hazard: Each of these kinds of resources may have built-in biases that affect the reliability of its information.

To pursue these questions further and add to our considerations about critical reading, let me present a more extensive illustration for you to analyze.

The Brady Problem

Here is an excerpt from a documentary website describing the life and work of Mathew B. Brady, the great nineteenth-century American photographer. The website was a class project by students of John Osborne, a professor or history at Dickinson College. This excerpt was primarily written by one of the students, Paul White. The whole text, which features many photos of and by Brady, outlines his life and argues for his importance as an innovative pioneer in the history of photography. I have not included in this excerpt all the photos and hypertext links that go along with it on the website. You can view these at http://www.dickinson.edu/~osborne/404_98/whitep.htm. Here is what this website says verbatim about the period in which Brady photographed scenes from the Civil War:

The War

Mathew Brady

In 1860, The American Civil War became one of the first wars ever documented by the camera. The stories that were being told of how gruesome the fighting was between the Union and Confederate Armies were now being told not by only by word of mouth, but by the photograph as well. Much of what America learned, and continues to learn today, about the war, is aided by the many pictures taken of it. Many of the images that have been left behind for historians to interpret were taken by Mathew Brady, who risked great fortune to document the war. Many of his closest relatives and friends advised the blinding photographer not to go, but he saw the need to turn his lens to a different subject. With the help of a traveling unit, which included many photographers and aides such as Gardener and Timothy O'Sullivan, Brady set out to copy onto film what many had been previously only hearing about. His intention to capture the war on film brought it to the home front very powerfully, and many of the pictures illustrated the horrors, truths and realities of the entire war.

I think that Brady attempted to capture these realities in many ways. He remained loyal to individual imaging, yet turned his attentions and subjects to military leaders, and individuals involved within the war. He photographed many different people, ranging from Confederate General R. E. Lee, to abolitionist Frederick Douglas. His efforts were entirely concentrated on individuals who were either inspired by or involved with the war. Brady took pictures of the dead at all battlefields, to illustrate what the killing looked like to those who have not had the displeasure of seeing such a sight. These pictures hit home the hardest, for both their graphic nature and extreme content.

Brady was a complete photographer. He didn't let his own emotions enter into his subjects, created a biased image, nor did he concentrate on one aspect of the war over certain others. That is to say, he felt that capturing every aspect of the war was essential in bringing the real story home. Books and films surrounding the war show pictures ranging from scenes of death to scenes of beauty. He captured it all, focusing on telling the entire story, rather than an individual one. . . .

Brady's group portraits show us more than just the group itself. It's as if he's trying to give us an idea of who these men were, and why they were there. Their order and discipline in the image tells us that Brady wanted them to look like true American heroes, who fight because they want to defend their beliefs. How can this be deduced? The images of Union regiments compared to those of Confederate are not all that different. In what they are wearing, there is a difference, but in what they are doing there isn't any. Both groups are fighters. Both groups are willing to die for their cause, representing an equality in his process. That is, he took pictures of both sides, and in doing so he showed that the two sides had more in common than might be actually recognized.

Brady was able to capture the human element as well in many images which showed soldiers outside of a formal setting, either relaxing, eating or other daily activities which might not have been considered important. To Brady however, they illustrated reality. . . .

Brady's reputation as a master photographer, as well as the art of war photography, grew tremendously after Bull Run. They gained respect from both the soldiers and the American people for their efforts to depict the war in images and their attempts to bring the realities of it to the home front. Brady and his men went under fire to capture a still image, proving how brave and courageous they were willing to be in order to take a picture. The conditions were equally as bad off the battlefield as well. Once Brady returned from Bull Run, he knew that in order to get the images taken and developed on sight he would need his 'what-sit' wagons to travel everywhere. They traveled over rough terrain at times carrying many glass-plates and valuable negatives which could have easily been damaged in the moving process. It's hard not to say Brady's efforts fall short of being miraculous.

Since Brady could not be at every battle, his hired hands traveled far lengths to reach certain battles, but yet under Brady's guise. From him, they knew what types of images to take, and they knew what type of picture Brady wanted them to bring home. Prior to Bull Run, Brady wasn't aware that he needed to move his studios to the battlefields, but once he stated to do so, he eventually brought the battlefields to his studios. He was one of the first 'on-sight' photojournalists. Men like O'Sullivan and Gardener helped to create many of Brady's images, but Brady helped to create men like O'Sullivan and Gardener as well.

I think Bull Run was the key moment in Brady's illustrious photographic career. It did a number of things for him and his profession, and eventually showed him what he would show the world in his images to come. Bull Run opened him up to the war, and it opened him up to the death that was inevitable through the war, and inescapable from his lens. After Bull Run, Brady was encouraged to expand his practice, and to open up studios surrounding the war as well as to hire other photographers to create his own type of army. It equally discouraged him from returning home as well, for once he knew the magnitude of what was to come, he saw great opportunity in traveling to cover the war. To his wife Julia's dismay, he spent little time back home concentrating on the studio life that once dominated him in the years prior to the war.

"My wife and most conservative friends had looked unfavorably upon this departure from commercial business to pictorial war correspondence; and I can only describe the destiny that overruled me by saying that, like Euphorion, I felt like I had to go. A spirit in my feet said 'GO' and I went."[1]

The Dead

"The pictures most heart rendering to make yet technically the easiest were those of the dead; for such battlefield coverage, motion was not a factor."
Dorothy Kunhardt

Following the Union defeat at Bull Run, Brady ventured down to a small river source in Maryland called Antietam Creek. There Brady would witness one of the deadliest battles of the Civil War, as well as one of the worst battles to ever take place on American soil. Here many Americans, both of Union

and confederate blood would meet their demise. Brady and his men took many images at Antietam, and they were so widely acclaimed that he opened up an exhibit in one of his New York Studios entitled "The Dead of Antietam."[2] Here he displayed his many photos of the war, and gave to his viewers their first taste of what images of the deceased actually looked like. In a way, it was like a 'photographic culture shock' for the public, because they showed mixed reviews once the exhibit went on display.

The images of the dead further beat the reality of the war into the minds of the people, and it showed what was happening to the men who left home to fight for their country. Brady's exhibits and the pictures were a painful reminder of what was happening on the battlefields.

Capturing war in images is mostly about combat. And how we view those images of combat, the images of the dead, is how we interpret it. It's also how the photographer interprets it.

"Combat, no matter how peripheral, how Pyrrhic, how purposeless, is the heart of war. It is what young boys glamorize, old men remember, poets celebrate, governments rally around, women cry about, and soldiers die in. It is also what photographers take pictures of."[3]

Pictures of the dead, no matter how chilling, or vivid in content, tell of the grim realities that war brings. Brady, when capturing the dead on the battlefields, not only captured this reality, but historically left a foundation for all historians to base their research and studies on how powerful of a war the Civil War was. His images of the dead were so personal, so frighteningly real, that he actually scared many people, and after the war was over, hardly anyone wanted to ever look at a Brady war image again, because it reminded them of what had happened to their sons, brothers, neighbors, etc.

Brady, after having produced his images of the dead, changed in many ways. First, many of his 'fans' somewhat turned against him at the end of the war, after he continued to display his pictures of the dead, from Antietam, to Gettysburg, Cold Harbor, and Fredericksburg, to name a few places. He went from a somewhat conservative still imagery, to taking on this larger role of picturing the sudden cataclysmic event which changed the faces of many of the images which were being produced. When the picture began to change, so too did the profession of photography. When Brady and other photographers saw what they were taking pictures of, it was such a serious change from individual portraits that people were now being affected personally by what they were seeing. It took the image of war, and the art of photography to a higher level. Moeller offers us this:

"Concurrent with the interest of capturing war in photography grew the desire to circulate those images. . . The Brady studio pictures of Antietam, 'literally stunned the American People' because of the photographs' relentless portrayal of the dead."[4]

These pictures of Antietam not only showed the realities, but also gave the viewing public an image of the human element, and to how this war was affecting those who fought in it. They were very graphic, and received much attention from the public and the media for that.

"For the people back home, photographs were the newsreels of the day—the only visual connections between the comparatively normal lives of most Americans during the war and the horrors of the battlefields. Of all the pictures taken, it was those of the dead and wounded that had the most effect, that made people realize the price of keeping the country whole."[5]

In a review of Brady's gallery, which showed the images of the Antietam fallen, gave this assertion in their review of his exhibit:

"Mr. Brady has done something to bring home to us the terrible reality and earnestness of war. If he has not brought bodies and laid them in our door-yards and along our streets, he has done something very like it."[6]

Again, we see the respect that Brady gets, and we see the attention to the war that his images of the dead were demanding. It was one of the first instances where "*the public's long nurtured belief that death on the battlefield was glorious and heroic.*"[7]

There should be a great deal said about how Brady changed the face of photography after entering the war. His coverage of the war stood as the first real account of war photojournalism, and set a standard for the coverage future wars would receive in images to come. The pictures that we have from the Civil War became a basis for which other wars would be photographed. The soldiers, the battlefields, the dead, all of these 'groups' were focal points in war photography to come. These images gained a substantial amount of popularity here, and gave photographers to follow an advantage in knowing what types of pictures to take. Credit for this should be given to Mathew Brady, and his many field hands who visually saw the type of image they wanted to create, and knew how the image would speak about the battle. Especially the images of the dead.

This image of a young, dead soldier at Petersburg is very

telling. From it, we see the soldier's innocence, as well as the pain in which he felt as he fell to the bottom of the trench to meet his final moments of life. It's also a sad image in how close is it to the viewer. We can see the pain in his facial expressions, and to those viewing this in one of Brady's galleries, the impact it had must have been quite powerful because of the seriousness of battle that the picture shows. His weapon is presumably propped up against his body, to illustrate the possible heroism that this soldier displayed by not giving up and setting his weapon down.

Many photographers, it is said, would position the bodies in the fashion that they saw would fit the need of capturing the realistic qualities of death. Alex Gardener is said to have carried a dead soldier over a course of 40 yards so he could prop his body against a specific spot at the Devil's Den, presumably to capture the essence of a single, dead sharpshooter. In response to the allegation that Gardener had manipulated the scene to help portray the sadness, he responded; "*The artist, in passing over the scene of the previous days' engagements, found in a lonely place the covert of a rebel sharpshooter, and photographed the scene presented . . .*"[8]

Whether or not this is true, many photographers not only saw the opportunity to cover the war in pictures, but they gained the knowledge of how powerful a certain scene 'might' be, so they would change it around to fit their own personal belief of how it should be seen. They were art historians themselves in this respect, because they knew what type of image to capture, even if the original scene had to be rearranged in order to do so. The scenes of the dead were key in capturing the public eye, and Brady and others took many images, simply because there were so many scenes of death itself.

During days between the fighting, officials would agree on truce days, so the dead could be buried. Photographers used these days to roam the battlefields and image the scenes of the dead while not being under constant fire. They would take pictures of the relatively 'new' dead, and what a tribute it is to their abilities to take images of what must have been possibly the most gruesome images that they had ever witnessed.

Notes

1. Dorothy Kunhardt. *Mathew Brady and His World* (Time-Life: Canada) 1977, p. 58.
2. Ken Burns. *The Civil War* 1994.
3. Moeller, Susan. *Shooting War* (New York: Basic Books) 1989.
4. Ibid., 24.
5. Kunhardt, 248.
6. Moeller, Susan. Excerpt from *New York Times* can be found on Civil War Documentary, film.
7. Moeller, 25.
8. Kunhardt, 248.

Osborne's website praises Brady's accomplishments in terms of his unprecedented method of bringing the realities of war home, and in terms of the personal courage it took for him to photograph the war. What other evidence of admiration comes through in this prose? The student writer does admit that other photographers were part of Brady's team, who "helped to create" the photographs, namely O'Sullivan and Gardener, whom he calls "hired hands." He raises the issue, toward the end of this excerpt, of whether some of the photos were faked in that bodies were repositioned by the photographer to enhance the effect, reporting that Gardener was "said to have carried a dead soldier . . . 40 yards." He then goes on to defend this practice by quoting Gardener's ambiguous denial and saying, "Whether or not this is true, many photographers . . . gained their knowledge of how powerful a certain scene 'might' be, so they would change it around to fit their own personal belief of how it should be seen." Are the images of war more able to portray realities when the bodies (possibly) were manipulated to fit the photographer's "personal beliefs"? We seem to be left with this question. Why do you think the website did not address it directly?

Confronted by the information in this website, we could easily wonder what is true about the photos in at least two ways: Who took them? Were the bodies moved for effect? With such questions in mind, we might decide to read further on the subject. Here, then, is a paragraph I found in a printed catalog of Mathew Brady's photographs entitled *Mathew Brady 55*, written by Mary Panzer, the curator of photographs at the National Portrait Gallery:

> **Bodies Near Dunker Church, Antietam, Maryland, 1862.** In September 1862. Confederates met Union troops in Maryland for what became the three bloodiest days of the war. Immediately afterwards, Alexander Gardner and a team of photographers documented the carnage in terms that all viewers found shocking. The *New York Times* reported that these images exerted a 'terrible fascination', and credited Brady with showing, for the first time, 'the terrible reality and earnestness of war . . . he has . . . brought bodies and laid them in our door-yards and along the streets'. Gardner soon left Brady to establish his own business, and his photographers produced some of the war's harshest and most memorable images. Brady, true to his romantic vision, recorded battlefields only after the corpses were gone.

Here we have another expert source telling us not only that Gardner (now without an *e*) took battlefield photos as part of a team but that he did so after quitting work for Brady—a different impression than Osborne's website gives of their relationship. What's more, we learn from this that Brady didn't take photographs of corpses at all. Now we seem to have conflicting expert opinions on the question of what Brady himself contributed. So, we decide to read even further on the subject.

Here is a passage taken from a book, entitled *Mathew Brady and His World*, by Dorothy Meserve Kunhardt and Philip B. Kunhardt, Jr., one of the sources cited in Osborne's website:

Mathew Brady was one of the commercial photographers covering parts of the War. Certainly he was not the best, nor the most prolific, nor the most important. Nevertheless, he was by far the most famous. And he was one of the very first to have the courage and initiative to think of moving a minature studio out into a combat area. An anonymous daguerreotypist had taken several battlefield pictures during the Mexican War, and an English photographer named Roger Fenton, working out of a crude horse-drawn van, covered soldiers and campsites during the Crimean War in 1855. Still, the very idea of photographic war coverage on a grand scale was audacious, to say the least. Brady helped to lead the way and showed that it was possible.

But his personal coverage was limited in scope, usually within easy range of the city of Washington, and he certainly never had "men in all parts of the army." Maybe "like Euphorion" he felt he "had to go" at first, but the spirit soon wore off. What remained was an unceasing and passionate desire to be the curator, if not the creator, of all the war pictures that could possibly be taken.

To this end Brady committed much of his resources, not only toward materials and supplies but toward courageous, artistic cameramen as well. In his employ at one time or another during the War were Alexander Gardner, Timothy O'Sullivan, George N. Barnard, T. C. Roche, Guy Foux, James F. Gibson, E. T. Whitney, David Knox, J. Reekie, S. F. Denny, Stanley Morrow, David Landy, John Wood, William Pywell, James Gardner and David Woodbury. It may have been, too, that an unheralded young black man named A. B. Foons, who often drove the wagon when Brady himself went out, also helped operate his camera.

Mathew Brady's definition of what made a Civil War picture a "Brady" was just as loose as it always had been in the portrait galleries—but with less justification. It included, of course, any picture taken when the proprietor was on the scene—actually persuading a general to pose, asking the wounded to be still for a minute, ordering gun batteries into different positions in order to improve the composition, helping the camera operator set up the equipment, framing the scene, running the show as he squinted through his thick, bluetinted glasses. But it also included any picture that was taken by any photographer who was on his payroll, whether Brady himself was around at the time or not.

The fact that he would give no mention to the actual picture-taker involved and insisted that all photographs carry only the credit "Photo by Brady" infuriated the men who worked for him. Many of them came and went, working for Brady until they got fed up with his $35-a-week wages, catching on with another sponsor for a while, maybe drifting back to Brady for another interval of frustration. Alexander Gardner, who always insisted that it was he and not Brady who first thought of covering the War, had his fill early. Gardner was frustrated by Brady's long stay in 1861 at the Washington gallery, from which the proprietor made his forays to nearby battlegrounds; and Gardner insisted that his own war pictures were not Brady's, since they had been taken with Gardner's own private equipment and on his own time. Gardner left Brady before the War was a year old.

After a span of time taking pictures for the Army of the Potomac, terminating when General McClellan was replaced, Gardner, along with his brother, opened a Washington gallery of his own on Seventh Street. It became a lucrative portrait and general assignment business; Gardner continued his war coverage as well. Timothy O'Sullivan, possibly the finest photographer to work in the War, left Brady to join Gardner's enterprise. So did Guy Foux. But to Brady, "operators" were expendable; there were always replacements.

Since Brady didn't have to be behind the camera, he enjoyed, when he was in the field, slipping into his own pictures and being recorded, almost always with his back toward the lens. Usually he would hurry back to make sure the public saw his work, either through prints, which were on exhibit at his galleries, or through reproduction in *Leslie's* or *Harper's* weekly magazine.

The plot thickens! Now we have discovered more information about why Gardner quit Brady and about Brady himself. What emerges here is far from the portrait of Mathew Brady we saw in Osborne's website. The Kunhardts emphasize Brady's commercialism and his attitude toward his employees, as well as his large ego.

Other conflicts—both of opinion and of fact—are raised by these three accounts. Whether we choose to believe one of them more than another is, of course, our right, but on what basis do we make the choice? My point here is not to judge the merits of any of these accounts but to ask you to think about reading. Given such conflicts, we as readers are put in the position of having to adjust our beliefs. But how? Is there a process we can go through as readers to measure our belief in the facts and opinions we read?

What sort of process am I talking about? Not one, I assure you, that will prevent you from ever being duped or that will tell you when a thing is true. Critical reading can do no more than keep you ask-

"Don't be so critical all the time!" Who hasn't heard or said that, when "being critical" means picking something apart or dismissing it? In the community of thinkers in college, however, this kind of negative act isn't what's meant by the terms *critical reading* and *critical thinking*. Being critical is a positive act involving respect for ideas and reasons. In this book, for the purposes of discussing argumentative writing, *critical reading* means evaluating what you read in such a way that you can adjust the degree of your agreement or disagreement to the quality of the reasons that support any idea.

ing about potentially good or bad reasons, so that when you face the question of whether to agree or disagree, you will be able to make a qualified decision based on your understanding of the quality of the reasons given. People who believe without caring about the quality of the reasons, as well as people who disbelieve without caring about the quality of the reasons, no matter *what* they believe, are, by this definition, uncritical. All of us are uncritical sometimes. We are more or less critical at different times. When we are reading, however, we should try to read as critically as we can. If we don't, we risk being misinformed and possibly coming to conclusions we cannot support.

When writers write, they do not simply string together sentences that all directly assert some information. As we saw in Chapter 1, writing takes its shape from the writer's intention. That is, writers want people to believe something. They write with an idea in mind, therefore, but their choice of things to say in addition to that idea depends on what they think people need to hear in order to believe it. Writing is purposeful and *strategic*. Writing that contains information, then also contains something put there in order to help you or encourage you to believe that that information is true.

A critical reader must, therefore, pay attention to more than *what* a piece of writing says. A critical reader must also consider *how* information is presented, and in what context. This is because a writer who thinks strategically is mindful of the *means* necessary to reach the *end* that he or she has in mind. This does not mean that writers cheat or want to deceive us. It simply means that writers intuitively understand that they must convince readers to believe them, and they make use of available means of persuasion accordingly. Information by itself is rarely the *end* of a piece of writing.

The process of finding out more and hearing a wider range of points of view is potentially endless, but even to begin it one must be motivated by a sense of the importance of making up one's mind based on the *best* reasons. It is up to us to seek different relevant views and then to evaluate those views according to the quality of the reasons they give in support of their conclusions, and not on the basis of the credibility of the source or the authority of the writer alone.

Reading and Belief

Some people are accustomed to think that facts must be either believed or disbelieved—as if belief were like a light switch with only two positions, on and off. My use of the Brady problem is intended to illustrate that belief does not have to operate as a simple yes or no choice, all or nothing. Belief can be more conditional; it can be something that we decide to have up to a point or to a degree. And so, the question we might ask ourselves while reading does not have to be "Should I believe it or not?" but instead "How seriously should I entertain this possibility?" This latter question implies that the belief we have in any given fact, or in any given idea, is not determined by whether it sounds right or whether the source is an authority. It means that our beliefs are determined by the reasons that justify them. Belief is not a mechanical action, brought about by invariable rules of nature. It is a human activity, the exercise of judgment.

The process of weighing beliefs against the quality of reasons is one that you already go through all the time, whether you are aware of it or not. We all do. The practice of critical reading is the exercise of this kind of judgment on purpose. By doing it, we protect ourselves from being led into belief for inadequate reasons, but at the same time we open up our minds to the possibility of arriving at belief for adequate ones. If we decide to grant or withhold assent based on the quality of the reasons that we are given, we admit at the same time that two things are possible: We admit that we might assent less in the future if we discover that the reasons are not so good after all, and we admit that we might assent more if we are ever presented with better reasons than we had formerly known. This attitude is not pure skepticism any more than it is pure credulity. It is somewhere in between. It is the attitude of an openminded thinker, of someone who wishes to be responsible for deciding for herself or himself what to believe. This attitude also implies a willingness to question one's own beliefs while at the same time remaining open to new and different ideas.

The practice of critical reading, then, can do more than protect us from jumping too quickly to conclusions. Because it is a process of examining reasons and measuring conclusions against them, it can provide us with a way to learn to live with uncertainty. Living with uncertainty is one of those skills we need to get along in this world, but it is also a skill that people do not talk about much. We have just seen that certainty is not easy to come by. It requires that we assume some responsibility for questioning what we read, which might entail a search for more information and better reasons than we are given in a single source. In other words, it requires independent inquiry and thought, which are carried out not only because we want to know what to believe but also because each of us alone must make up his or her own mind.

If absolute, permanent belief is not available about many matters that concern us, we must adjust to this situation and accept it. It can be a situation to be enjoyed, not lamented, it is what makes thinking and learning an adventure. More inquiry is always possible. New ideas or reasons may turn up. This keeps our minds alert and active. It makes us want to continue to learn because we are more able to accept new ideas. We become less susceptible to the tactics of people who would like to do our thinking for us. Instead of the easy convictions that come from narrow-mindedness, this process offers us the possibility of continuing to think about things that matter to us.

Critical reading, then, is something we practice in order to acknowledge that we belong to a community of inquiring minds, as I called it earlier—a discourse community in which inquiry and argument are valued for their ability to keep us thinking and talking to each other about ideas that matter.

Some Considerations for Critical Reading

The preceding section has offered you some philosophical ideas about reading and writing, about education, on which this book is based. You are free, in fact encouraged, to question them. But now we must get practical in our thinking about critical reading.

Here are some questions that a critical reader might consider in order to arrive at an adequate basis for deciding how much to give or withhold assent. Asking the questions will not, of course, guarantee answers. It can only serve to guide further thinking.

- **What is the writer's purpose?** What is this writer trying to do to the reader? What is the single most important idea in the writing, the one that makes everything else in it necessary? This central idea (or thesis) may or may not be stated explicitly by the writer. It may or may not be obvious.

- **What question does the writing answer?** The writer's intended audience is assumed to share a concern for some question, which the essay serves to answer in some way. The question may or may not be explicit or obvious. Do I share this concern? Should I?

- **Why does the writer think this question is important?** There must be some reason the writer has chosen this question to answer. What difference does it make to the writer that the question be resolved? What about the writing tells me this?

- **How persuadable am I?** Do I already have my mind made up on this question? How willing am I to listen to another point of view? If I agree with the author, can I maintain some critical distance and not agree with the reasons just because I already agree with the conclusion? What untested reactions do I have to the writer's thesis?

- **What are the writer's reasons?** What ideas does the writer advance in defense of the thesis? What ideas are advanced in defense of *those* ideas?

- **Where does the reasoning stop?** What reasons are asserted as if they are self-evident? Although some reasons are supported by a further line of reasoning, it is impossible for all of them to be. If the reasoning depends on these ideas being believed without further support, do I believe them?

- **Are the reasons adequate?** Not all reasons actually support the conclusions they seem to support. What actually connects the reasons to the conclusions?

- **What responsibility does the writer take for the verifiability of information?** If the writer cites facts, studies, experiences, or sources, is there an adequate basis for checking up on them, or does the writer expect me simply to take his or her word for them?

- **What has the writer done to put me in a receptive frame of mind?** Not all parts of a writing have the strictly logical function of supporting a thesis. Some aspects of the composition, especially its style, will function to create confidence in the writer or a special bond between the writer and the reader. How do I react to these features?

- **What am I going to do about it?** If a critical reader is engaged in measuring assent, then I should know how I might be changed by having read and thought about these ideas. To what extent must I adjust my thinking? Do these ideas have relevance to my thinking about other questions? Are there connections between these ideas and other things I believe? What are the consequences or practical effects for me of believing or doubting?

Perhaps you already consider many of these questions when you read, even if you never become self-consciously deliberate about doing so. They are not intended as a checklist, to proceed through in mechanical fashion. Use them as a basis for more thought.

Questions for Thought, Discussion, and Writing

1. Have you ever had the experience of believing something you read and then discovering later that it was not true? What did this experience teach you about reading? Do you read differently as a result? How so?

2. Have you ever read something that someone told you was bad for you? Was it? How do you know? How about something that someone said would be good for you?

3. Can you think of any ideas that you agree with only to a certain degree? What has your agreement to do with the quality of the reasons you have heard in support of these ideas?

4. In general, how would you define a *good reason*? Find examples of good reasons and bad ones to illustrate what you mean. Does everyone in your class agree with your examples?

5. As you read an essay assigned in class, or one you find yourself, use the questions at the end of this chapter to guide your critical reading. For a particular reading, write short answers to each of the questions. Does your conscious attempt to apply these critical reading questions provide you with ideas for an essay of your own? Do they open up areas in which you wish to conduct further inquiry?

chapter

3

The Deep Structure of Reasoning

Opposing Terms

Where do arguments come from? One answer to this question is that arguments are generated by ideas in opposition. Before we go on to talk about ideas and how they form the basis for structuring argumentative writing, let's consider the idea of opposition itself. Where does opposition come from? Perhaps, the answer that comes most readily to mind is that it comes from differences or conflicts among people, but let's consider for a moment the way that differentiation and opposition are deeply embedded in language, providing the basic material out of which all arguments arise. Meaning itself would be impossible without differentiation; a word names one thing, not another. The word *table* has meaning because it distinguishes one kind of furniture from other kinds.

Opposition is a special form of differentiation. Let's consider it more fully.

The poet Richard Wilbur writes about a family word game in which someone says a word and another has to make up an opposite for that word. Wilbur then makes poems out of the words:

> What is the opposite of *hat?*
> It isn't hard to answer that.
> It's *shoes,* for shoes and hat together
> Protect our two extremes from weather.

> The opposite of *doughnut?* Wait
> A minute while I meditate.
> This isn't easy. Ah, I've found it!
> *A cookie with a hole around it.*

> The opposite of *spit,* I'd say,
> Would be *a narrow cove* or *bay.*
> (There is another sense of spit,
> But I refuse to think of it.
> It stands opposed to *all refined
> and decent instincts of mankind!*)

The fun of this game is in thinking up a reason that something can be seen as the opposite of something else. Play the game yourself. What is the opposite of *chair*? Hmm. It depends. Is it *couch*? Or is it *floor*? Or is it *bicycle*? Nouns that name concrete things don't generally have opposites, even though they can be contrasted with other words for things:

tree	in contrast to	bush
		lumber
		building

These contrasting words could be seen in opposition to the word *tree* in different circumstances. *Tree* and *bush* might be seen in opposition in the context of landscaping. *Tree* and *lumber* are opposed in the context of raw material versus product. *Tree* and *building* might be said to be opposed in the sense that one is natural and the other artificial. In each case, it's the qualities assigned to the tree, or the context in which it is seen, that are opposed to other qualities, not the tree itself.

Opposition, then, is not really a condition of specific things, or words for specific things, but of abstract concepts that might be applied to things. Some nouns that name things do seem to have opposites, such as:

circle	square
land	ocean
city	countryside

Yet in such cases, these are not concrete things so much as they are qualities of concrete things. At yet a higher level of abstraction, words, unlike the nouns used to name specific things or qualities of things, name concepts, like *love*. Such concepts are understood not because we can point to them but because we can name and define them in terms of other concepts. Opposition is inherent in abstract terms because for any such term naming a concept there is a term that may be used potentially to name its negation or absence, like *hate* in relation to the concept *love*.

A few more examples are:

motion	stillness
sound	silence
beauty	ugliness
intelligence	stupidity
grace	clumsiness
wealth	poverty

Abstract terms seem to come to our minds and exist in our awareness already paired with opposing terms. Such pairs of terms are used to define each other. They are known to us because we understand them in terms of the opposite concepts with which we pair them. Such pairings may be called *dialectical oppositions,* when we understand one of the terms by defining it in opposition to the other term, as in, for example:

deep	shallow
joy	sadness
sacred	profane
lost	found
clear	obscure
loyalty	betrayal
sharp	dull
power	weakness
friend	enemy
pleasure	pain

We understand each term only in relation to the other: *Deep* is understood relative to *shallow,* or *clear* relative to *obscure,* and so forth. The meaning of the term is somehow not inherent in the term itself without the contrasting term to define it by comparison or negation. Language seems to have an infinite number of dialectical oppositions, pairs of words that are understood as opposed concepts. If you look up an abstract word in the dictionary, it will often be found to have several opposites, called *antonyms.* Dialectical opposites are those antonyms we understand through negation, each word forming a necessary part of the definition of the other. In the previous examples, *power* is defined as the absence of weakness and *weakness* as the absence of power. Something that is sharp cannot be said to be dull at the same time, because each of the two concepts is understood as the quality of not being the other.

Assigning Value to Terms

We often associate dialectical pairings with qualities of "good" or "bad," which is, of course, a basic dialectical opposition itself. Sometimes such positive and negative associations are purely cultural, as in the following oppositions:

rich	poor
introversion	extroversion
beauty	ugliness
conflict	agreement

To see how we tend to associate positively and negatively with such oppositions, try putting each pair into these sentences:

_____ is better than _____.
_____ is worse than _____.

In most cases, one sentence or the other will feel right. But think about circumstances in which reversing the terms in the sentence might be closer to the truth.

Certain philosophical pairings of words in our language do not have inherent or cultural negative and positive poles. It is impossible to say of these that one is "better than" the other, apart from their application to particular conditions. Here are some examples of what I mean by such dialectical pairs:

nature	nurture
society	individual
reason	emotion
past	future
active	passive
natural	artificial
plain	ornate
essential	accidental
general	abstract
means	ends
cause	effect
part	whole
subjective	objective
theory	practice
central	marginal
universal	particular

Only a particular application of these terms to a circumstance will tell us whether one or the other half of such a pair seems to be better than the other. For example, even though neither *objective* nor *subjective* seems inherently better, I may think that it's important to be subjective when judging a painting I might choose to buy but objective when judging candidates for whom to vote. Either term can carry the quality of good or bad depending on the situation.

Assigning value to dialectical oppositions is a basic precondition to the formulation of arguments. Such pairings orient us to ideas: When ideas are in conflict, it is generally because underlying those ideas is a dialectical opposition of some kind, and when we choose one idea over another conflicting idea, it is because we have placed a positive or negative value on the terms of that opposition. In a given circumstance, we associate ourselves, orient our thoughts, with one term or the other of a dialectical pairing.

I do not mean to give you the impression that dialectical terms lead us to think of argument as on either one "side" of an issue or another. We think in terms of dialectical oppositions, but we employ them to serve a wide range of positions, and it is the range of oppositions we have to choose from and the way we associate them (as in the following discussion) that permits any number of positions to be possible. In any argumentative situation, a wide spectrum of potential positions might be taken, not just the choice of one side or its opposite. I am talking about the dialectically opposed terms we use to construct a position, not opposed positions as such. We make use of dialectical terms freely to construct positions. For instance, I may see a particular issue in terms of the dialectical opposition between *justice* and *injustice*, and that will define my position, but on the same issue I might take a different position by framing it in terms of the dialectical opposition between *justice* and *mercy* instead. In one set of circumstances, *beauty* may be opposed to *ugliness*, but in a different circumstance it may be opposed to *truth*. One's position is not predetermined by dialectical oppositions, only made possible by them.

Let me illustrate dialectical oppositions at work in an argument that addresses a complex issue and can't be reduced to a simple "side."

If you have not read Martin Luther King, Jr.'s famous "Letter from Birmingham Jail" (It can be found online at http://www.stanford.edu/group/king/popular_requests/.), please do so at this point. In this letter King makes use of a number of fundamental dialectical pairings, including the distinction between *justice* and *injustice*, as in his references to *just* and *unjust* laws. This dialectical opposition comes to our minds already associated with a positive and a negative polarity. King makes use of this ready-made preference for justice over injustice in his argument that his direct actions in the Birmingham demonstrations, even though against the law, were necessary and therefore right. The dialectical distinction he creates between *direct* action and *indirect* action becomes linked to these values, and the idea of direct action is thereby associated with the value of justice. The situation in which King found himself helped to define for him the opposition between direct action and indirect negotiation, but this pairing is not necessarily already associated with a positive or negative quality: In some situations negotiation is better than direct action; in others direct action is better. King must ally himself with one or the other, in his present circumstance, and he does so by linking the opposition of *direct* action and *indirect* negotiation with the opposition of *justice* and *injustice*. That is, he argues that direct action is necessary in this situation in order to create justice. Notice how in this argument King must also reduce our sense of a strict dialectical opposition between *legal* and *illegal* acts. Also notice that in taking a position against the eight clergy who wrote him the letter to which he responds based on the dialectical opposition between legal and illegal acts, he takes a position with them in his belief that their motives are *sincere*, as dialectically opposed to *insincere*, and in his appeal to shared faith in God.

These are not just word games; King provides the reasons for these associations and disassociations, which are important to his thinking about civil rights issues. But without the oppositions already provided by the dialectical nature of abstract language, he could not provide those reasons in order to get his beliefs across.

If you were to read other writers on the same question addressed by King (from Plato to Thoreau), you would find that similar oppositions precondition the development of the argument. Obeying the law and disobeying the law function as the basic dialectically opposed concepts, but different ways of understanding these concepts, and for choosing one in preference to the other, might result from linking them to other dialectical oppositions, such as:

freedom	slavery
the good of the society	the good of the individual
the good	the expedient
ends	means
violence	nonviolence
wisdom	foolishness
body	mind (or soul)
male	female

What kinds of argument might result?

On Dialectic

The argumentative process of making such distinctions and using them to debate conflicting ideas is itself often called *dialectic*, the process of reasoning from basic distinctions. Dialectical argument is often seen as a process that involves reasoning about the consequences of making certain distinctions. Reasoning from basic distinctions implies a kind of interior dialog, the ability to pursue an idea by asking and answering questions about it. Dialectical reasoning pays attention to the arguments made on different sides of any question. It seeks the best reasons, not just those that support one side. This kind of internal debate is a quality of all argumentation, as I am using that term in this book (based on a dialectical opposition of *inquiry* and *fighting*). We engage in reasoned inquiry in the presence of opposing views, or with an imaginary other who challenges our thinking by representing a different dialectical preference.

In this sense, as this book shows in different ways, reasoning is itself a communal process, not just because we reason together but because we reason in response to others' views. These views are both opposed and not opposed to our own. Our ability to imagine what ideas might oppose our thinking is what motivates us to reason, whereas our knowledge of what ideas might agree with our thinking enables us to know where our reasoning must begin and end. Thus, dialectic somehow operates in the very fabric of our thinking. And both agreement and disagreement (one of the basic dialectical oppositions on which this book is based) are necessary to generate the thinking we do.

The Interplay of Dualisms

To explore further how we make distinctions and link them to dialectical pairings, let's go back briefly to Richard Wilbur's game of opposites. As we have already seen, when we make up opposites for words that are not dialectical, words that do not naturally have opposites, we find that our choice is somehow affected by context or perspective. For example, if I ask, "What is the opposite of *shirt?*" a variety of answers are possible depending on the context in which the nondialectical term *shirt* is considered. In the context of pickup basketball games, the opposite of *shirt* is *skin.* In the context of an individual's apparel, the opposite of *shirt* might be *pants.* In the context of boys' and girls' clothing, the opposite of *shirt* might be said to be *blouse.* From the perspective of one's choice of a particular garment, the opposite of *shirt* might be *tank top.* Notice that in each case the very meaning of *shirt* is slightly different. Our understanding of the term changes when we see it in relation to these other terms.

Here's another example. This time ask yourself what context or perspective determines whether each potential opposite seems appropriate.

The opposite of *photograph* is   painting
                                                movie
                                                negative
                                                interpretation
                                                memory
                                                hearsay
                                                postcard

When you imagine a context in which each of these terms might be opposed to *photograph,* you are, in effect, constructing an argument about what the term means. Try playing this game with other nondialectical terms.

In the case of dialectical terms, where opposites are somehow paired in our minds, context may also affect our understanding of the meaning of one or the other term. Let's consider, for example, the meaning of the term *freedom.* *Freedom* is paired conceptually with its opposite: *bondage* or *constraint* or *limitation*—terms that themselves are defined as a lack of freedom of some kind. But what kind? In what contexts might different terms be appropriately said to be the opposite of *freedom?* What, for instance, is the opposite of *free* in each of these sentences or expressions?

Here is your free gift.

You are free to choose only from the items on the menu.

You have ten minutes of free time.

Freedom ends where responsibility begins.

"Free at last, free at last, thank God Almighty, I'm free at last."

"Freedom's just another word for nothin' left to lose."

You are pretty free with your criticism.

He believes in free love.

He's a free agent.

I'm free and easy.

I'm home free.

Do you have a free hand?

In each case, does the meaning of *free* change? Is *freedom* the opposite of *responsibility*, or are they part of each other? Whole philosophical or political systems are built around different answers to this question. *Freedom* means one thing when contrasted to the literal condition of slavery, another when contrasted to social or economic oppression, something else when contrasted with a lack of opportunity or means to take a certain action, and another thing when contrasted to lack of permission to use the car on Saturday night. It seems, then, as if the answer to the question "What is freedom, really?" might be that it depends on what you mean by the opposite of *freedom*.

Dialectical oppositions may themselves provide the context from which we view the meaning of other oppositions, as we saw in the case of King's letter. In such a way, dialectical oppositions form perspectives. Take, for example, the dialectical pair *intellect/emotion*. How does your understanding of the relationship between these concepts change when you look at the distinction in terms of other dialectical pairs, such as the following?

science	religion
objectivity	subjectivity
male	female
art	craft
fact	value

Linking one side of such an opposition with either intellect or emotion creates an association and signifies a preference. From such linkages, if you feel drawn to them, positions follow that give rise to arguments. You can see this by playing with the word *mere* in sentences that combine such dialectical terms:

Science requires intellect, whereas religion is *mere* emotion.

Religion values emotion over *mere* intellect.

True art derives from emotion; a craft is the exercise of *mere* intellect.

Facts must be true, not *merely* believed.*

Arguments are built on the basis of a process similar to this; each of these stated preferences could be supported with further evidence.

Many of the most difficult and divisive arguments that take place around us derive from the association of one set of dialectical terms with another set of irreconcilable dialectical opposites. For instance, *evolution* and *creation*, as pure concepts, may not be necessarily opposed to each other, but looked at from the perspective of the dialectical pair *science/religion*, they are put into

*This exercise is adapted from Wayne C. Booth, *Modern Dogma and the Rhetoric of Assent* (Chicago: The University of Chicago Press, 1974) 17–18.

seemingly irreconcilable opposition. Similarly, *electric chair* and *lethal injection* are not opposites when they are seen as both on the same side of the opposition between *death* and *life* sentences. But when seen in the context of the dialectical pair *humane/inhumane*, they can be put into opposition. *Capital* and *corporal* punishment are put into seemingly irreconcilable opposition when associated with the dialectical pair of *revenge/mercy*. Can you think of other examples of terms that are put into opposition by framing them in the context of dialectical pairs?

There is a kind of free play among dialectical pairs if they are considered only in the abstract. But when we encounter them in the context of serious debates about matters that are important to us, a great deal is at stake when we create, use, and assign value to distinctions based on dialectical oppositions. We make such associations freely and without rules to guide us. The dialectical oppositions of language are available to be used by all of us, no matter what so-called side we take in any conflict of ideas. And we cannot avoid using them.

To return to the *evolution/creation* opposition that is so intractably part of our cultural debates, I recently read an exchange of letters to the editor in our local newspaper in response to articles about the debate over a school board's adoption of science textbooks. One writer tried to make his audience believe that the opposition between creationism and evolutionary theory in this debate is a false distinction because the two can be seen to be compatible if only we make another distinction: between *how* and *why*. Science deals with how questions, this writer argued, whereas religion deals with why questions. If seen this way, he wrote, science and religion do not conflict because each deals with different questions. But in a few days, another letter appeared in answer to this letter, saying that the distinction between *how* and *why* is itself a false distinction because when looked at from the point of view of complete understanding, as opposed to partial understanding, the two questions are not opposed but part of the same whole. Thus, the first writer used a distinction between knowing *how* and knowing *why* to undo a previous distinction, whereas the second writer used a distinction between *complete* knowledge and *partial* knowledge to undo that one.

It's interesting, and sometimes frustrating, to see distinctions arise and collapse in association with various dialectical oppositions. Argument, the process of trying to find the best reasons to support an idea, cannot do without distinctions of this kind, and underlying all arguments, at some level, are various dialectical oppositions. The term *opposition* itself—which is the opposite of . . . what? *harmony? oneness? sameness?*—might suggest to you that arguments always break down into one side or the other. But the interplay among dialectical oppositions of all kinds makes it possible for there to be many sides to any question, not just two, based on the ways one ascribes qualities to or sees things in terms of many kinds of dialectical relationships. We find ourselves in agreement with an argument when we identify with all of the choices made by a writer in putting dialectical pairings together. We find ourselves in disagreement with some part of it when we cannot identify with the way any or some of those distinctions and associations are made.

Some debates in our society, such as the evolution versus creation controversy I discussed above, seem unable to find common ground because the most basic dialectical oppositions on which the arguments are constructed cannot be shared. For example, debates about abortion are notorious for sometimes failing to make sense to people who disagree: The so-called right-to-life argument sees the issue in terms of the opposition *life* and *death* of another human, or between *God's* authority and *humans'*, whereas the so-called freedom-of-choice argument sees the issue in terms of an opposition between *freedom of choice* and *lack of control* over one's own body, or between an *individual's* authority and the *government's*. In order to find any shared ground of agreement from which to conduct mutual inquiry—as opposed to totally missing each other's point—such oppositions have to be reassociated with other sharable oppositions that change the values identified with those terms. This is an especially difficult process when beliefs are attached to the language's most fundamental dialectical pairings, such as *good/evil, right/wrong, appearance/reality.**

I have argued in this chapter that all arguments rely on distinctions, and choosing among distinctions depends on associations with underlying dialectical oppositions. Where do arguments come from, then? In one sense, they come from conflicts that are already present among words in our language. Such conflicts generate arguments in the sense that they give rise to the way distinctions are created. But it's people, of course, who associate themselves with one side or another of dialectical oppositions. So, of course, arguments come from people too. But people who disagree do so because language makes it possible by providing them with dialectical terms that function in their thinking. If these oppositions already exist in language, it's possible to say that although we use language to make arguments, it is also the case that language uses us. That is, ready-made oppositions exist in language that can seem so natural and commonsensical that we are not even aware of them.

Seeing language itself as the source of argument can help us to see that when we struggle to make a case for our ideas, we are not struggling *against* other people but to gain control over our terms, the language we use. Understanding the underlying oppositions that give rise to argument is an attempt to think with and about language rather than have it do our thinking for us. This is a task we share with all others, even those with whom we disagree.

It is possible to become more conscious of the role dialectical oppositions have in our thinking. In this way we might also gain more control of the distinctions we make use of when we compose a reasoned argument. So we need to return to consideration of the basic structural elements of arguments: questions, answers, and reasons. As we do so, think about how

*If you wish to pursue this idea further, I recommend Chaim Perelman's discussion of "The Dissociation of Ideas," in *The Realm of Rhetoric* (Notre Dame, IN: University of Notre Dame Press, 1982) 126 ff., as a good place to begin.

the arguments you read as examples, and even the arguments I make about argument, rely on fundamental distinctions and associations with dialectical opposed pairs of terms. In the next chapter, I link the basic dialectical pairing *ethical / unethical* to others as a basis for making a case for ethical argument.

Questions for Thought, Discussion, and Writing

1. Make a list of dialectical oppositions that have not already been cited in this chapter. Can you link or associate these pairs with other dialectical oppositions? What perspectives or ideas are suggested by these associations?

2. Choose a piece of argumentative writing from a newspaper or magazine, or another class, and analyze the way its reasoning is based on dialectical oppositions or fundamental distinctions. How does the reasoning also link those distinctions to others? What happens to your understanding of or agreement with that reasoning if you imagine that those associations are reversed or replaced by others?

3. Write a dialog between two (or more) characters engaged in a campus or civic controversy. Identify the dialectical oppositions that you want to use to develop the conversation between them. Do you find it difficult to give each participant an equally reasonable voice? Also ask yourself whether your characters are engaged in mutual inquiry or whether they seek to outmaneuver and defeat each other's argument.

4. What dialectical opposition is implied by the last sentence in question 3? How does that opposition function in the way you are invited to engage in argumentation in this book?

chapter

4

Ethical Argument

Ideas in Conflict

Members of a discourse community (such as college or your writing class) agree about many issues but also disagree about other issues of mutual interest. When members of the community care about whether a disagreement is resolved, they look for ways to cooperate and to reason toward the best possible answer to shared questions. You are engaged in such an inquiry whenever you talk to anyone about a problem you share and try to work out a solution. You are engaged in argumentative writing whenever you use writing to respond (whether formally or informally) to a difference of opinion, trying to find support for what you think is a good answer.

The word *argument* itself can be an obstacle to engaging in the process of reasoned inquiry I am inviting you to practice in this book, because that term is also used to identify a cultural phenomenon that emphasizes threatening debate over rational dialog. In her book, *The Argument Culture: Moving from Debate to Dialogue*, Deborah Tannen argues that a warlike atmosphere in our culture leads us to see all issues in terms of polarized sides, or strictly pro and con positions.[1] This produces an adversarial condition in which ideas are debated. Complex issues of public concern are often reduced to only two sides, each of which is seen as trying to destroy the other. The common assumption informing this phenomenon, Tannen argues, is that opposition is seen as the best way to get to the truth. But, as Tannen explains, this oppositional frame can make it seem that victory over the opposition is more important than mutual understanding and collaborative inquiry. When argument is more about winning than about seeking solutions to problems, Tannen argues, everyone loses. In her book, Tannen advocates a change in cultural values, placing the value of engaging in dialog over the value of winning a debate.

I certainly agree with Tannen's attempt to redefine the term *argument*. It is important to our culture to seek dialog to reach mutual understanding.

[1]New York, Ballantine Books, 1998.

We cannot do away with opposing claims or viewpoints; we must engage them.

But *how* we respond to opposition and use it in our communication with each other is up to us.

The word *argument* in the context of argumentative writing in college does not mean a verbal battle between opponents, each of whom desires to silence the other. It means, instead, the search for reasons that will bring about cooperation among people who differ in how they view ideas but who nevertheless need to discover grounds for agreement. Argumentative writing, then, may be seen as a process of *reasonable inquiry into the best grounds for agreement between a writer and an audience who have a mutual concern to answer a question.*

"In moving away from a narrow view of debate, we need not give up conflict and criticism altogether. Quite the contrary, we can develop more varied—and more constructive—ways of expressing opposition and negotiating agreement.

We need to use our imaginations and ingenuity to find different ways to seek truth, and gain knowledge, and add them to our arsenal—or should I say, to the ingredients for our stew. It will take creativity to find ways to blunt the most dangerous blades of the argument culture. It's a challenge we must undertake, because our public and private lives are at stake."

—Deborah Tannen, *The Argument Culture*

The Ethical Turn

The distinction between argument as persuasion and argument as inquiry suggests differences in approach that might be called *ethical*. Whereas argument as persuasion seems to justify the use of any argumentative means that are effective, argument as inquiry justifies only argumentative means that are fair, honest, and reasonable. If the goal is a search for the best grounds for agreement, then it is not consistent with that goal to engage in misleading arguments, withholding or slanting critical information, or substituting techniques like name-calling for giving good reasons. Thus, the approach to argumentation in this book is meant to be ethical, since it invites you to focus on finding and communicating effectively the very best reasons. At the end of Chapter 1, I used the word *ethical* to describe what I called an "earned conclusion." Here, I want to encourage you to consider other aspects of ethical argument.

As Tannen's critique of our "argument culture" makes clear, we are subjected to forms of argument every day that we might wish to judge as unethical. Much advertising and many politicians lie, or at best distort or spin what they know to be the truth, in order to persuade us. Public debate frequently takes the form of degrading or demonizing those who disagree, or misrepresenting others' views. It often seeks to outshout and to silence opposing voices. It may be angry, disrespectful, or threatening. Much of what we encounter in our culture as argument is a kind of verbal aggression. Much of the language we use to discuss argument is therefore borrowed from the language of war:

We have conflicts of opinion, we attack and defend positions, we marshal our evidence, we battle it out.[2] We speak of the battle of the sexes, the war on drugs, the cable wars.

It's no surprise, then, that we are often tempted to use misleading or manipulative means ourselves, and I think it's fair to say that we have all done so at various times. I know I have. My purpose in asking you to think about ethical alternatives to the more debased forms of persuasive discourse in our culture is not to turn us all into saints, or perfect arguers. This chapter is an invitation for you to consider ethical alternatives to the kinds of argument that predominate when the *only* purpose for arguing is to win at any cost.

Most of you are probably familiar with extreme forms of argument practiced on television, radio and films, or in print. Examples like the shouting matches on *Jerry Springer*, or the way Bill O'Reilly tells people with different opinions to "shut up," or the ways in which Michael Moore or Rush Limbaugh employ techniques of persuasion to incite strong feelings among those who are already on their side, could lead one to conclude that hostile forms of argument have become a form of entertainment. It is doubtful that many people watch or read such performers open-mindedly, willing to be persuaded of beliefs they do not already hold. These entertainers never seem to admit of the possibility of being wrong, or that others who disagree might have good reasons for doing so. It seems, therefore, that their purpose is not inquiry or even persuasion but rather a kind of celebration of group identity. "We," the intended viewers, are unified in our belief that "they" are wrong and we are right, and hence most people seek out such performances to feel good about beliefs they already have; that's why I called them *entertainment*. Indeed, they can be entertaining, like watching choreographed violence in a film, even when we are not part of the implied audience of believers.

I recently read some on-line transcripts from episodes of *Crossfire,* a television show in which representatives of the conservative right and the liberal left debate current issues. I found that typically the debaters do not listen to each other. While they often ask questions, they seem not to want to hear the answers, so the opposition generally doesn't bother to answer them. Most of the statements made in the form of dialog are not dialogic; the participants don't respond to each other, and often interrupt each other instead. Half-completed statements are common. Although there is some turn-taking, often one person is speaking, or shouting, at the same time as another. In the transcripts, these moments are referred to as "crosstalk," a term that indicates that two or more people are talking at once so that none of them is being heard by anyone and even the transcriber can't tell what's being said. Can you follow the arguments being made in this excerpt from *Crossfire* about "America's Food Fight"?[3]

---

[2]For a more extensive analysis of the argument-as-war metaphor, see George Lakoff and Mark Johnson, *Metaphors We Live By* (Chicago: University of Chicago Press, 1980), 3–7, 61–65.
[3]http://www.cnn.com/TRANSCRIPTS/0403/10/cf.00.html (aired 10 March, 2004)

BANZHAF: Tucker, read the rest of—read the rest of the opinion. He says McDonald's should be liable because people go in there thinking that a Chicken McNugget . . .

CARLSON: Actually, he doesn't say that.

BANZHAF: Yes, he does.

CARLSON: I don't know what you're talking about. You know that's not true. (CROSSTALK)

BANZHAF: You don't remember the (CROSSTALK)

BANZHAF: I read the opinion. You haven't read it. (CROSSTALK)

ROGERS: A fried piece of chicken is good for you? Who believes that?

BEGALA: Well, you know what—what's not on here. If we were to go into the grocery store and buy any kind of packaged product, it would say the percentage of fat. It would say carbohydrates. (CROSSTALK)

ROGERS: You can get all that.

BEGALA: No, I can't.

ROGERS: Absolutely.

BEGALA: Why not—not to tell you how to do your job, but I am a taxpayer, so you guys do work for me. (CROSSTALK)

BEGALA: Why doesn't Congress make these big corporations put a little logo on here, a little label that says, here's how much fat, how much salt, just arm us with information? (APPLAUSE)

ROGERS: You can get that at the counter. (CROSSTALK)

ROGERS: If we do that, will he stop suing Girl Scouts? That's what I want to know.

BANZHAF: Oh, come on. (CROSSTALK)

BEGALA: Why not label the food?

ROGERS: You get this wacky label kind of thing going on. This year alone, this year in Michigan, they had a wacky label contest for lawsuits, of which we all pay for. Everybody pays for that, every car, every tool for your home, every ladder.

BANZHAF: Why not take the information off the food then, Congressman?

ROGERS: Well, let me tell you. Well, it was a hook, fish hooks. This was the winning prize. Fish hooks came out and said, harmful if swallowed. Thank you very much. I really appreciate that. You've done a lot for your country.

Although such exchanges may be amusing to watch, or perhaps get our blood boiling, crosstalk hardly seems to be an effective or rational way to argue. In reading such transcripts, I also noticed that although many assertions were made, few attempts were made to offer reasons to believe them, as if it were enough to take a position without having to justify it. In place of reasoning, I found many instances of name-calling and *ad hominem* attacks in which the opposition was labeled or condemned rather than refuted, for instance as "a bunch of liberals," or "that gang of ultraconservatives," or "you hypocrite," or "you artful dodger," or "the kind of insane people who talk like that." Other examples are sometimes more extreme, and indeed more creative. This sort of thing may feel stimulating to the participants and the viewing audience, but it doesn't make anyone's ideas any less or more valid.

This is argument as spectacle, a kind of theatrical performance we have come to accept as common practice in our public debates. In popular media and movies, argument is often accompanied by anger, obscenity, or the quick use of force or weapons to "resolve" differences. In some cases, we may find the message of a violent film to be anti-violence. In our daily encounters, however, such verbal or physical violence often goes along with, or perhaps is caused by, the assumption that some disagreements cannot be resolved in any other way, or that people who hold certain ideas are "bad" people who need to be kept separate, or even eliminated. As Tannen illustrates in her book, reasonable communication also breaks down when positions are labeled as belonging to one of two allegedly opposed ideologies—like conservative/liberal, macho/feminist, religious/atheistic. If some ideologies are assumed to be beyond reasons and a matter of gut feeling alone, we may feel no responsibility to argue reasonably. For some, "opinions," as opposed to facts, cannot be defended rationally anyway, just "felt." Some distrust reason because they think it is used only to rationalize a deep desire for self-interest or power. Such assumptions may be used to justify hostile forms of argument that are at best amusing and at worst a poor foundation for arriving at conclusions.

The Fairness Principle

The ethical dimension of such forms of argumentation becomes clearer if we think of speech actions as in the same class as other actions. That is, we use words to perform actions in relation to other people. Our sense of whether an action is right or wrong, even though there is no easy way to tell the difference in many situations, involves our sense of how it affects others. How we act is also a model for the behavior we expect from others, since their behavior affects us. It is from this that we acknowledge that we should act responsibly. Although we often act out of self-interest, it is equally true that we often set aside self-interest in certain situations in which we have an interest in the general welfare of the community with which we interact. In the case of speech actions, we are similarly responsible. If we used words only to get our way, how would this affect how others treat us? You can think of many situations— a dispute with a loved one comes to mind—in which the benefit of "winning" an argument is less than the benefit of trying to reach mutual understanding.

What and how we choose to argue derives in part from values that we hold or admire. We are motivated by such values to find some ideas more compelling than others. Those same values form the basis of many of our ethical choices, whether to act in one way or another toward other people. We also know that such values may be in conflict, and this may motivate us to want to engage in trying to change others' minds. Often, we feel good about being "right" and to have that acknowledged by the agreement of others. It can feel threatening to acknowledge the possibility of other views being just as reasonable as our own. But such feelings need not motivate us to say whatever it takes to win at the potential cost of another value, getting along with others.

The role of values in argument suggests that any argumentative situation is also an ethical situation. We choose to act according to our sense of how we affect others and who benefits. Consider, for instance, a range of environments in which the same argument might take place—an argument, say, about the benefits of marijuana as a medical drug. The question may be argued in a political campaign as a matter of public policy, in a conference of medical researchers as a matter of factual effectiveness in certain circumstances, in a family as a matter of how to help a loved one in pain, in a courtroom as a matter of guilt or innocence according to prevailing law, or in school as an exercise in argumentative writing or debate. In what ways do the stakes change in each case? How does the situation affect what values, and whose, determine the ways participants argue? How differently might participants argue depending on who is affected by the outcome? We might choose to argue differently depending on the answers to these questions in different situations. Such a choice would be an ethical one.

It's not easy to make rules for ethical conduct, and so we shouldn't be surprised to learn that there are no strict rules for ethical argument. In a few isolated circumstances, speech actions such as lying, distortion, name-calling, or demonization are appropriate or necessary—although the idea that these actions are unfair seems generally true to most of us. Such actions certainly feel unfair when they are used against us.

What is *fair*? We've all felt that something was not fair, and sometimes what we meant was simply that it wasn't what we wanted. This is a selfish sense of fairness that we outgrow as we mature, learning instead that what is fair isn't just what is good for us but what somehow applies even-handedly to everyone in the same circumstances. *Fairness* belongs to a cluster of concepts that includes *equity* and *justice*. One way in which Western culture expresses fairness is through the Golden Rule: "Do unto others as you would have them do unto you." Similarly, philosophers may evaluate an action on the basis of whether it can be universalized—that is, by asking whether any particular act is consistent with the way you would want everyone else to behave if it were a universal rule.

There are as many possible speech actions as there are people and situations, so universal rules, even if we accept them, would be difficult to apply to particular circumstances. What to do or say in a particular, unique, complex situation cannot always be deduced from a general rule, and so ethics involves the exercise of judgment. As in other actions we perform, we must make choices among possible speech actions. Making such choices on the basis of fairness, equity, and justice is acting ethically, even when we cannot know for sure which action is right in some universal sense.

It is normally considered unfair to hold other people to standards of conduct that we ourselves feel no obligation to follow. I like to use the term *exceptionalism* to refer to the idea that although one disapproves of an act if performed by others, it is okay to do it oneself, maybe just this once. As a political and religious concept, exceptionalism may justify anything from the practices of the Inquisition or genocide, to U.S. military aggression or discriminatory laws. Rhetorical exceptionalism is everywhere, in the form of speech actions one performs even as one denies those same actions to others. For instance, if I were to make the sweeping claim that "all meaning is impossible," I would be making an exception for the meaning of my claim itself. I once heard someone lament, "I hate clichés; why can't people just tell it like it is?" It is likewise exceptionalist to call one's opponent a "name-caller," or to argue that "we are inclusive, they are exclusive." While such ironies occur frequently in public discourse, the kind of exceptionalism we need to be most careful about is the belief that our own position is too important to risk losing and therefore we are justified in using any rhetorical means whatsoever, including those we would disapprove of others using. But to use this exceptionalist rationale is to act as if a particular idea and its success are finally more important than the quality of the discourse we depend on to make any case whatsoever. That is the rationalization some have used to justify lies, deliberate misrepresentations of others' views, outshouting others, the substitution of slogans for reasons, and all the other means of persuasion we might identify with an unhealthy or polluted argumentative culture. Once again, the Golden Rule seems to be the best ethical principle we have to rely on to make choices in argument. Do not make yourself an exception to the ways you want others to argue with you. When we do make ourselves exceptions to those ideals, we justify others doing so too, with the result that verbal aggression is more likely to replace nonviolent, reasonable attempts to earn agreement.

Some Ethical Precepts

Here are some ethical principles that might be used as a basis for our choices as we argue or disagree with others. I have deliberately not phrased them as rules but as acknowledgments we might make or as ideas to consider as we respond to others' arguments and make our own.

No matter what we disagree about, we share a vastly larger number of agreements. Situations of conflict focus on differences, making it easy to neglect the similarities that must also exist to bring about those situations. A number of agreements necessarily underlie all disagreements, whether we are aware of them or not, such as a shared capacity for language and reason, and a shared belief that it is valuable to contact other minds through communication. It is always possible to find *something* any two people agree on, no matter how strongly they disagree about a specific issue. More abstractly, we share experiences and beliefs that enable us to get along in the world, like feeling heat and cold, or a belief in gravity, or a desire for human contact. My colleague, James Crosswhite, has added to the list this way:

> There is a whole . . . set of agreements that must also be in place before argumentation can proceed. We need not simply a language, we need also agreement on some common facts, truths, values, hierarchies of value—and our relations with one another here are very powerfully ethically charged and very complex. We often need agreements about technical expertise and when to defer to it, about the standards for what counts as knowledge, about the proper way to interpret and present data, about definitions, about genres and their purposes, about when something is clear and when it is not.[4]

Admitting to all such possible and necessary agreements reminds us that what is at stake when we disagree with anyone is only part of the total realm of our relationship.

As we engage in argument, our purpose is not to silence each others' voice on any matter. No argument can eliminate an idea, it can only complicate it. Even if we changed the minds of people who held certain ideas, or silenced those people, the ideas themselves would continue to be available for anyone to think. Even as we attempt to persuade another to a view we hold dear, we would not attempt to change a mind unless we valued that mind and its capacity for thought, like our own. The act of arguing with someone acknowledges that person's ability to reason and to decide. We implicitly grant a kind of freedom to those with whom we choose to argue rationally. Disagreement is unavoidable, but even more importantly it is valuable, since if it were eliminated our own ability to think freely would go with it. Thinking is a communal activity; we do it in response to others' ideas. We need to hear ideas in order to have one.

Disagreement is necessary to the overall well-being of our culture. If we perform our argumentation as if the goal is to establish our ideas while destroying others, then we seem to be implying that our vision of the best culture is one in which everyone thinks one way and believes the same thing. But there is evidence all around us that we need each other's disagreements to keep our discourse community healthy and vital, which includes the challenge of ideas that rub us the wrong way and therefore challenge us to come up with better reasons. Advocacy flourishes in an environment of diversity, the tolerance and coexistence of multiple points of view and ways to live, for the sake of everyone's ability to thrive. While these differences bring about disagreement, they also underscore the necessity of a way of negotiating disagreements that does not lead to the total dominance of a single idea or viewpoint. The interplay of agreements and disagreements forms the dialectic of an open society. Think of

[4]*Ethics and Argumentation,* (Eugene: University of Oregon Center for the Teaching of Writing, 2000) 23.

a discourse community as an ecosystem in which the ability of any idea to thrive depends on the continued existence of different kinds of ideas. Some are in conflict with one another; many are not. Not all ideas must be argued; they can simply coexist, like two species. When they must be argued, they can mutually benefit.

As we enter into discussions of our disagreements, it's always possible that our own mind might be changed in the process. This principle is related to the distinction made earlier between argument as persuasion and argument as inquiry. Persuasion is one-directional and unilateral (one person persuades others to believe a foregone conclusion), while inquiry is reciprocal and bilateral (the ideas of all participants are relevant to reaching a new conclusion). Of course, there are times when the two may appear to be nearly the same, or when the ideal practice of inquiry simply does not recommend itself because too much is at stake. We each have certain issues that we are less willing to consider with open minds. We all have deep commitments and loyalties that form part of our deep ethical make up, whether they are based on religious faith, love, or experience. Sometimes, the need to *win* the argument is great because we perceive the conclusion as too important to risk losing. When much is at stake and our convictions are harder to give up, our willingness to be persuaded may even matter most, since we always face a choice of being open-or close-minded on any question. How open-minded do we want others to be about their convictions, so we can engage in mutual understanding and inquiry? It's best to know when we have made the choice to be obstinate in our belief on purpose. By acknowledging that even some of our most certain convictions might be shaken, we are kept from adopting arguments we know are unfair to the convictions of others. It's then that we ought to feel most required to use the kinds of arguments we would have others use to persuade us.

Any claim or conclusion we wish to argue might turn out to be wrong. Even something so simple as knowing that we have been wrong in the past ought to tell us that we could be wrong again. But belief has a way of feeling permanent and inevitable, so we must remind ourselves also that we came to the conviction in the first place because of acts of persuasion, and that acts of persuasion other than those we have experienced are always possible. I'm not saying that we must be skeptical and relativist in order to practice ethical argument, only that we can acknowledge that our beliefs, however strong, are contingent on other beliefs and subject to conditions. If I have not yet heard all the possible reasons for refuting an idea (and I never will have), then I don't really know what might be said to make me change my mind. This principle therefore relates to the discussion of degrees of belief in Chapter 2.

Our beliefs, conclusions, claims, assertions are only as good as the quality of the case that can be made for them. Unless we hold opinions for no reason at all, we think we hold them for good reasons, and not for bad reasons. This in itself suggests that better or worse reasons are possible and obliges us to keep trying to make better ones. Thus, we exchange arguments in order to measure them against the best reasoning available, whether our own or someone else's.

It's therefore important to judge another's claims in the context of that person's stated reasons for believing them. Here I am invoking what has been called *motivism*,[5] the belief that we can know why a person has made a claim based not on the reasons that person asserts but on the so-called real motives that are always unstated. If I think people use reasons only in order to rationalize beliefs that are actually based on psychological, social, or political drives, then I don't have to listen to anyone's stated reasons or take those reasons seriously. Whatever people may say their reasons are, I know why they "really" believe that. We often doubt politicians' statements, for example, simply because we think they will say anything in order to gain votes. No wonder people on *Crossfire* don't listen to each other; they already have the other person's position explained away, insofar as that person is already seen as having an ulterior motive. Motivism seems therefore strongly related to paranoia. Are we a paranoid culture, I ask motivistically? Up to a point, perhaps.

> "What we call reasons can always be seen through as rationalizations or superstructures or disguises or wishful thinking. . . . I call this dogma *motivism*, for want of a better term, and I call motivism a dogma not because I think that all or most value choices are made on the basis of fully conscious and 'scientifically cogent reasoning,' but because I find many people assuming, without argument, that *none* of them ever can be. 'Look for the hidden motive' has . . . been a slogan in many disciplines, and the unexamined assumption has been that if you can find it . . . you have explained away whatever 'surface reasons' anyone offers for beliefs or actions."
>
> —Wayne C. Booth, *Modern Dogma and the Rhetoric of Assent*

We therefore have a responsibility to be sure we understand what others are saying before we set out to refute or challenge them. Here I can do no better than to adopt a principle from counselling psychology[6]. Understanding is demonstrable only if one is able to repeat someone else's position and reasons back to them in such a way that they say, "Yes, that's exactly what I mean." Understanding is more of a challenge than we are accustomed to make it when we rush to refute or ascribe ideas to people who have never actually uttered them. Taking the time to listen and to understand what others say, in this basic sense, is hard, but necessary if our arguments are to communicate across differences of opinion. A failure to understand can also lead to unnecessary arguments in situations where we think we disagree but in fact only misinterpret another's position.

---

[5] I am borrowing the term from Wayne C. Booth, *Modern Dogma and the Rhetoric of Assent* (Chicago: University of Chicago Press, 1974) 24ff.
[6] See Carl Rogers, "Communication: Its Blocking and Its Facilitation (1951)," *Rogerian Rhetoric: Collaborative Rhetoric for Oral and Written Communication*, Nathaniel Teich, ed. (Ablex Publishing, 1992) 27–33.

Our audience is always potentially larger than our intended audience. This principle might at first seem to conflict with the idea of a discourse community I introduced in Chapter 1. But remember that all communities function in relation to other communities; they cannot be considered in isolation from other communities. Of course, when you write you must "know your audience," a useful rhetorical principle, but in isolation this principle begs an ethical question. If I think of my audience as comprising identifiable individuals with particular traits, not to mention particular beliefs, I am more inclined to make my choice of rhetorical strategies as appeals to those particularities. If I am arguing for only one person, I can design psychological ploys or devise premises based on my knowledge of that person's fears and desires or idiosyncratic beliefs. With an audience of two people, some of those strategies are no longer available to me. With an audience of ever-increasing numbers, what is left for me to use? Only the very best reasons I can. Although it is not possible to conceive a literal universal audience, in attempting to universalize one's appeals one is compelled toward forms of rationality that are not subject to the particularities of one's tribe.

The students whose essays appear in the Appendix of this book wrote them in response to a unique situation, a discussion among their peers of ideas they had all encountered in their reading. These students developed their reasoning in connection with the ideas expressed by others in that discussion. Yet now, as those essays appear to a wider audience of readers of this book, that reasoning is subject to a wider range of reader responses. Although no writer can predict all possible responses, inquiry is carried out both within and beyond the boundaries of any particular discourse community, such as a classroom. I wrote this book, for instance, with college writing students as its primary audience, in the discourse community we share by virtue of writing in and for college. But this means that the teachers of those students are necessarily part of my audience as well, even though their collective interests and needs are somewhat different from the students. And then there are my colleagues who are also scholars and theorists of college composition and argumentation—their knowledge and interests also affect how I write this book. And then there is the possibility of people outside this discourse community picking up this book for whatever reason; how has my understanding of their possible purposes affected how I write here?

Making Ethical Choices

Living up to these ideals is hard, and we may never do so completely, but that should not deter us from trying. Imagine a world in which all of these principles were forgotten and no one attempted to live up to them. Is that the world as you understand it today? It would at least be a world in which all arguments became so deeply polarized that no one could hope to reach anyone with differing views by reasoned words, and only force would be left. There are places in the world where disagreements have reached this point, but thankfully there are many others where at least some attempt is made to practice these ideals. What practical applications do these ideals suggest?

The principles just discussed can be applied to your writing in many ways, depending on the particular circumstances in which you argue. As I list a few examples of such applications, consider what kind of situation might encourage such a choice, and what reasons you might have for making that choice:

- You can openly acknowledge what you have in common with those with whom you have a difference of opinion.

- You can try to restate others' ideas in ways that are most likely to seem fair and accurate to them before trying to argue against those ideas or reasons.

- You can try to address others' best reasons for their positions, rather than their worst ones in order to more easily refute them.

- You can refrain from characterizing the motives that presumably underlie others' positions, and focus instead on the adequacy of the reasons they actually give.

- You can acknowledge that although you disagree with an idea, you do not consider a person bad or even unjustified for holding it.

- You can show how, although you still wish to argue a certain idea, your mind has been changed in some way as a result of encountering conflicting ideas.

- You can adjust your ideas to leave room in them for others' positions, perhaps through compromise, or by asserting your ideas conditionally and provisionally rather than categorically.

- You can acknowledge the limitations of your own ideas, or the conditions under which they might not be true.

- You can revise your thinking and writing by asking whether the particular way in which you have chosen to argue ought to be used by others in situations in which they argue with you.

In what other ways could your writing reflect your attempt to apply the ethical principles outlined in this chapter?

Those principles are, like all ethical guidelines, ideals. As such, it's not always clear how they apply to specific situations, and there may be times when they don't seem to apply at all. This suggests two further considerations.

First, if you decide not to follow one of these principles, do so for a good reason after making a deliberate decision. Such decisions will be rare if you are interested in trying to make your arguments fair and honest. You may have a favorite example of an argument you consider good precisely because it defies one of these principles—and in that case you should be able to articulate why it is an ethical argument after all. When you decide to set aside any of these principles, ask yourself whether you are still engaged in inquiry or whether your writing is doing something else.

Second, it may be humanly impossible to follow all of these principles at once. Most of us have habits of speech and writing that are hard to break, and everyone fails sometimes to live up to some ideal. If we gained some of our habits from watching *Jerry Springer* or *Crossfire*, it will be difficult to replace them with new habits. This can happen only with new models and by practicing different ways. Nevertheless, another ethical consideration to keep in mind is that when we encounter argumentative appeals we consider unethical, or when we make them, we should probably forgive others' and our own all-too-human lapses. No ethical system can neglect to make room for the imperfections of our behaviors, verbal or otherwise. Some of those imperfections result in laws and punishments for those who break them; others simply call for greater tolerance. We are fortunate to have freedom of speech in our culture; we cannot be jailed for what we say. But we take responsibility for what we say, nonetheless, and judge others for what they say. But how much responsibility we take and how harshly we judge is up to us.

Are you perhaps thinking something like this: "Why should I follow any principles for ethical argument when other people don't? I will lose all my arguments. Isn't it fair to fight others on their own terms?" These questions cannot be answered definitively, but if you think of speech actions the way you think about other actions, a perspective on these questions may emerge: Do the same questions apply, for you, to using firearms, or to spitting on people, or to cheating on your love partner? The questions ought to raise even deeper ones about personal integrity as well as the responsibilities we possess for others. No one has answered all such questions once and for all, but it is ethical to keep thinking about them.

Questions for Thought, Discussion, and Writing

1. Think of activities other than war that could provide metaphors for characterizing argument. Could argument be compared, for instance, with gardening, or with photosynthesis, or with dance? Explain how those metaphors and others you come up with might alter our understanding and practice of argument.

2. Find an example of writing that you consider to use unethical means of argument (in a newspaper, in a book, in the media, in your own previous writing, or even in this textbook!), and describe what makes those means unethical. What alternative ways of making the case would you suggest?

3. In my critique of *Crossfire* on page 44, I said, "most of the statements made in the form of dialog and are not dialogic." What does this distinction mean to you? Can you find other examples of this distinction?

4. Read some transcripts from *Crossfire* programs at http://www.cnn.com/ TRANSCRIPTS/cf.html, and give examples of places in which the participants engage in what you consider to be ethical argument. Explain why.

5. The abstract concepts *ethical* and *unethical* constitute a dialectical opposition of the kind discussed in Chapter 3. To what other dialectical oppositions is this one linked in the present chapter (for instance, *fairness/ unfairness, inquiry/persuasion, particular/universal*)? How do these associations further the arguments made here?

6. Find an example of exceptionalism used in an argument, a case in which the author breaks a rule that he or she would have others obey. Is it justified?

7. Which of the nine ethical principles outlined in this chapter do you find the hardest to apply? Which ones resonate most meaningfully for you? Why?

8. Can you think of specific argumentative situations in which it would be ethically justified for a writer to violate any of these nine principles? What features of that situation make such a justification possible?

9. Do you agree today with every position you held five years ago? Think of an example of a conviction you once held strongly but no longer do. What process of thought brought about this change?

10. As an exercise, consider that you are involved in developing a new drug to cure lung cancer. What ethical decisions would be involved in making an argument in the following situations? Remember, lives may be at stake.
    - You are a scientist who does basic drug research.
    - You are a scientist hired by a pharmaceutical company to conduct tests.
    - You are an executive of a pharmaceutical company representing your product to the Food and Drug Administration.
    - You are employed by that company to market the new drug.
    - You are a sales representative talking to a doctor.
    - You are a doctor talking to a patient.
    - You are a politician debating laws to regulate the cost of prescription drugs.

    What do the differences tell you about the nature of ethical choice?

chapter

5

Asking Questions, Generating Ideas

An Idea Worth Writing About

In the previous Chapter, I defined argumentative writing as a process of reasonable inquiry into the best grounds for agreement between a writer and an audience who have a mutual concern to answer a question. This definition is not confined to the academic essay, of course. You have probably written arguments in letters or other informal situations whenever you felt the need to explain or support your ideas. The argumentative *essay* (the word comes from the French for "attempt") is a more formal composition that attempts to deal reasonably with significant ideas. It is the form that college writing usually takes, simply because in an essay a writer encounters ideas directly, for the sake of coming to a new understanding. This process goes on in college for the sake of a larger aim: to help you deal reasonably with diverse ideas wherever you may encounter them.

A significant idea is not necessarily any idea that you happen to come up with. Some ideas are so conventional that they cannot be said to be ours. Some are trivial. Some might seem like good ideas for a moment but turn out to be silly after a bit of thought. Ideas of these kinds occur to everyone. But when we set out to *write* about an idea, it is generally not one of these. We write because we have an idea that is worth writing about. It is one that the writer thinks should matter to other people and that the writer cares enough about to discuss. This means that the writer also thinks that others can be led to share the idea and that the writer, therefore, accepts the burden of communication. If an idea is worth writing about, it must be worth communicating effectively.

Ideas in Context: Audience

Ideas worth writing about do not exist in a vacuum: Writing—even in a diary— is meant to be read, and writers imagine their words entering into dialog with readers when they sit down to write. As I type these words, I focus on the question that governs the beginning of any writing process: Who is my audience, and what is our shared concern? You know that in order to communicate an idea effectively, you need to consider your audience. But have you ever thought about the possibility that you need to consider your audience in order to know what your ideas *are?*

Any idea you choose to argue is to some degree determined by your audience, those members of your discourse community whom you are addressing in your writing. The intention of any piece of argumentative writing combines what the writer has to say and what the audience needs to hear. What is at issue for the audience and the writer both? You are free, of course, to choose to argue anything you like, in an absolute sense, but it is only when you find your audience that you really face the necessity of reasoning well. If I were to argue that "a moon colony should be used for the purpose of manufacturing perfect golf balls" to an audience that in no way cares whether I am right or wrong, then it would hardly matter whether I based my case on good or bad reasons. (Remember Alice and the Cheshire Cat?) But if I argue it in a situation where some people believe that moon colonies should not be used for commercial purposes or that perfect golf balls are a useless commodity, then the reasons I choose will make all the difference in whether I am listened to or not.

Your knowledge of your audience can never be complete, of course. Not only does an audience usually consist of more than one person having more than one set of interests and beliefs, but it may also consist of people who are entirely unknown. The question of who constitutes an audience is not a simple one, nor should it be made to seem simple. It is one of those matters about which you need to make a judgment, using whatever knowledge there is, without being able to arrive at certainty. You do not have to think of your audience as particular people with individual characteristics, nor do you have to invent imaginary readers who function as straw men to be blown over by incomplete reasoning. You can write, instead, to a more general audience assumed to be made up of people who share your argumentative situation, who share the question at issue, and who are capable of reasoning in response to your assertions. Whether you think of this general audience as an extension of the beliefs of a particular person or as a composite of possible points of view, the relevant characteristics of that audience are characteristics that somehow make a difference for how the argument is conducted. If you were arguing about your right-to-life stance, for instance, you would probably not think about the relevant characteristics of your audience in terms of hair color or nationality, but you might think of your readers in terms of religious beliefs or social class.

When you write for an audience, you take on a kind of obligation to that audience that does not exist if you write simply for yourself or if you write just for your instructor or for a grade. We have all done this kind of writing, and it can be valuable—but to write without an audience can often feel as though you are writing without a purpose. Once you have an audience in mind, your purpose is clear: You write for an audience that shares your concerns (but perhaps not your views).

Questions at Issue

It may seem strange to think about a thesis as a response to a question, but if you think about writing as a social act, as a way of entering into discussion about an issue, then the idea that a thesis responds to a question may begin to make more sense. As members of any number of discourse communities, we constantly face questions which we must think about before we respond. The questions we confront as members of communities take many shapes: Is assisted suicide really murder? Does bilingual education slow the process of assimilation for non-English-speaking public elementary students? Should property taxes be raised to fund higher education? Is Hamlet's decision to avenge his father's death a good one? These are not simple questions by any means, but they are worth writing about when they reflect the concerns of particular communities.

Questions like these do not have easy answers; they require careful thought from the members of the communities to which they are posed. Clearly, not all community members would respond to these questions in the same way. As a property owner, I may not like the idea that my taxes could be raised to support local schools. If I have children who attend those schools, my attitude may be different. And what if I am a teacher in a public school? As you can see, a single question may lead me to consider several positions from within my own discourse community, questions that ultimately will help shape my response to the question of whether or not property taxes should be raised to fund education.

Questions like these are said to be *at issue* because to answer them requires inquiry into grounds for shared assent. Different kinds of questions call for different kinds of answers and for answers that take different shapes.

Stasis: Kinds of Questions at Issue

The kind of thesis you compose and use as the basis for your essay will depend on the kind of question that is at issue for you and your audience. Whether a question is at issue depends on the particular situation you are in when you feel compelled to state your case. To understand this situation, it helps to know what sort of question really separates you and your audience, because if the situation calls for you to answer one kind of question and you answer another kind instead, you may not be successfully addressing the audience you mean to address.

Questions at issue may be seen as one or another of these six basic kinds:

Questions of fact arise from the reader's need to know "Does this [whatever it is] exist?"

Questions of definition arise from the reader's need to know "What is it?"

Questions of interpretation arise from the reader's need to know "What does it signify?"

Questions of value arise from the reader's need to know "Is it good?"

Questions of consequence arise from the reader's need to know "Will this cause that to happen?"

Questions of policy arise from the reader's need to know "What should be done about it?"

These are sometimes called *stasis questions*. The *stasis* of any argument is the specific point on which the controversy rests, that point on which one person says "yes" but another says "no" or "I'm not sure." You have often discovered such points when you have listened to someone else's argument and found yourself in agreement with some parts of it but not others. You might have said "Yes, but . . ." and pursued your disagreement in the context of other parts of the argument where you already agreed. The question on which you found yourself doubting was the stasis question, or the *question at issue.*

In any particular argumentative situation, questions of one kind or

> *Stasis,* in English, means a stable state, a point of balance. Similarly, in argumentative writing, the term is used to identify the place where two ideas come into conflict, the meeting point of two balanced assertions. In classical rhetoric, *stasis* (or *status,* in Latin, meaning "place") referred to elaborate systems designed to assist orators in identifying the primary issue to be debated in any particular situation, leading to the discovery of appropriate arguments. The questions here are a more practical version of those systems, which often became unnecessarily complex.

another will be at issue while others may not be. In a discussion of civil disobedience, for instance, controversy may arise over the meaning of the term itself—or it may not. A writer may misjudge the issue by choosing a definitional thesis (such as "Civil disobedience applies only to laws that are unjust," or "Any law is unjust that imposes the will of a minority on the actions of another minority") in a situation where a question of consequence is what, in fact, divides the audience. In his essay "Civil Disobedience," (the text is available at http://eserver.org/thoreau/civil.html..) Henry David Thoreau wrote:

> Unjust laws exist; shall we be content to obey them, or shall we endeavor to amend them, and obey them until we have succeeded, or shall we transgress them at once?

By putting the question in this way, Thoreau assumed that the question of definition (what makes a law unjust?) and the question of value (is an unjust law good?) were not at issue, but that the question of policy (what should we do about unjust laws?) is the one that needed his attention.

More than one kind of question may be at issue, of course, in a particular argumentative situation, and questions of one kind may have to be answered before one can ask questions of another. But the writer who wishes to make a genuine contribution to an inquiry may be aided by thinking about the kind of question that defines the situation. "What is really at issue here? Are we questioning how to *define* a concept, or whether an idea (or action) is *good*, or whether a certain consequence will *result*, or what we *should do* about it?" Trying to place the question in this way is one means by which the writer may meet the audience. Answering the wrong kind of question in any situation will lead to missing the audience—talking at cross-purposes or saying the obvious. You don't want your readers to say, "Sure, but so what?" Ultimately, the question you decide to respond to gives you and your audience a sense of where your essay is headed and what to expect along the way.

Kinds of Inquiry

Different kinds of stasis questions represent different argumentative situations and call for different kinds of inquiry. When *questions of fact* are at issue, it generally means that readers need to be given information or that they require a demonstration that some fact is "in fact" the case. The arguments of science are often of this kind. "At what temperature does water freeze?" is a question of fact, as is "Will this antifreeze work in my car over the winter?" Situations in which questions of fact are at issue are those in which there is an unknown to be discovered.

> When was *Othello* first performed?
>
> Who is credited with the discovery of X-rays?
>
> Is it possible to build a bridge here?
>
> What was the final vote on Measure 6?

Such questions have in common the determinacy of their possible answers. In each case, the answer is a matter of verifiable fact. If the answer could not be verified somehow, then the question must remain unanswered. The answers to questions of fact are either correct or incorrect, true or false, yes or no. Such questions will be more or less interesting—either important or trivial—depending on the subject matter.

There is no absolute test of whether a question of fact is worth pursuing for its own sake. In matters of literature, say, or political science, such questions may have less inherent interest than they would in matters of, say, chemistry. I might find an answer to any of these questions and then find myself asking, "So what?" At that point I would have discovered that the question I had been pursuing was only a doorway into a question of larger significance, a question of a different sort.

When *questions of definition* are at issue, it generally means that the audience does not accept a particular meaning for a word or concept. Although it might seem as if such questions are easily answered by consulting the dictionary, many questions of definition are not answered so easily if they are actually at issue. Definitions may separate people who know what the dictionary says but who must inquire into shared meanings that no dictionary can contain. For instance, if I do not know what *law* means, I can look it up. But if I ask, "What are the different meanings of *law* in Martin Luther King, Jr.'s 'Letter from Birmingham Jail'?" the answer can be discovered only by examining instances of the word in the text itself, which may not define the word for us. Arguments sometimes hinge on definitions that cannot be resolved by verification in the dictionary.

Is Chuck Yeager an astronaut?

Is this film pornographic?

Is abortion murder?

In such cases, the answer depends not only on the meanings of the words but also on the dialectical oppositions the words may imply and on whether certain circumstances match those meanings and oppositions. Such questions may hide deeper issues. Like questions of fact, questions of definition may be ends in themselves or may lead to different kinds of questions.

Questions of definition and questions of interpretation are similar and often overlap. When *questions of interpretation* are at issue, it means that more than the meaning of a word is in doubt; the significance of something needs explaining. Interpretations may apply to the meaning of many words or the significance of events, actions, structures, or concepts. Interpretations can never be answered by consulting a reference work because they refer to what something means to the interpreter.

Is Othello an Aristotelian tragic hero?

Will this new bridge represent the concern of our community for the environment, or will it show others how wasteful we are?

Does the result of this election signify a mandate for all of the candidate's policies?

Does this film advocate the use of violence as a means of social change?

Questions of interpretation generally are at issue when there is a difference in point of view. Interpretations involve looking at a phenomenon from a particular perspective or through the lens of a particular dialectical opposition. Hence, arguments about interpretation often require that the point of view itself be articulated or defended.

Questions of interpretation arise in most fields, especially when the subject of inquiry is discourse or human action. That Hannah Arendt called evil a "banality" is a fact I can verify by citing her work. What she meant, however, is a question with which historians and social theorists have had to struggle. Anthropologists may seek to interpret a ritual act or a social relationship. Sociologists may seek to interpret data collected in surveys. Questions of interpretation result whenever the significance of a word, an idea, an event, or a fact is not self-evident.

Does the potential uncertainty of questions of interpretation make them less important than questions of fact? We have seen just the opposite. Questions of interpretation often attempt to answer the "So what?" questions that matters of fact can raise. Yet, they seem equivocal because they cannot be answered with the certainty of questions of fact. An idea can often have more significance to our understanding as it becomes less certain. As we attempt to go beyond facts and to establish interpretations, we are dealing with our own relation to the subject matter as much as we are with the raw data. What we learn about when we interpret is twofold: We learn about the subject, and we learn about ourselves.

Questions of value are similar to questions of interpretation. When questions of value are at issue, it generally means that people agree on the meaning of something but differ on whether it is "good" or "bad." Like interpretation, then, value depends on one's point of view or the system of values that informs one's judgment. Some standard of good is used as the measure: thus arguments about questions of value often require one to articulate standards. "Is this essay worth an *A*?" The answer obviously depends on whose standards of judgment are being used. Yours may differ from your teacher's, and each of you will judge accordingly. Any argument about the issue will have to address both those standards and the features of the essay that they apply to, a question of interpretation. Questions of value nearly always depend on answers to questions of interpretation.

Although some standard of good and bad is at issue in value questions, other words are generally used to communicate a sense of value. *Value terms* are words that already imply a judgment of good and bad. Thus, the assertion *"Huckleberry Finn* contains only racist stereotypes," although offered as a neutral interpretation, would generally imply that racist stereotypes are not good. The statement "This film is not pornographic, it is erotic," although seeming to answer a question of interpretation or definition, invokes a dialectical opposition based on value. Questions of definition and interpretation can be questions of value in disguise.

Questions of consequence are at issue when people find themselves disagreeing or wondering about cause and effect. Answering questions about what causes some occurrence or what result some event will have requires interpretation. "This bridge will help the economy of our city by encouraging more construction of homes across the river." This statement makes two *causal* interpretations. Causality is subject to varying degrees of certainty. "Will the bridge encourage more home building?" is a question that might not be as difficult to answer, or as likely to be at issue, as the question "Will more homes across the river help or hurt our city's economy?" Answering either question will require argument about causes and their probabilities.

> Do opinion polls discourage people from voting?
>
> What is the effect of too much television on children?
>
> Will tax exemptions on capital gains stimulate investments?
>
> Can the slaughter of elephants be stopped by banning the sale of all ivory?

Speculations, rather than controlled experiments, are necessary to determine reasonable answers to such questions. Yet, like scientific experiments, those speculations must consider which variables make the difference. Thus, most speculations about cause and effect are conditional: "It depends on . . ." or "Yes, if. . . ." Arguments about probable causes generally acknowledge that certain conditions must prevail and seek to demonstrate that they do. For instance, to argue that the banning of the sale of ivory would end the slaughter of elephants, you would have to show a causal link between the sale of ivory and this slaughter. *If* ivory comes only from the illegal slaughter of elephants, and *if* that is the only reason elephants are slaughtered, then banning the sale of ivory might have this effect. In making this case, it would be your responsibility to show that these conditions pertained.

Because most questions of consequence, unless strictly scientific, can be answered only conditionally, it might seem as if they are useless to argue. Think, however, of the vast number of questions of consequence that must be argued if we are to know how to solve important problems in our lives and in society. We seek to solve such problems using the best reasoning we can construct, even if it does not constitute absolute certainty.

When *questions of policy* are at issue, it generally means that readers differ on whether, or how, to take a particular action. Such questions are answered with a recommendation, a prescription, or a preference for some action. Questions of policy thus arise from situations in which alternative actions are possible, and the problem confronting those for whom such questions are at issue is which of the alternatives is best. You can see why such answers also are conditional, because they depend on acknowledging that the action will achieve its end (a question of consequence) and that the end is desirable (a question of value).

> Should television networks voluntarily refrain from announcing voting results in the East until the polls close in the West? Should Congress vote to force them to do so?
>
> Should this bridge be built? Should properly taxes be used to pay for it?
>
> Should the school board remove *Huckleberry Finn* from the school library?

How should we respond to this action?

Should AIDS prevention information be distributed to children? What form should it take?

Policy questions, like questions of consequence, must be answered conditionally. If the action will bring about a specific result, and if that result is desired, then it follows that the action should take place. But it does not necessarily follow absolutely. Who should perform it? Will negative results accompany the positive one? Are there other, better, ways to achieve the same end? Such considerations always complicate policy issues.

As we have seen, questions of fact, definition, interpretation, value, consequence, and policy are interrelated. No argument is likely to be confined to only one kind of question. Arguing for an answer to one kind of question can imply that other kinds of questions are already answered. In any argumentative situation, some questions will not be at issue while others will define the stasis of the argument. This is why it is helpful to ask what *kind* of question is really at issue.

For instance, if you chose to argue that "the university should send AIDS information to all students," your thesis would answer a question of policy. But it would also presuppose that your audience shared that kind of question with you and that other kinds of questions were not at issue. The discourse community might be divided not on the policy question but on a question of consequence, such as "Will this particular piece of information be effective in educating students about AIDS?" You may not be in agreement with your audience on a question of interpretation, such as "Is the university responsible for AIDS education?" or of value, such as "Is AIDS education important enough to justify the expense?" Questions of fact may need to be settled first, such as "Can the university afford this?" or "Do the students already know everything the information provides?" And so forth. Knowing whether a particular kind of question is at issue requires an understanding of what the people in the discourse community are actually saying to each other, what they already agree about, and what they desire to find agreement about. The complex network of issues and stances that characterizes any real controversy is a little easier to understand by thinking about the kind (or kinds) of questions that are actually at issue.

Visual Argument

The discussion of argument in this chapter has focused on argument that occurs in words, but we should reflect also on the kinds of arguments that involve visual images, how they are similar and how they differ from exclusively verbal ones. Consider, for instance, this image, which illustrated a magazine article about obesity in America.

This image has à thesis. It makes a claim. Just like a sentence that makes an assertion, it has parts, even though we do not experience them in a particular order as we do a sentence. Visually, we more often take in the idea as a whole, but we get our sense of that whole by noticing particulars. Also like a verbal assertion, the image is understood to be making a claim in the context of other information. To fully understand the nature of the thesis being asserted here, we have to know already Grant Wood's famous painting *American Gothic*, which this image parodies. If we know that painting, the visual impact of the original is part of what we experience when we see this version. The person who produced this visual argument relied on the audience being aware of this context.

Can you put the argument being made by this image into words? Doing so entails both a gain and a loss. The thesis of the image, since it is not in words, could be stated in a variety of ways, depending perhaps on how it grabs you, and each way of stating it would constitute a different verbal claim:

Americans are overweight.

The average American is overweight.

Overweight Americans are proud of it.

Overweight Americans worship food.

The economic practices of the farming industry cause obesity.

. . . and so forth. Images might be said to be inherently ambiguous in this way because of the nature of images as nonverbal. They work effectively, in part, because of their ambiguity. At the same time, these attempts to put the thesis into words rob the image of its power; they all seem reductive. The verbal statements are ineffective compared to the impact of the visual statement. The image is more than an assertion of a claim; it is a complete experience of an attitude.

As we saw in Chapter 2, the impact of a visual thesis results from someone's selection and arrangement of details. In the above image, the table fork (replacing Grant Wood's hay fork) comes as a surprise, and it was put there for that purpose. Some surprises, however, may be accidental, since it is the nature of visual images to be rich in details. The photo of the women drinking in Chapter 2 contains details to which you might respond, even though the photographer or the editors may not have intended them as part of the message. In assessing visual arguments, we may need to distinguish between details that are relevant to the thesis and those that are not.

Visual arguments may be distinguished according to the kinds of stasis questions they answer. The following image is an editorial cartoon from the World War II era:

I presume that image makes a policy argument about the war in the Pacific, asserting visually that President Roosevelt should send General Douglas MacArthur after General Tojo. How does this argument work to make that claim effectively? It employs the metaphor of war as chess. It puts Roosevelt in a dominant posture (the cartoon is intended for Americans). It caricatures Tojo not only in racial terms but in terms of his apparent bewilderment and comparative lack of skill at chess. Notice, too, that in order for the cartoon to make its claim, it needs to add the word "CHECK," in case we didn't read the visual clues clearly. We are often helped to interpret visual images by the addition of language.

Here is another editorial cartoon from the more recent "war on terror."

Without the words, this image would be more difficult to interpret as an argument. Here the visual and verbal statements work together to produce a thesis, in this case a consequence argument. It seems to be making the claim that Bin Laden's actions have had the unintended consequence of harming the whole religion of Islam. Yet the cartoon derives its power from having echoes of deeper meaning. It also suggests that those who react against Islam, or take Islam as the enemy (which could include many Americans), are mistaking the true cause for a false one. In each of these two interpretations, our understanding of the thesis depends on our sense of what question at issue is being addressed. Part of the power of visual communication is that the answer can be both at once.

It is also therefore possible for visual information to make several arguments at the same time. We are most accustomed to this complexity when we see information being presented graphically. Consider, for example, this chart, taken from a U.S. government website:

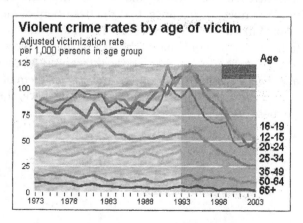

Here is evidence that might be used to draw a variety of conclusions, and the compiler of the chart seems not to be making any particular claim. Here are some possible conclusions this information might encourage (others may occur to you):

fact Since 1993, violent crime rates have fallen most among the 12–15 age group.

interpretation At age 65, you become relatively safe from violent crime.

value The decade of the 1990s was a violent one.

consequence The election of Bill Clinton in 1992 resulted in a decline in violent crime.

policy Successful measures to decrease violent crime must be continued.

All such conclusions are subject to counterarguments, perhaps even using the same data. The information provided by the chart is itself subject to interpretation: What is meant by "violent crime"? How were the data collected? How was the National Crime Victimization Survey redesigned after 1994? As in the case of strictly verbal arguments, we assess the potential conclusions based on the clarity, reliability, and relevance of the evidence.

Even though visual images in our culture often seem to be making no claim, they nevertheless convey *stance*, as I used the term earlier to mean an attitude toward a subject. Much daily communication occurs nonverbally—for instance, in familiar icons like these:

We understand such symbols because, like words, they have acquired arbitrary meaning. We know, for instance, that the deer symbol means "watch out for deer" not "kill the next deer you see." The stance taken by such symbols relates to the regulation of behavior; they tell us what we are supposed to do and not supposed to do. In other words, they argue. Many visual icons of this kind are available to us by computer, and we use them often in email communication to convey stance and attitude—for instance, the emoticons or smileys like these:

:-)   :-*   {(:-)   :-)~

There are dictionaries online that identify the meanings of such icons, in case we haven't kept up with the innovations.

Information is often presented with an even stronger stance, as in the use of so-called infographics, like this chart:

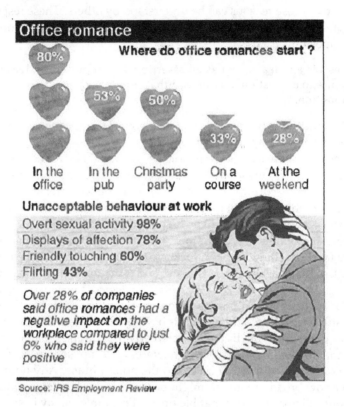

Deciding what is information and what is illustration can sometimes be difficult in infographics. But even the details that do not constitute the information in the chart are selling that information in a particular way. On the subject of visual argument, I probably don't even need to mention advertising, since you already know that the images there are designed to persuade you to purchase a product. The kinds of visual appeal found in advertising range from associating the product with other desirable things to overt appeals to nonverbal but nevertheless unambiguous appeals to our sexual desires or financial greed. The advertising industry knows better than anyone how to argue psychologically— that is, by appealing to desire or fear through visual images—except possibly the government!

What a Thesis Does

Responding to a significant question at issue presents a writer with certain responsibilities: to be sure that sufficient reasons exist for believing an idea and to be sure that those reasons can be understood by others. These responsibilities are present throughout the writing process. They begin when one thinks about composing a thesis.

> A thesis is an idea, stated as an assertion, that represents a reasoned response to a question at issue and that serves as the central idea of a composition.

Each of the terms of this definition has special significance for the process of composing a good argumentative essay.

A thesis is an idea. . . . Some people use the word *idea* to mean something like topic or subject, phrases that indicate an *area* of potential interest, such as "economics" or a "cure for cancer" or "my first encounter with Professor Smith." These phrases might be said to be broad or narrow subjects, but they are not yet ideas because they do not say anything *about* economics or *about* a cancer cure or *about* the first time I met Smith. Perhaps you have had a teacher who was fond of telling you to narrow your subject. Such advice misses the point, unless that teacher also pushed you to come up with an idea by saying something about your subject. The noun *economics* is not an idea. The narrowed (or focused) noun phrase "economic conditions in South Africa in 1875" is still not an idea. "Economics is bull" *is* an idea—although, of course, not a very good one. The difference between noun phrases that are not ideas and statements that are ideas lies in the verb. Ideas are sentences; they complete a thought by connecting a verb to the noun phrase. Any noun phrase, no matter how broad or narrow, might become the basis of many ideas, even totally contradictory or incompatible ones. "Economics is my best class" is a very different idea from "Economics is bull," and yet both apparently share the same subject.

A thesis is . . . stated as an assertion. Not all ideas are stated with the intention of asserting something. Even though an idea must be a complete sentence, not all sentences are uttered for the purpose of asserting a proposition. "Go away" is certainly a sentence that communicates, but it does not seem to be proposing anything as true. It expresses a desire but does not put forth a claim. "I guess I'll take a walk." "What a day for baseball!" "Please tell me how to get to the geology building." "Gimme a break!" Sentences, ideas, can perform many other actions besides asserting.

To assert is to claim that some condition is the case. Each of the nonassertions above could be made into assertions by making them into such claims. "A walk would be good for me right now." "Sunny days are best for baseball." "Geology is to the left of Art." Assertions propose ideas to which one might respond, "No, that's not the case," or "Yes, that is the case." As you can see, making assertions implies that one believes in what one has just said. To seem to assert without belief would be a different kind of action: to lie or to joke. Assertions imply a willingness to defend an idea against the possibility that it might not be the case.

A thesis . . . represents a reasoned response to a question at issue. An assertion is worth writing about when not everyone already believes it and when people should care whether to believe it or not. A thesis answers a question, in other words, that people are really asking because they do not already share the answer. As we saw previously, all assertions answer a stasis question of some kind. Not all assertions answer a question at issue. Consider these assertions and the questions to which they are answers:

It's raining.	Is it raining?
Today is election day.	Is today election day?
You should vote "no" on Measure 6.	Should I vote "yes" or "no" on Measure 6?
Measure 6 will violate your constitutional right to own a handgun.	Will Measure 6 violate my constitutional right to own a handgun?
The Constitution does not make handgun ownership a right.	Does the Constitution make handgun ownership a right?

Are the questions to which these assertions respond *at issue?* You're right if you answer "it depends." It depends on who is asking them and why. It depends on the context in which the question is asked. A thesis is a response to a *situation*, which includes a community of people who, for their own reasons, are addressing certain questions. There are situations in which these questions might constitute questions at issue, and there are other situations in which they would not. The difference is whether the answer calls for argumentation. Is there doubt whether the answer should be believed? If I assert that "it's raining" in a situation where the question is not at issue—where no one cares whether it's raining or not or where everyone is satisfied by my mere assertion—then there is no issue to be argued. If I assert that "today is election day" in a situation where everyone already knows it, then there is no issue. In this case, however, the question at issue might become, "What, then, should we do about it?" and argument might ensue over whether it's worth going out in the rain to vote. Then again, it might not, if that question is not at issue. If I am talking to some friends who have already decided to vote against Measure 6, then my statement "You should vote 'no' on Measure 6" would not be at issue, although my statement "Measure 6 will violate your constitutional right to own a handgun" might be at issue if those friends were divided on *why* Measure 6 should be defeated. If I were addressing an audience of uncommitted voters, my assertion "Measure 6 will violate your constitutional right to own a handgun" might address a question at issue. But if that audience happened to believe that the Constitution does not provide citizens with such a right, then I would have missed them with my arguments because I chose to address the wrong question. I would have to back up and address the question of whether there is, in fact, such a right. Only by finding the question at issue and arguing for an assertion that answers it do I find my audience.

The judgment of whether you have focused on such a question must be made by thinking about your audience. What do they already believe? What answers do they share with you? On what issue are you divided? To what assertions of yours will they say, "Yes, but . . ."? Such questions help you decide whether to argue this assertion or that one, and the decision can change from situation to situation, from audience to audience.

As a reasoned response to a question at issue, a thesis cannot be taken for granted. It is determined by a process of inquiry into the question. A stance that does not emerge from inquiry is sometimes called a knee-jerk response to indicate that it is formed as a reaction without thinking. Keeping a critical reader in mind is one way to be sure you give a thesis adequate consideration before asserting it unequivocally. And then you may find that a qualified assertion is better than an unqualified one.

A thesis . . . will serve as the central idea of a composition. This final part of the definition points us forward, toward the process of development by which a thesis becomes an essay. The last two parts of the definition, one pointing backward and one pointing forward, suggest that a thesis has two functions that stand at the center of your thinking about what you will write. It represents the result of a process of inquiry, and it represents the beginning of a process of putting together sentences and paragraphs to make a whole essay. As a beginning, a thesis provides a basis for further thinking you must do to produce a fully developed argument. If a thesis is reasonable in the sense that it emerges from your deliberations about what assertion to argue, it should also be reasonable in the sense of being able to be supported by reasons.

We have already seen how the thesis stands for the whole composition, in a way, and represents its overall intention. This means that the parts of a composition are, in some sense, implicit parts of its thesis. As a complete idea, a thesis has several parts, and identifying them is a basis of planning what the essay must say and how it must say it.

For example, suppose I have decided to argue that:

> Hydroelectric power provides an acceptable alternative to nuclear energy in supplying present power needs.

Assuming that the assertion satisfies the definition of a thesis in other ways (although it may not), consider how it points forward to an essay. Its parts must become parts of that essay, because that essay would not be complete without satisfying certain demands the thesis makes. The thesis calls for the essay to describe hydroelectric power and nuclear energy, and also to compare them according to how each satisfies "present power needs," which must also be described. Finally, the essay must make the essential connection that is asserted in its verb phrase, "provides an acceptable alternative to." This will necessarily entail a discussion of *how* hydroelectric power is preferable to nuclear power, probably by showing that it has some benefit that nuclear power lacks or that it avoids some risk that nuclear power creates, or maybe both. There are further parts that this essay might contain, of course, but these constitute the essential elements that an essay written from *this* thesis must contain in order to be complete. (This process is the subject of Chapter 7).

This example illustrates that any thesis statement creates responsibilities and provides the basis for fulfilling them. You are free to choose your thesis or to change it at any time, but, having done so, you become responsible for somehow developing the essential parts of your thesis and for *earning* it. There are limitless kinds of possible thesis statements, but all have essential parts that must be developed and connections that must be made.

Knowing precisely what your thesis is helps you to think about what to include and what not to include in your essay. It will help you to distinguish between details that are necessary and those that are superfluous. Of course, no rule will tell you exactly what details are necessary and sufficient to make a complete essay, because every thesis makes its own unique demands. But a precise thesis makes the choices easier to recognize.

The Need for Precision

In the stasis section of this chapter, we saw that different ways of asking a question can lead to different kinds of inquiry. Likewise, the way a thesis is phrased can be very important. Different ways of asserting the same stance can lead to different ways of developing an essay. Hence, you should be ready to ask yourself, "Is this precisely the question?" and "Is this precisely what I want to say?" You should be concerned about the precision of your language as you think about questions at issue and thesis statements.

Let's look at a couple of the examples I used to illustrate questions of consequence and see how they might be rephrased more precisely. The question "Do opinion polls discourage people from voting?" seems very general, not because the issue itself is a large one but because the terms are imprecise. Anyone seriously asking such a question would probably intend it to refer to a specific context in which certain kinds of opinion polls occur. But it's hard to tell what is meant when the question remains so vaguely worded. Changing the wording to make it more precise would change the nature of the issue, as in the following possibilities:

Does the early publishing of exit poll results discourage people from voting?

Do people think that opinion polls accurately predict the outcome of elections?

Do opinion polls actually change public opinion?

Do opinion polls encourage a bandwagon effect that makes it impossible for an underdog to win?

Other ways of stating the question are possible. Each of them implies a different meaning for the original question. Any of them could have been intended by the original question. So, until a more precise form of the question is found, it isn't clear exactly what the issue is.

Similarly, the question "What is the effect of too much television on children?" is imprecise. Some people would call this a loaded question because the answer is implied: "Too much television" is already a bad thing, and bad effects are what "too much television" must have. But to make a distinction, the issue probably depends instead on saying what the effect of a *precise* amount of television is. The inquiry might in fact need to address the kind of television and not just its sheer quantity. Also, the issue may need to be defined in terms of some children (i.e., preschoolers) and not others. It all depends on what the members of the discourse community are actually trying to decide. Thus, any of these rephrasings, and others, are possible:

Does lengthy exposure to violent programming cause antisocial behavior in preteens? (What is "lengthy exposure"? What does *violent* mean? What is "antisocial behavior"? Which "preteens"—in which social conditions? . . .)

Do cartoons about consumer products confuse children about the difference between advertising and entertainment? (All such cartoons or those of a certain kind? What does *confuse* mean here? What is "the difference between advertising and entertainment"? . . .)

My further questions about each of these rephrasings indicate that precision is a relative matter. Readers can always ask for clarification. The wording of a question or a thesis statement is precise enough when both you and your reader understand it to mean the same thing. You can't know with certainty, of course, when this will be, so you have to anticipate as many questions as possible and clarify as necessary. When you are part of an argumentative situation that calls for you to write what you think, the effort of drafting and redrafting possible questions at issue and thesis statements for precision is worth it in helping you think clearly about your argument.

Generating Questions About Fiction

For this course, you will probably read mostly nonfiction argumentative essays and develop questions at issue in response to those essays. But how do we understand an author's argument when it is presented through a fictional text? Asking this question assumes that fictional works—short stories, novels, plays, poems, and films—actually do convey arguments. Remember that even though you are writing academic essays to make your arguments, all writing is an act of communication intended to have an effect on an audience. This means that all writing, even fiction, conveys a *kind* of argument.

The best way to understand the arguments made in fiction is to consider one of the main differences between essays and stories: Whereas a nonfiction essay presents an argument that is given *directly* to the audience, a fictional story presents a plot with characters to whom we respond and through whom a complex argument is made *indirectly*. This indirectness makes the arguments presented in fiction harder for us to respond to because we usually can't locate claims or infer a thesis. We respond sympathetically or unsympathetically to characters and their actions rather than to reasons.

Disagreements about how to understand a fictional argument arise from potential for ambiguity. For example, in the course of a story we may begin to care about a character who eventually goes off to fight in a war. One reader might make an assertion about the novelist's argument: "This author is glorifying war because she gets us to care about a character and, as a result, we respect his decision to go to war." Another reader might object with a more convincing argument, pointing out aspects of the story the other reader has failed to consider: "No, the author doesn't glorify war because the author lets us see that the character is thinking negatively about war at the same time as he goes. In other words, the author is critiquing war because he's showing how strong the pressures are on an individual if they can make someone who is opposed to war decide to fight despite those objections."

These assertions could be developed in an essay with a close look at the elements of the story: How do we know that we are supposed to respect one character and not another? How does the author guide us to have these reactions and feelings? How is the argument complicated when an author leads us to care equally about two characters who disagree in a story? Answering these questions will help guide these two readers in supporting their assertions about the argument conveyed in the story. The question at issue for these two readers is based on *understanding* because both share a common concern. They both want to answer the question "what argument about war is being made by the author of this novel?" But what if our second reader convinces the first reader that the novel does actually critique the war? If they agree on an understanding of the novel, then they might move to a question at issue based on what Wayne C. Booth calls *overstanding*.

A question at issue that leads to overstanding must be based on a shared common ground of understanding: In this case, our readers agree that the author of the novel is critiquing war. At this point, they can move from questions of interpretation to questions of value, consequence, definition, or policy. A possible question at issue in terms of overstanding might be asked in this way: "Is the argument made as convincingly as it could be?" In answering this question, our two readers might again disagree. One might argue that even though the critique is clear, it isn't as convincing as it could be because the character doesn't die in the war. The reader might argue, "If the author wants to critique war, that critique is limited because the main character we care about lives. As a result, we never have to experience the emotions of sorrow and despair that real people experience when they lose someone they care about."

This reader's argument is based on the idea that emotions must be appealed to in a way that corresponds with emotional responses to similar events in the real world. Our second reader might respond in several ways arguing that the novel does effectively critique war. First, he could argue that other characters we do care about in the novel do die and as a result, we experience the necessary emotions of revulsion to war. This argument would be based on the shared assumption that those emotions are necessary for the argument to be effective. The question at issue is whether the novel appeals to those emotions in the reader. However, our second reader might question this concept itself by agreeing that those emotions are never invoked in the reader while arguing that the author doesn't need to use this emotional appeal to make his argument.

We can consider another type of question that involves overstanding: "*Should* the author be making this argument?" This question leads us to evaluate a fictional argument even if we agree that the argument is well made. For example, we might agree that a novelist is advocating the use of violence. And we might agree that the argument is conveyed as well as possible. Still, we might want to overstand by pointing out the ethical problems with writing novels that make this kind of argument. On the other hand, we might argue that a novel critiques war but doesn't make that critique as well as it could. Still, we could argue that flawed arguments such as this one are better than convincing arguments that we find ethically wrong.

Stasis questions that come from reading fiction can lead to argumentative essays about issues that are important to our discourse community, a community that includes readers of novels and stories and viewers of fictional works in movies and other forms. These kinds of arguments affect how we respond to ideas as much as direct arguments do, and we can think about them in similar ways.

Revising a Thesis

The process of rethinking and redrafting a thesis is important because it helps you to confront questions in your thinking while changes still can be easily made. It is much easier to rephrase a thesis statement until it works than it is to try to revise a whole essay that has gone off in a confusing direction because it is based on a poor thesis. You cannot predict every feature of an essay in advance, of course, but you can at least have the advantage of thinking through potential directions that an essay might take. Revising a thesis carefully can help you to avoid premature commitments to ideas that may not work out.

You can use these questions as a guide to revising possible thesis statements:

- Is it an *idea?* Does it state, in a complete sentence, an *assertion?*

- Does it answer a question that is really *at issue* for the audience? (What *kind* of question is it?)

- Does the thesis say exactly what I mean? Are the terms I use precise and clear?

- Has it developed out of a process of reasoning? Have I considered each side of the issue adequately?

- Can it be developed reasonably?

A thesis that satisfies these conditions helps you to see clearly what responsibilities you must meet as you compose an essay in support of it.

Attempting to revise your thesis using these questions will have its payoff in a more coherent, better-argued essay. But it will also prove to be difficult if you feel locked into your ideas and can't change your mind. We feel close to our own ideas, and it's hard to think of them as things to be manipulated and fiddled with, like a clay sculpture. It helps to remember that just because they sound clear and convincing to us, a reader will not necessarily come at them with the same familiarity. I recommend going over these questions with a friend in your class, or as part of a workshop in class where others ask these questions about your thesis statement and you ask them about theirs. Get others' points of view. Try out suggestions. Change the wording just to see how it sounds. Let yourself play with the idea in order to get used to feeling less locked into the version of your thinking that emerged on the first attempt.

Nothing can guarantee that you will come up with a good thesis. How we have good ideas is simply part of the intuitive mystery of the mind, and no rules can be written to account for it. But trying out a thesis and then thinking about rewriting it—with the five criteria in mind—is one way to keep your thinking alive and focused in a productive direction.

Questions for Thought, Discussion, and Writing

1. Identify the thesis of a piece of argumentative writing (or a visual argument) and then ask yourself who the intended or implied audience of that thesis is. What else about that writing (or visual image) confirms or refutes your answer?

2. What kind of stasis question is each of the following? How do you know? Under what circumstances might each be at issue? What related kinds of questions might also be at issue in each case?

    a. Are groups that use dangerous drugs in religious ceremonies exempt from laws against use of those drugs?

    b. Do college administrations have the right to censor the contents of student newspapers?

    c. What makes a real marriage?

    d. Are scientific experiments that cause pain to animals necessary?

    e. Do grades inhibit learning?

    f. Does giving large amounts of money to a college entitle the donor to tell the college how to use that money?

    g. Is mandatory drug testing for athletes wrong?

3. Say whether you think the following statements fit the definition of a thesis. Why or why not? If they could be improved, what would the writer have to think about?

    a. I want to write my paper about sports and society and how it should be changed.

    b. Some people just don't know how to take a joke.

    c. I wish people would stop bugging me about what I'm going to do with my life, so I can find out.

    d. The widespread use of surveillance cameras in public places has increased people's fear.

    e. The use of *he* and *man* to refer to both men and women is sexist.

    f. *The Federalist Papers* should be read by all students before they graduate from high school.

    g. All teaching will someday be done by computers, leading to a more effective education for all students.

4. What responsibilities does a writer accept in choosing any of these statements as a thesis? What parts would an essay about each of them have to contain to be complete?

    a. Legalization of marijuana would give young people greater confidence in government.

    b. Procrastination, more than any other cause, leads good students to perform badly on assignments.

    c. Belief in a CIA conspiracy to murder President Kennedy has led critics of the Warren Report to misinterpret its findings.

    d. Overpopulation is a greater threat to world peace than nuclear proliferation.

    e. Eradicating cigarette smoking by the year 2020 should be a priority of the U.S. government.

    f. A clear conscience is not necessary for happiness.

5. After you have discussed an issue in class, construct a thesis that represents your response to that discussion—that is, something you have to say that addresses some question that was at issue for the class. Considering the five criteria on page 77, revise that thesis until you think it would provide you with a good basis for writing what you have to say in the form of an argumentative essay. Then show that thesis to other members of the class for whom the question was also at issue, and see whether their responses lead you to want to make further revisions.

6

Giving Reasons

What a Reason Does

A reason is any idea that functions to support another idea. It is nothing more than the answer to an implicit question, "Why?" It invites the reader to agree with one statement by linking it to another statement that explains why it is true. A reason, then, is anything one might say after *because* or before *therefore*. Reasons, of course, do not have to be connected to conclusions by such words. They can imply such a relationship simply by being asserted along with the conclusion.

> The present arms control negotiations do not go far enough.

> These negotiations do not include discussion of biological and chemical weapons.

These two assertions are connected by an implicit *because*. If they were presented in reverse order, they would seem to be connected by an implicit *therefore*. Any assertion can function as a reason.

> The current administration is not really serious about arms control.

> The present arms control negotiations do not go far enough.

Here, the same assertion that functioned as a conclusion takes on the role of a reason when put beside a different assertion.

No idea is necessarily a reason or a conclusion until it is put into relation with another idea. *Reasoning is a process of creating relationships between ideas in such a way that belief in one is intended to follow as a consequence of belief in another.*

Statements that explain why without actually arguing in support of another statement are also called *reasons*. For instance, if I said, "I want to go to the mountains for my vacation *because* I have hay fever and need to get away from the grass seed pollens," I would have explained my reason, but I would not have given a reason to believe that it is in fact the case that "I want to go the mountains." Of course, no such argument is needed in this case; an explanation will suffice.

Before going any deeper into the question of how reasons work, I want to clarify one possible confusion that results from the ambiguity of the word *reason*. The word can refer to an explanation of cause or motive, or it can refer to a statement that argues for belief. This distinction is important, because in talking about reasoning in this chapter I am focusing on the second meaning.

Here is an assertion:

> The Supreme Court has made it harder for African Americans to achieve representation in Congress.

If I responded to this assertion by asking "Why?" I might be asking either for an explanation or for a reason to believe the assertion. In answer to my questions, I might get answers of either sort:

> Because the Court is inherently racist.

or

> Because the Court has repealed voter's rights legislation.

The first reason answers the question "Why has the Court made it harder for African Americans to achieve representation?" or "What are its motives?" The second reason answers the question "Why should I believe that assertion is true?" Both of these are reasons. Each is potentially important. But only the latter reason argues directly for the assertion to be believed. So when I said that "Reasoning is a process of creating relationships between ideas in such a way that belief in one is intended to follow as a consequence of belief in another," I did not use *reasoning* to refer to the kinds of explanations we often introduce with the word *because*. I am referring to those *because* statements that answer the implicit question, "Why should I believe that that assertion is the case?"

In this sense, any assertion can function either as a conclusion or as a reason, because any assertion that is used to substantiate another (answering "Why is it true?") can also be substantiated by another reason. Here, for instance, is a paragraph in which some of the sentences seem to have this dual function:

> Ours is a paradoxical world. The achievements which are its glory threaten to destroy it. The nations with the highest standard of living, the greatest capacity to take care of their people economically, the broadest education, and the most enlightened morality and religion exhibit the least capacity to avoid mutual destruction in war. It would seem that the more civilized we become the more incapable of maintaining civilizations we are.[1]

[1] F. S. C. Northrop, *The Meeting of East and West* (New York: Macmillan, 1946) 1.

This writer has made a series of assertions without labeling them as reasons or conclusions by adding connective phrases. But we experience the sentences as functioning logically anyway, simply by understanding what one sentence has to do with another. After analyzing these relationships, we could make them explicit (at the expense, perhaps, of the dignity of the author's prose):

> Ours is a paradoxical world. *How do I know this? Because* the achievements which are its glory threaten to destroy it. *I think this is the case because* the nations with the highest standard of living, the greatest capacity to take care of their people economically, the broadest education, and the most enlightened morality and religion exhibit the least capacity to avoid mutual destruction in war. It would, *therefore*, seem that the more civilized we become the more incapable of maintaining civilization we are.

The first sentence is supported by a reason in sentence two, which in turn becomes the conclusion of another, more detailed reason in sentence three. The last sentence is a conclusion based on the reasons offered in sentences two and three, which is itself a reason explaining the general assertion in the first sentence. People often speak of writing as having a "line of reasoning" because the sentences of prose are often held together in this way; one reason gives rise to the need for another. Reasoning is the glue that holds the ideas together.

As this example also illustrates, any reason, because it is an assertion, can be supported by another. But a writer cannot keep supporting reasons with reasons forever. This passage comes at the beginning of a book that offers much more specific support for these general claims as it goes along. But, however much support is given, it must stop somewhere. At some point, the writer must decide to stop answering the question "Why?" A line of reasoning must result from consideration of what assertions to support and what reasons to develop, because it cannot, obviously, support and develop all potential lines of reasoning that might be followed. Of all the potential reasons for asserting that "Ours is a paradoxical world," this writer had to choose those he thought best, based on his sense of his audience. The reasoning available to be used always exceeds the scope of a piece of writing. Once he chose a line of reasoning, the author had to decide how far to pursue it. Writers make such decisions by asking themselves what makes a good reason and how far it must be developed. In order to pursue one line of reasoning, we have to give up the pursuit of some other. Our problem as writers of arguments is to decide which of many possible lines are worth pursuing and which are not. This consideration, in relation to a thesis, will be what determines the shape, or structure, of the composition.

The Enthymeme: Connecting Reasons and Conclusions

At this point, we need a name for the relationship created between a reason and a conclusion. I will call this combination of assertions an *enthymeme,* a term adopted from classical rhetoric. It is more open and flexible than any of the terms I might have adopted from formal logic. For many people, *logic* suggests mathematical formulas and rules that must be followed. For the purpose of gaining more control of the logical process that underlies our writing, it is sufficient to think of reasoning as a creative, generative process rather than a system of prescribed rules and formulas. We reason all the time without trying to follow any rules or fit our thoughts into predefined patterns or stopping to consider whether those connections conform to logical models. I use the term *enthymeme* to refer to any combination of ideas in which a conclusion of any kind is supported by a reason.

Enthymeme was used by the Greek philosopher Aristotle when, in his treatise on rhetoric, he needed a word to describe how reasoning works informally in our every-day arguments, where we do not necessarily use the mathematically rigid forms of logic. In Greek, the term combines *en* = *into* and *thymos* = *soul* to suggest the way that reasoned language is able to produce belief. Aristotle called the enthymeme the "body (or substance) of proof" and said it was the rhetorical version of the logical syllogism. The ideas we argue rhetorically, for Aristotle, are those that "are capable of admitting two possibilities" and so exist in the realm of the probable rather than the universally true. Thus, what makes the enthymeme different from the logical syllogism is that in ordinary discourse the enthymeme contains statements that are contingent rather than universally true, it does not have to assert all of the underlying premises of the reasoning, which are understood, and its validity is based on making reasonable connections for the audience rather than strictly valid inferences. In this book, the enthymeme is a generative form designed to help a writer bridge the gap between his or her reasoning and the beliefs of the audience, as discussed further in Chapter 7.

Enthymemes occur throughout our discourse whenever we connect ideas in this way:

Idea 1   *because*   Idea 2

or

Idea 1   *therefore*   Idea 2

In the first case, Idea 1 is the conclusion. In the second case, Idea 2 is the conclusion. The following pairings of ideas are each enthymemes because they connect a conclusion to a reason:

The toxic waste disposal business is a noble career goal, because a healthy environment in the future will depend on proper elimination of harmful chemicals.

Free the monkeys now! (We need the laughs.)

We have to win this election. So vote early and vote often!

As the examples show, the conclusion-reason model by itself does not guarantee that an enthymeme makes connections that are reasonable. Some ideas can be put into such a relationship and seem unreasonable, whereas others seem reasonable. What makes the difference? What makes some enthymemes seem compelling? What makes a conclusion seem to follow?

Connecting the Enthymeme and the Audience

The relationship created between a reason and a conclusion is not self-contained. It makes implicit reference to other ideas that help to bind the reason to the conclusion, making it seem to follow. Before discussing serious examples of this process, let me give you a nonsense one, just to show how it works:

Suppose two moms are talking about the man one of their daughters is dating. One says, "That boy Jason, he stays out too late at night." The other replies, "And that's why he'll never be wealthy." Has the second parent jumped to a conclusion? Well, that depends. It depends on whether the two ideas these two moms have asserted are connected by a third idea, which neither of them actually said. Of course, that idea is the proverb "Early to bed, early to rise, makes a man healthy, wealthy, and wise." If these parents both believe that proverb is true, then the second mom may not be jumping as far as it first seemed. She asserted a reason, but it only seems like a reason if we perceive and accept that connecting truth. The second mom's statement assumed that this truth was shared between the two of them. She didn't have to say it out loud. It was implicit in her reasoning.

So, the inferential process at work in the second mom's thinking is something like this:

Stated reason: Jason stays out late at night.

Unstated assumption: Early to bed, early to rise, makes a man healthy, wealthy, and wise.

Stated conclusion: Jason won't ever be wealthy.

As long as this unstated assumption is a matter of agreement, the reason seems like a reason. As soon as the assumption is denied, or if it is not shared at the outset, then the reason seems like no reason at all.

When enthymemes are asserted, they imply more than they say because reasons somehow appeal to assumptions that constitute the given condition behind the reasoning. Enthymemes therefore can be said to derive from beliefs that the particular audience is assumed already to have accepted as given. The choice of one reason or another to support a conclusion results from an understanding of what sorts of agreements can be assumed in one's audience.

If I were to argue, for instance, that "America is in great shape," I could draw on a wide variety of potential reasons to use as support for this assertion.

If I chose to support it by saying "because hamburger consumption grows by 10 percent every year," I would be making a very risky assumption (as well as imagining a very uncritical reader who would share it). I would be basing my reasoning on the implied precondition that consumption of hamburgers is an index to a country's well-being. If I chose to support the assertion by arguing "because our products set the trends in international markets," I would be assuming my reader already believed that "Any country that sets the trends for other countries' markets must be in great shape"—also a risky assumption. If I chose to argue the assertion by saying "because national unemployment has fallen to 6 percent," I might be basing my reasoning on an assumption that is somewhat more likely to be acceptable to a critical audience, that falling rates of unemployment signify national health. This is not a complete argument, of course, but it is on somewhat firmer ground.

Here is an example of enthymemes used in an actual argument, in a brief passage from Martin Luther King, Jr.'s "Letter from Birmingham Jail."

> A law is unjust if it is inflicted on a minority that, as a result of being denied the right to vote, had no part in enacting or devising the law. Who can say that the legislature of Alabama which set up the state's segregation laws was democratically elected? Throughout Alabama all sorts of devious methods are used to prevent Negroes from becoming registered voters, and there are some counties in which, even though Negroes constitute a majority of the population, not a single Negro is registered. Can any law enacted under such circumstances be considered democratically structured?

Having already seen that certain dialectical oppositions are at work here (in Chapter 3), let's now consider the logic of King's case. King's reasoning supports the conclusion that Alabama's segregation laws are unjust. This conclusion is itself unstated, but we perceive it because the reasoning makes it seem to follow. That reasoning depends on enthymemes that also work on the basis of assumptions, either stated or unstated:

Conclusion: Alabama's segregation laws are unjust.

Reason: Those laws are inflicted on a minority that had no role in enacting them.

Assumption: Any law that is inflicted on a minority that had no role in enacting it is an unjust law.

The reason here is itself the conclusion of another enthymeme:

Conclusion: African Americans had no role in enacting Alabama's segregation laws.

Reason: African Americans were prevented from voting for the state legislature.

Assumption: Anyone prevented from voting for the legislature has no role in enacting laws passed by that legislature.

Real arguments, like King's, are often hard to reduce to the underlying enthymemes from which they derive their reasoning. But the enthymemes are there, nevertheless, providing the basis on which the argument's actual sentences are formed. The enthymemes represent the reasoning of the argument, even though that reasoning may be explicit or implicit, directly or indirectly conveyed in the language of the argument.

I have thus far talked about enthymemes as a basic structure of reasoning. I have distinguished three kinds of statements that make up enthymemes: conclusion, stated reason, and unstated reason or assumption. In the sections that follow, I explain how principles of informal reasoning can help you to think about selecting a line of reasoning, and then how you can test its logic.

Informal Reasoning

In our various discourse communities, we rarely demand a standard of proof as rigorous as that which pertains in science and mathematics. Some people think we ought to demand such a standard, but they are not always able to define it. The mathematical truth that $9 + 5 = 14$ is expressed in symbols that are assumed to mean exactly the same thing to everyone. The quantities referred to by the numbers and the operations referred to by the symbols are said to come very close to this degree of certainty: "Water is wet." Obviously. But the statement is self-evident; that is, it needs no evidence other than itself. It is so obvious that no one would argue with it. And if anyone did decide to argue with it, testing its self-evidence, they would begin by asking "What do these words mean?" This is one of the ways that lawyers are taught to think of the so-called self-evident in language. It seems self-evident that, if there is a law against spitting on the sidewalk, and if somebody spits on the sidewalk, he or she has broken that law. Yet this person's lawyer might ask us to ponder the unpleasant (and deceptively simple) question "What is spit?" before rendering judgment. We might, in the process, discover that what seemed obvious is not.

When we reason about ideas that are not self-evident and when we use ordinary language (rather than mathematical symbols) to do it, we must think of reasoning as an activity *guided* by a sense of probability but not *governed* by rules of valid inference. In other words, rather than mathematical formulas to tell us whether our reasons lead to true belief in our conclusions, we rely instead on our sense that they *seem* to support conclusions with more or less certainty. Although rules guide our sense that $9 + 5 = 14$, no such rules are available to us to account fully for our belief in (or disbelief of) statements about most actual questions at issue, statements such as "Computer simulations can replace tests on live animals in medical research" or "Politicians' private conduct is an important measure of their suitability for public office." In the world of real issues that demand real answers from us, we must settle for agreement based on the best available reasons rather than expect perfectly reliable methods of reaching conclusions.

Here are two key points about the enthymeme and informal reasoning:

1. Enthymemes express what we think here and now, and why we think so, rather than permanent, stable, unambiguous truths. They express our reasoning concerning questions of interpretation, value, consequence, and policy in the absence of a mathematically perfect system of logic to apply to such questions.
2. Enthymemes are not, therefore, to be judged according to a mathematical standard as either valid or invalid. They make more or less adequate, weaker or stronger, arguments relative to the knowledge and beliefs of the intended audience.

All real arguments probably seem somewhat sloppy compared to the elegant and strict proofs of geometry. But this does not mean that we cannot talk with some precision about how they work and apply some standards to how we judge them. These standards are matters of judgment. We have already applied one such standard in the preceding chapter: An argument must address a question that is actually at issue or it will not seem relevant to its intended audience.

Exploring the Audience Connection

Another kind of informal connection between reasoning and its audience is the direction in which the reasoning moves, up or down a ladder of abstraction. Does it move from the general to the particular or from the particular to the general? Neither way is better nor yields more reliable conclusions. Different circumstances might call for one or the other kind of reasoning. If members of the discourse community are connected by the assumption of certain general principles, then those principles can be used as a basis for reasoning toward more specific conclusions. If specific facts or details can be taken for granted by the members of a different discourse community, then those may be used as a basis for reasoning toward more general principles. The choice depends on what one thinks the audience already knows.

It is possible for a reason to be stated in the form of a general principle from which a more specific conclusion is derived. It is also possible for a reason to be stated in the form of a specific instance from which a more general conclusion follows. In these examples of each kind of enthymeme, consider what the audience is assumed to believe already that might have helped to determine the direction the enthymeme moves:

From General to Specific

1. Grades should be abolished because the purpose of education is to teach people, not to rank them.

2. Handguns should not be outlawed because the Second Amendment of the U.S. Constitution establishes the right to bear arms.
3. War would be less likely if women outnumbered men in the Senate because women seek compromise more readily than men do.

From Specific to General

1. Grades do not accurately assess what students have learned because test scores reveal only a small part of the knowledge a student may have.
2. Handgun ownership should be unregulated because many people have protected themselves from violent assault using unlicensed handguns.
3. More women need to be elected to the Senate because 95 percent of women in state legislatures voted pro-choice.

Of course, *general* and *specific* (a dialectical pair) are relative to each other. No statement is inherently either general or specific, although it may seem so when compared to another statement. Thus, the conclusion that "The Olympic Games promote world peace" could be said to be general in relation to this reason:

> because countries with incompatible types of government must learn to compete in athletics using the same rules.

but specific in relation to this one:

> because world peace is made more likely whenever countries cooperate to bring about international events.

You may already have noticed from these enthymemes that when specific reasons are stated, general principles tend to be assumed, and vice versa. Here's a simple example:

Conclusion: Rap music is designed to shock parents ...

Stated reason: ... because its lyrics advocate teenage sexuality.

Assumption: Parents are shocked by lyrics that advocate teenage sexuality.

This argument is based on the specific kinds of lyrics contained in the songs and would be developed by showing how those lyrics do in fact advocate teenage sexuality. The audience does not need any more evidence that such lyrics are shocking to parents. But this emphasis assumes a certain kind of audience. Consider the difference if the stated reason is changed from the specific one to the general one:

Conclusion: Rap music is designed to shock parents ...

Stated reason: ... because parents are shocked by lyrics that advocate teenage sexuality.

Assumption: Rap lyrics advocate teenage sexuality.

This argument assumes an audience that already knows what the lyrics advocate but does not already agree about what does and does not shock parents. Thus, some reasons might need to be developed, whereas others can be allowed to remain undeveloped because they are assumed. This decision depends on whether the audience is most likely to agree on the general principle or on the specific facts. Of course, developing both kinds of reasons is often necessary.

When it is the general principle that can be assumed and the specific reason that must be developed, the reason is sometimes said to define the *burden of proof*. The term probably brings to mind a courtroom because in court settings the law itself is not on trial and forms the general principle of most arguments, so the facts and whether they fit the general law must be argued:

Conclusion: Sidney S. must pay child support to Sylvia R.

Stated reason (burden of proof): Sidney is the natural father of Suzie R., Sylvia's two-year-old daughter.

Assumption: The law requires men to pay child support to mothers of children they father.

If Sylvia's lawyer can establish that Sidney is the natural father, the conclusion will follow. If Sidney's lawyer can show that he is not, the conclusion will not follow. Neither spends any time arguing that the assumption is or is not true. (They will leave that argument for an appeal to the Supreme Court.)

The concept of burden of proof functions in other kinds of arguments, too, even though the proof called for may not be a factual kind.

Conclusion: State education money should not be used to fund intercollegiate athletics ...

Stated reason (burden of proof): ... because intercollegiate athletics has a negative effect on the education of the students.

Assumption: State education money shouldn't pay for anything that has a negative effect on the education of students.

In any real situation in which this argument would be proposed, the stated reason would have to be developed and the assumption would probably need no further explanation. (Once again, this depends, of course, on the audience.) But although this reason establishes the burden of proof, the statement cannot be proved except to offer more reasons. *Burden of proof* can simply mean the responsibility to develop the argument further. In the following section, I consider some of the ways in which this responsibility may be met. Conclusions are reached by means of reasons that are meant to *appeal* to the audience.

Kinds of Appeal

When we talk about wanting to reach an audience with our argument, we sometimes say we want to appeal to them. Another way to discuss informal, practical reasoning is to distinguish reasons according to the *kind* of appeal they make. Now that I have talked about the role assumptions play in making our reasons sound like reasons, let's explore what kinds of reasons are available to us.

In general, we can distinguish three kinds of appeal:

- the appeal to authority
- the appeal to emotion
- the appeal to the logic of the case

The first kind seeks to establish belief in an assertion by referring the audience to the credibility of a source. Appeals of this kind range from the writer's establishment of his or her own expertise to citations from others who are assumed to be believable on a given subject. It is a common form of reasoning, and it takes its power from our willingness to grant superior credibility to others based on their credentials. Such appeals depend on our willingness to accept an idea based on *who* says so.

The second kind of reason, the appeal to emotion, seeks to establish belief in an assertion by referring somehow to the reader's desires. Appeals of this kind can range from the writer's outright manipulation of the reader's feelings to the construction of reasons out of shared moral principles such as justice or mercy. This is also a common form of reasoning, and it takes its power from our willingness to grant superior credibility to ideas that correspond to our preference for what ought to be true.

The third kind of reason, the appeal to the logic of the case, seeks to establish belief in an assertion by showing it to be a necessary consequence of belief in some other idea or ideas. Appeals of this kind can range from the use of proven experimental data to the suggestion that one idea follows directly from the acceptance of another one. This common form of reasoning takes its power from the sense of necessity that accompanies logical inferences. Such appeals differ from the first and second kinds in that the conclusion seems to follow and to remain valid no matter who says it or whether we wish it were true.

It might seem from this description that the third kind of reasoning is the best. To be sure, it seems to be the purest kind of reasoning, insofar as it does not depend on the seemingly irrelevant considerations such as accepting authority or submitting to emotion. But these considerations often enter into our reasoning, to a greater or lesser degree depending on the kind of conclusion we are arguing. One could probably not persuade a mother and father that their love for a child is irrelevant to their reasoning about the child's education. An art critic could probably not be persuaded that emotion is irrelevant to his or her reasoning about the qualities of a painting. And although we may all want to question authority at times, we all probably accept it as reasonable at other times, as when we admit someone else's expertise. Even arguments that seem purely logical often seem to deserve more or less belief based on their source or on how well they accord with our desires.

Perhaps the best way to demonstrate how these appeals work is to discuss a few examples of enthymemes of each kind.

Appeals to Authority

Appeals to authority establish an idea based on the credibility of its source. Thus, each of these examples, in its own way, is an appeal of this sort:

An exciting game of tennis relieves stress because it works for me.

An exciting game of tennis relieves stress because it says so in Dr. Merit's *How to Relieve Stress.*

An exciting game of tennis relieves stress because several studies have shown it.

Here are three reasons put forth in support of the same assertion. These lines of reasoning might be developed further. Each suggests a different kind of discussion, however, and we must decide initially whether the basic reasoning underlying that potential development is sound. If we were to make this decision on the principle that appeals to authority are never sound, none of the examples could be said to provide a good reason for believing the conclusion. But, in fact, they provide adequate reasons for accepting the conclusion in certain circumstances.

If, for instance, the question at issue is whether tennis ever relieves stress, the testimony of a single individual that it does, as in the first example, would be one way of answering that question convincingly. Once that testimony had been given, who would dispute the fact that, for that individual, the claim holds true? This issue would be better supported by the reasoning in the first example than the reasoning established in the second example because the best judge of whether one's own stress has been relieved is oneself, not the writer of a popular self-help book. But Dr. Merit's authority to make a general claim about the value of tennis for others may be greater than the authority of any single amateur based on a few Sundays on the court. If the issue is how best to relieve stress, the reasoning in the second example might be more adequate than in the first. This would depend, of course, on how credible Dr. Merit is. Why should I take his word for it? Because he signs himself "Dr."? Certainly not. I should take his word for it based only on what he has to say for himself. If all Merit has to say is that he has enjoyed many rousing tennis games and felt better afterward, then he could hardly be trusted as an authority on what other people ought to do. But if Merit's reasoning proceeds along the lines suggested in the third example, his authority might become more credible—as credible, at least, as the authors of the studies he cites.

Anyone can *say* that something is true "because several studies have shown it," but the speaker's authority is then only as good as the authority of those studies, whatever they are. Sloppy studies based on inconclusive samples or weighted by inappropriate assumptions need not *show* any such thing, even if that is what they conclude. Here, then, is an appeal to authority that is appropriate only if the studies themselves are reliable. Such an argument would have to depart from its appeal to authority and talk about the nature of the studies themselves. Studies can be used as appeals to authority, or they can be used as appeals to the logic of the case. As mere authorities, studies will generally provide weak support. As a context for discussing the reasons the studies themselves offer in support of a conclusion, their use can be quite appropriate.

The appeal to authority provides appropriate or inappropriate reasons, depending on whether someone's special knowledge, or testimony, is relevant to the issue. Some issues call for such reasoning. It is important to consider, however, whether a conclusion would continue to be true no matter who asserted it—and if that is the case, authority might provide relevant reasons that are nevertheless insufficient. Suppose I were to argue, for instance, that

U.S. foreign policy is inconsistent. My political science professor said so.

I could, in that statement, be said to have chosen a more appropriate appeal to authority than if I had chosen to argue the same conclusion by saying "Julia Roberts said so." My political science professor can probably be expected to know more about the subject than Julia Roberts does. But the appeal to authority is not my only choice and probably not the best one. The issue underlying the assertion is not one that calls for anyone's testimony. It calls for an explanation of what it is *about* U.S. foreign policy that makes it inconsistent, independent of what my professor or anyone else might say. If I can read the newspaper, chances are I can offer this explanation without having to find an expert to agree with me.

Appeals to Emotion

We are sometimes taught that reason and emotion are opposites, and indeed they can function as dialectical pairs, as I illustrated in Chapter 3. By contrasting emotion with reasoning, the emotional appeal can be made to seem unreasonable. There's an old joke ridiculing emotional appeals: A man accused of murdering his mother and father asks the court for mercy *because* he is an orphan. But emotional appeals may be a perfectly legitimate form of reasoning. After all, it is possible to argue reasonably that mercy is justified. Emotion, in this context, refers to a range of human responses that is much broader than what we might mean in casual utterances such as "stop being so emotional." In the case of issues having to do with what is right and just, appealing to emotion is unavoidable because our sense of right and justice is a feeling as well as an abstract belief. Our feelings inevitably, and properly, enter into our sense of what we *should* believe. Some value statements may legitimately function to arouse our consciences. We rarely respond well to arguments that seem to us cold and objective, or devoid of human feeling.

So, appeals to emotion provide appropriate reasons in certain circumstances. But, like appeals to authority, they do not generally offer the best support available unless the issue specifically makes the reader's desires relevant. Here are three examples of reasons offered in support of a single conclusion:

> Students should support the clerical workers' strike by boycotting classes because only scabs will go to class during the strike.

> Students should support the clerical workers' strike by boycotting classes because joining just causes shows courage.

> Students should support the clerical workers' strike by boycotting classes because the clerical workers are underpaid.

In different ways, each of these reasons appeals to the reader's desire. The first example is a kind of threat, and it appeals to the reader's desire not to be thought of as a scab. This kind of name-calling would probably not be effective, but there is a power, nonetheless, in reasons that act on the fears of the audience. "You should not go into Kasstle Park alone at night because if you do you may be a victim of a mugger." This is not an unreasonable statement, even if it uses a strategy similar to the scab argument. What makes that argument seem inappropriate, however, is that the issue—whether or not students should boycott classes—is not answered by such a threat, the way the issue of whether or not one should venture alone into Kasstle Park at night is answered by noting the potential danger. *Victim* is a term applied to people who are mugged, whereas *scab* is a label used to denigrate people who disagree. No one would choose to be a victim, but people can decide for reasons of their own not to participate in the boycott.

Just as the first example appeals to emotion by threatening the reader with a derogatory label, the second example works by flattering the reader with a positive image. The reasoning connects a desired image on the part of the reader with a desired action on the part of the writer. As a reason for believing that students should join a boycott of classes, however, the appeal is weak. It may flatter the reader into thinking that he or she can be a courageous defender of a just cause, but it does not provide support for the justice of the cause itself. The reader is asked to take part in a cause to be courageous, as if any cause would do. This answers the question of why students might *want* to join the clerical workers, but it does so in a way that serves the appearance of the students more than the cause itself.

In the third example, unlike the second, the reasoning answers the issue by referring to the needs of the workers. Hence, the third example seems to contain reasoning that is more relevant to the issue. The justness of the cause, not the reader's desire to escape or to acquire a particular image, is the basis of the appeal. However, that reasoning is also based on an appeal to emotion in that it arouses the reader's sympathy. Why, in other words, is the fact that the workers are underpaid a good reason to support them? It is a good reason because we desire that people should not be underpaid; we want fairness. Thus, although the reasoning seems more logical, it nevertheless depends on the reader's sense of compassion and a preference for fair treatment of the clerical workers. It may not be as blatant an appeal for sympathy as arguing that the workers cannot afford to feed their families, but it is the same kind of appeal.

Appeals to the Logic of the Case

Appeals to the logic of the case derive one idea from another independent of the writer's authority and the reader's sympathy. The use of this kind of reason does not guarantee that the specific reason chosen will be appropriate, of course. Although no such guarantee exists, one can test the logical adequacy of a reason by looking at its relevance and connection to the claim. You may already have encountered this kind of testing in the logic of a valid syllogism. However, because of the kinds of questions the enthymeme addresses, we are interested here more in the relative strength and weakness of lines of reasoning than we are in the kind of strict mathematical validity sought by formal systems of logic.

Actual discourse rarely comes in the neat categorical statements of formal logic (even though such logic may underlie the reasoning). The principles for exploring the logic of a case that we will use are *relevance, connectedness, relative precision,* and *circularity.* In each case, it is the relation of the unstated assumption to the reason and conclusion that is being explored. As readers and arguers, we usually understand such assumptions based on our intuitive sense that our conclusions are connected to our reasons by the bridge of obvious truths. Yet, as you saw in the discussion of dialectic in Chapter 3, much of what underlies our reasoning is not obvious to us. Being as precise as possible about the way the unstated assumption is working makes your reasoning clearer to you and to your audience. The following four techniques for evaluating the logic of an enthymeme are not meant as formulas for mechanically processing your arguments but rather as considerations that may help you to explore the implications of your own reasoning and revise your thinking.

Relevance and Connectedness

It is possible for a line of reasoning to contain true or acceptable claims and yet fail because those claims do not connect with each other. Here is an obvious example:

Lambs are not good pets because people eat meat.

The difficulty is that the reason and the conclusion seem to address different issues. The reason says nothing about the qualities important in a good pet but rather speaks to people's culinary preferences. Although the two might be related within the broad topic of people's relation to animals, they lack direct relevance to each other.

Most arguments in actual discourse are less obvious than this nonsensical example. Here is a realistic example of an enthymeme in which a lack of relevance makes the relation between the reason and conclusion seem too remote:

> Commercial television threatens to diminish the intellectual standards of American society because most people would rather watch television than read.

The conclusion says that the threat to diminished intellectual standards is television. The reason given does not say anything about *why* television is such a threat. The question at issue answered by this enthymeme is: "What threatens the intellectual standards of American society?" If commercial television is the answer, then the reason must be about television as well. The stated reason is about how most people prefer one kind of activity or another, not what television does. Although that reason is related to the topic, it is not directly relevant to the question at issue or to the conclusion. After all, if these same people read nothing but magazines about celebrities and trendy fashions, their intellectual standards might be as low or lower than if they watched television.

Here is a revision of the television enthymeme that attempts to make a more relevant connection between reason and conclusion but that may not yet be adequate:

> Commercial television threatens to diminish the intellectual standards of American society because it portrays people who value only money and status.

The reason does address the nature of television and therefore has more relevance to the issue, although the way it makes the connection may still be too remote. There is an assumption linking them: Things that portray people who value only money and status diminish intellectual standards. Yet the connection between the reason and conclusion could be stronger. If it is the case that television portrays people who value only money and status (and, of course, such a generalization is itself too sweeping), this by itself has no obvious relevance to television's threat to intellectual standards. The conclusion is about what television does to intellectual standards. The reason is about what television portrays. But the enthymeme does not make a connection between portrayals on television and the effect on intellectual standards. The unstated assumption may be clearer, but the causal connection could still be made more explicit.

This next revision of the television enthymeme attempts to improve the connection between reason and conclusion:

> Commercial television threatens to diminish the intellectual standards of American society because it demands no thought from the viewer.

This example uses a reason with more potential to explain why the effect of television on the viewer is a threat to intellectual standards; it seeks to connect the conclusion not only to the nature of television but also to the nature of television's audience. It thus provides a better reason than the first two because its relevance is direct and apparent. If it were to be developed by showing how television places no demand on thought and by showing how this affects intellectual standards, then this reason might provide the basis for a reasonable argument about the effects of television on society. It is an argument that you may have heard in one form or another. It is one that a few authorities have used to convince people, emotionally, of television's dangerous qualities. It may be an argument that contributes to making television better. At any rate, although it may have all of these functions, it is an argument based on the logic of the case, independent of who says it and whether or not we want to believe it. This argument will be convincing or not depending on how well each of the aspects of its logic can be developed.

Relative Precision

Unintentionally ambiguous language is a great source of humor—as, for instance, in those lists of allegedly real headlines that circulate on the Internet:

> Grandmother of Eight Makes Hole in One
>
> Experts Say School Bus Passengers Should Be Belted
>
> Court to Try Shooting Defendant
>
> Man Sent Back to Jail for Not Finishing Sentence

Words that may be taken more than one way can also create unintentional misunderstanding.

> "Shall we eat at Chez Ray tonight?"
>
> "I have no reservations."
>
> "Well, then, I guess we'll have to go somewhere else."

You know a lot of jokes based on these kinds of ambiguities. The kind of misunderstanding we need to be concerned with in argumentative writing is that which comes from reasoning in language that is simply too broad to allow the writer's explicit meaning to come through. For instance, if someone wrote this enthymeme

> Student protesters should be expelled because they disrupt the educational process.

we would probably object that the reasoning should not apply to all student protesters because most acts of protest do not have such an effect. The phrase is too broad to specify which acts of protest are at issue. And we might go on to object to this argument by saying that for us the educational process should include exposure to protests and even participating in them. The term *student protesters* is too general, and the term *educational process* is too vague.

Let's return briefly to the revised enthymeme about television and ask whether its terms are precise enough to communicate a specific argument.

Commercial television threatens to diminish the intellectual standards of American society because it demands no thought from the viewer.

As potential members of the audience for this argument, we might ask, "What are these intellectual standards?" There are different kinds of intellectual processes, from those measured by IQ tests or SAT scores to more practical kinds of intelligence about health, financial management, and human relationships. Anytime anyone says something like, "Wow, that was a dumb thing to do," or "I wish I'd thought of that," that speaker is actually applying an intellectual standard. But it may not be similar at all to what the writer of the enthymeme has in mind. That writer may have a specific kind of intellectual standard in mind, but the language in the enthymeme is so broad that the audience cannot know what it is. In the absence of more specific language, the audience has to fill in that space with a standard that may or may not be what the author has in mind.

Overgeneralization can also be a problem when particular characteristics are misapplied to a larger group. Consider the group "American society" in the commercial television enthymeme. This group of people is so large as to be difficult to make any specific claim about, and formulating an accurate description of such a large number of people would be very difficult to do. Many kinds of people watch commercial television. How likely is it that all those watching will bring to their viewing the same expectations or be affected by it in the same way? The experiences of people of different ages, socioeconomic groups, and educational backgrounds are likely to be different. Lumping a variety of people together in a category that is so large that relevant differences are ignored weakens the claim.

The misapplication of particular characteristics to a large group is often the basis of prejudicial thinking, whether the characteristic is positive or negative. When forming a claim about a group of people, examine carefully who it is that comes to mind. Are there exceptions in the group that could undermine the claim about it?

The assumption that links reason and conclusion can also be overgeneralized to the point that its application is too broad. Here's an enthymeme I once read in a campus newspaper:

Beer should be sold in our student union because it will provide additional revenue for the student body.

The assumption linking the reason and conclusion seems to be this: Anything that will provide additional revenue for the student body should be sold. Examples that could be used to challenge the validity of this assumption come to mind easily: Should cocaine and marijuana be sold too? They would also provide revenue. The assumption connecting the reason and conclusion cannot be applied as a principle in this argument without committing the writer to unintended positions. What qualifications or distinctions might make this enthymeme more appropriate? The language has to become more precise in order for the logic to work as the writer intends.

The implied assumption underlying any given piece of reasoning may itself be too sweeping and require qualification. Another example I encountered recently is this argument from a letter to the editor written in support of the mandatory teaching of creation theory in biology classes:

> Evolution can only be considered a theory and not a proven fact because no one was there to witness it.

The assumption underlying this reasoning seems to be something like this: Nothing can be considered a fact if no one was there to witness it. How many exceptions to this idea could a critical reader come up with? Would they include creation itself? At any rate, the assumption is so general and vague that it seems a weak foundation for the argument. Revising the reasoning would be a matter of qualifying the language of the stated reason until it rested on firmer shared ground. In order to make such a revision of your own reasoning, you must consider carefully the potential applications of the implied assumption on which your enthymeme is based.

Circular Reasoning

Circular reasoning, also known as a *tautology*, appears to be reasoning when in fact it is only the repetition of the same idea in both reason and conclusion. Circular enthymemes end up exactly where they began, usually because they contain terms that are no more than redefinitions:

> Weapons of mass destruction should be banned because they are used to kill a lot of people at once.

The reason is not actually a reason because it merely redefines the term *weapon of mass destruction* without offering support for the claim. The assumption is nothing but a restatement of the same thing also: Whatever kills a lot of people at once should be banned. We aren't getting anywhere with this logic.

When an enthymeme has this kind of circularity, the cause is often the presence of a definition in the reasoning rather than a new claim that adds a different term to the reasoning.

> French cooking is high in fat because it uses a lot of sauces made with butter.
>
> **Implied assumption:** Butter is fat.

This is not actually reasoning as much as it is explaining, and the implied audience is not in need of a reason (there is no question at issue) but an explanation.

Circularity often results from the use of the verb *to be* because that verb asserts equivalency or definition. Consider this nonsensical circular enthymeme:

Time is the root of all evil because it is money.

The terms in this enthymeme are all interchangeable because underlying the logic is no more than the proverbial equations "Time is money" and "Money is the root of all evil." There is no line of reasoning to connect one idea to the next that is more than a restatement of the equivalency of two of the terms.

In circular reasoning, then, the reason simply reproduces the claim in one form or another:

The accountant is a crook because he embezzled money.

This agency's practices will harm the environment because its emissions standards contribute to air pollution.

Lack of regular raises will lower the worker's morale because staying at the same pay makes people discontented.

As with the nonsensical example, the terms all redefine each other and could be interchanged.

Revising an enthymeme that seems to be circular is easier if you are aware of the possibility that some of the terms may simply be redefinitions. If the reason and the conclusion actually state the same thing in different language, then the enthymeme is incomplete and the support for one's idea is lacking. If that seems to be the case, rewrite the enthymeme so that only one claim is made, and then write a new *because* clause that answers the question "Why should I believe that that claim is true?"

Questions for Thought, Discussion, and Writing

1. In the following passages, which sentences are reasons and which are conclusions? Do some sentences have both functions? Which ones that you describe as reasons offer explanations of the conclusion, and which offer justifications for believing the conclusion?
   a. I like reading detective novels. They keep me looking for interesting possibilities, like a game of chess. I never can guess the right solution, though. The writers are clever. I'm also too gullible. But it's fun to be fooled. It wouldn't be a challenge if I always knew "whodunit."
   b. The narrator of "The Turn of the Screw" is unreliable. It isn't possible to tell whether to trust what we are told. Henry James seems to want his reader to wonder whether the events really happened or whether they occur only in the minds of the characters. But which characters? The reader must be meant to wonder which of the characters can trust

their own impressions. I think it's a story about the ambiguity of appearance and reality.
c. Sixty-seven percent of the people surveyed said that they are not influenced by advertising with irrelevant sexual content. This does not, however, mean that such an influence is not more common. If we accept the possibility that there is a subliminal appeal in advertising, some of those who say that they are not influenced might be influenced without knowing it. Survey techniques alone cannot test hypotheses about subconscious knowledge.

2. What kinds of appeal (emotion, authority, or the logic of the case) are being made in each of the reasons offered here? How appropriate is the choice of each kind of appeal? Why?
   a. Salaries for state employees should be based on comparable worth because women workers, on the average, earn lower wages than men.
   b. A recent study showed that cocaine users are no more likely than anyone else to experiment with heroin. But only a fool would accept this as a green light to use coke.
   c. When you consider the extent to which the computer is used in all parts of our lives, it becomes obvious that computer literacy should be taught in elementary grades.
   d. We need leaders who are not afraid to tell the truth. Without them, this country is doomed.
   e. The newspaper decided to print pictures of men who went into adult bookstores in our town, hoping to humiliate them into staying away and by this means force the stores to close. The question is whether the newspaper is guilty of invasion of privacy or whether freedom of the press can include this kind of action. I think the paper has the right but would be wise not to use it. The public's trust in the press is undermined when it abuses its freedoms, just as the booksellers lose respect when they take the First Amendment too far. In both cases, the First Amendment is pushed far enough to risk a backlash that could destroy it.

3. Reconstruct the assumptions that connect the following reasons and conclusions.
   a. The student union should be allowed to sell beer because this would create more revenue to support student activities.
   b. Boxers frequently suffer permanent injury as a result of the impact of brain tissue hitting the inside of the skull. Yet some people continue to call this a sport. It's not a sport; it's a brutal entertainment spectacle. It should be outlawed.
   c. As long as the nation's laws are written and voted on by a majority of whites, the laws that send minorities to prison in greater numbers than whites are political laws. This makes political prisoners out of people who have done no more than follow their consciences in matters that they have not been able to change with their votes.
   d. The only way a politician can get elected is by telling people what they want to hear. No honest person can win enough votes to get into office.

      e. If the Constitution hadn't guaranteed people the right to pursue happiness, Americans might not be as selfish as they are.

4. Having decided on a thesis for your next essay, turn it into an enthymeme by adding a *because* clause that you might offer as a major reason for justifying that thesis. If, in the process of doing so, you find that you need to revise the thesis itself, go ahead. After you have composed this enthymeme, bring it to class for a discussion of the reasoning it uses, according to any of the concepts in this chapter.

5. Having read an essay in the appendix or from another source, consider the following questions:

      a. What enthymemes does the writer use?

      b. Can you identify appeals to authority, emotion, and the logic of the case? Does the reasoning tend to move from specific to general or from general to specific, or does it stay on the same level? How are these kinds of reasoning combined?

      c. Has the author overgeneralized from the evidence, made use of overly general assumptions, or fallen into circular reasoning?

      d. What do such analyses tell you about the author's view of the audience for which the essay is composed?

      e. Finally, are you convinced by the writer's reasoning? What about that reasoning has succeeded in changing or failed to change your mind?

chapter

7

Developing Structures

The Structural Enthymeme

A thesis statement in the form of an enthymeme can provide you with a bridge between the process of thinking about your argument and the process of developing it into the parts of an essay. It can help you to think about and to revise the whole argument in advance. An enthymeme composed to represent the whole argument (the conclusion and the major reason chosen to argue it) will not only help to ensure that the reasoning is adequate to your argumentative situation but also point the way toward structural possibilities in the essay itself.

Once you have discovered a thesis that represents the conclusion of your essay, you can begin to think about potential reasons. Obviously, many reasons are possible. What you seek at this point is a reason that might function as the central or main rational basis for arriving at the conclusion. Putting that reason together with the thesis will make the whole thesis statement into an enthymeme. So now, the whole essay, rather than being based on an assertion alone, can be said to be based on reasoning that you have already developed in response to a question at issue for your audience. If the assumption underlying that reasoning is an idea that you judge your audience as willing to accept without further argumentation, then your essay will also have the advantage of developing out of common ground between you and your audience. So let's now consider the enthymeme as a *generative* principle that can help you to give shape to an entire essay.

A thesis statement in the shape of an enthymeme has the following basic but elastic form:

Assertion 1 (thesis)   *because*   Assertion 2 (reason)

Each of these assertions is a complete idea. The first one is your conclusion, and the second one is the main reason you have chosen to support that conclusion. I call Assertion 2 a *because clause* since together the two assertions can be phrased as a single sentence. If the thesis statement is in this form, you should be able to reconstruct the assumption and by that means ensure that you have thought about the potential connection of your reasoning to the beliefs of your readers. As we saw in the previous chapter, that assumption is there whether you write it out or not. But it is necessary for you to know what it is if you want to be sure that your reasoning, as well as the issue, finds the audience.

The task, simply stated, is to find the best reason you can to support your idea. I don't mean that there is only one "best" reason for every idea, but our choice of reasons determines the directions in which our thoughts move. The because clause, then, should provide a clear direction in answer to the question "Why should my reader believe that my thesis is true?" Of course, an honest search for such an answer might result in the need to rethink the thesis itself. In fact, it often does. We view our ideas more critically when we carry out a sincere search for good reasons.

The task can be guided by criteria for an adequate because clause, like those presented in Chapter 5, to help guide the search for an adequate thesis (see page 77). Once you have used those criteria to help you to decide on a thesis, the following considerations can guide your search for a because clause:

- Is the because clause a complete, precisely stated idea?
- Does it represent a central reason for answering the question "What makes the thesis true?"
- Is the implied assumption one my audience can be expected to accept without further argument? (This means, of course, the same audience for whom the question answered by the thesis is at issue.)
- Have I explored the adequacy of my reasoning in terms of the relevance and connectedness of the because clause, the relative precision of all the terms, and the need to go beyond circular reasoning?

These four criteria do not guarantee an airtight argument, of course. In practical, informal argumentation about the kinds of issues that call for our best reasoning, there may be no such thing as proof beyond doubt. But the conscious attempt to apply these criteria to your own enthymeme can help you to create a fully developed line of reasoning designed to meet the needs of your intended audience. Having satisfied yourself that the enthymeme you have written and revised meets these criteria, you can begin to explore ways in which you might expand the elements of that reasoning into a more fully developed essay.

Using these criteria as a basis for revising your enthymeme will pay off in the process of drafting an essay that moves in the directions your reasoning establishes. The application of these questions to your reasoning can help you from being too easily satisfied with your thinking, which is important because if you write for critical readers, they will give your reasoning the same kind of close attention. Your application of these criteria doesn't have to follow a prescribed order. They are considerations for you to use, when they apply, as you revise an enthymeme. It also helps to have others' views in this process, because sometimes it is hard for us to see critically into our own reasoning, which always seems obvious to ourselves. For this reason, your teacher may schedule thesis workshops in class or otherwise have you look at enthymemes written by classmates. If not, you can do this yourself with the help of a friend whom you know to be a good critical reader.

From Enthymeme to Structure

Let's examine in more detail how a thesis statement, in the form of a well-thought-out enthymeme, provides you with the major parts that hold the structure of your composition together. By thinking through the enthymeme, you give yourself a basis for thinking about structure. The shape that your essay takes will, therefore, be the shape of your reasoning, a structure you generate to fit the argument you chose to develop. You need rely on no model essay form to find that shape. Your reasoning generates the shape of your essay.

> If the term *enthymeme* just seems too cumbersome and academic for you—and you aren't alone—try using the term *reasoned thesis* wherever you find the big fat Greek e-word in this chapter. It means the same thing: a form you can use to articulate and revise the underlying reasoning from which the wholly developed argument emerges and that helps you to make the structure of your essay both adequate and coherent.

In the broadest sense, the parts of the enthymeme can be thought of as the largest units of an essay's structure. They can be diagrammed as follows:

Enthymeme		Structure
(question at issue)	→	beginning
(assumption) because clause	→	middle
assertion	→	end

The enthymeme, having emerged from thinking about your ideas and reasons, can now be looked at as the source for the specific functions of these large structural parts—specific because each enthymeme has its own requirements. These requirements can be understood by thinking of the structure of an essay as the fulfillment of the logical relationships in the enthymeme;

Beginning: The reader is introduced to a problem that is of interest because it requires a solution. *The question at issue.*

Middle: The solution to the problem depends on the reader and writer sharing a common understanding. *The assumption.*

Given this understanding, an answer to the problem can be developed if a condition can be shown to be the case. *The because clause.*

End: Given the assumption and the condition just developed, the solution follows. *The assertion.*

Needless to say, these parts can be as long or as short as the specific case requires. They do not correspond to paragraphs; this could be the structure of an essay, a chapter, or a book. Within these parts, many kinds of sentences and transitions can occur as they are called for. But these basic functions are common to essays that *take a reader through a developing line of reasoning toward an earned conclusion*. These elements, in turn, help you to select and order other elements of thought.

The actual order of these elements grows out of what you have to say. The enthymeme can therefore help to guide this growth, but it does not determine what form the essay must take. The enthymeme suggests structural possibilities because it connects ideas through reasoning. Consequently, any enthymeme may give rise to different structures for essays, depending on the writer's choices and how the writer sees those connections.

An actual essay has many more parts than the enthymeme from which its structure derives. This is because as the essay moves through the reasoning of the enthymeme, other things must happen. Terms may need to be explained. Distinctions may need to be offered. Further reasons may need to be gone into. Examples may need to be used for clarity. Transitions may need to be composed. At any point that a reader may be expected to question, to object, or to be confused, the writer should find a way to help the reader along. Such considerations arise when the writer attempts to develop the basic reasoning of the enthymeme in such a way that a reader will be able to follow that reasoning clearly.

Outlines of Ideas

An enthymeme can help you to guide the development of your essay's structure by suggesting an outline of ideas. I do not mean an outline having blank spaces with labels such as 1.A.b., to be filled in with a few words—an outline with subdivisions and brief headings. I mean, rather, a sequence of sentences that represents the progress of thought in the essay, the ideas in the order in which they will arise in the essay. Having produced such an outline of ideas, you can use it to help to define further responsibilities you might face as the essay unfolds.

There is no single way of generating a structure of ideas from the parts of an enthymeme, and there is no formula that tells you how to do it. You can learn it only by doing it. But to help to make this process clearer, I will provide examples of possible structures that might be generated from an enthymeme. This will give you some sense of the range of possibilities implicit in the enthymeme. The enthymeme is not meant to restrict thought to a narrow linear chain but to help to stimulate thought. In each case, I illustrate the structure of the essay as an outline of ideas.

Suppose I have composed the following structural enthymeme to represent my argument:

The study of myths helps us to understand the social roles of women in history

because

it reveals how the myths of the past have molded the attitudes of successive generations and preserved social order.*

This reasoning implies a question at issue and an assumption, both of which connect it to its intended audience. The question at issue (a question of consequence) might be stated this way:

Can the study of myths help us to understand the social roles of women in history?

The assumption that holds the reasoning together might be stated like this:

The study of whatever has molded the attitudes of successive generations and preserved social order will be helpful in understanding the social role of women in history.

Writing out the enthymeme, the question at issue, and the assumption is useful in trying to make decisions about structure. Having written them out, I can ask myself, "Does the assumption need to be included and explained, or can it remain unstated?" In the present case, I might well decide that the assumption does not need to be put into the essay at all. I can also ask myself, "Should the question at issue be stated? Should it be developed? Is it obvious to the reader why it is at issue? Should I start with it?" In this case, I might think that it needs to be explained and that it might make a good place to start. Furthermore, I can (and should) ask myself, "What parts does an essay need to have in order to earn this thesis by means of this reasoning?" In this case, I might sketch out a small list.

The essay must

- show some myths.
- show how those myths molded the attitudes of successive generations.
- show how those myths preserved social order.
- connect those attitudes to the social role of women in history.
- show that those attitudes are preserved as part of the social order.

---

*This basic reasoning, though not the structures or examples that follow, is adapted from Sarah B. Pomeroy, *Goddesses, Whores, Wives, and Slaves* (New York: Shocken Books, 1975).

My choice to argue this enthymeme and not some other has made me feel responsible to do these things. Of course, my list of responsibilities might be longer. But any structural enthymeme contains such responsibilities, and they consist of explaining the parts of the enthymeme and connecting them. Furthermore, I can ask myself, "Should I put the conclusion at the beginning of the essay, or should I save it for later?"

Considerations of this sort enable me to make some structural decisions. I can see that several potential structures are implicit in this enthymeme. The following three outlines of ideas might result from such considerations.

Outline 1

Our understanding of the social roles of women in history can be enhanced by the study of myth.

. . .

How? By seeing first that myths of the past molded the attitudes of successive generations.

. . .

For example, in the myth of Atalanta, her father abandoned her in the forest because he wanted a son.

. . .

This myth suggests that female children were less desirable than male children.

. . .

Also, in Homer, female goddesses direct the actions of the men at war.

. . .

These stories allow men to blame their actions on women.

. . .

These attitudes are reflected in the historical role of women as both socially inferior to men and the cause of men's misfortunes.

. . .

Second, we can see that myths of the past also preserved the social order such attitudes created.

. . .

For example, Athena was the goddess of wisdom, peace, and war. She was worshiped, and the city of Athens was dedicated to her.

. . .

She was part of the religion, and civil order was seen as part of a sacred order.

…

Social roles could not be questioned without questioning sacred order.

…

Consequently, we can see how the social role of women in history was so difficult to escape. It was seen as divinely ordered. Men had an excuse to maintain the role of female inferiority and did not have to take the blame themselves.

Outline 2

Women feature prominently in ancient myths.

…

For example, the myth of Atalanta …

…

The goddesses in Homer …

…

The worship of Athena …

…

What attitudes toward women do these myths teach?

…

That they are inferior to men.

…

That they are to blame for men's actions.

…

That the civil order was seen as part of a sacred order.

…

What do these myths have to do with the continuation of social roles for women in later history?

…

They serve to instill these attitudes.

…

They preserved the social role of women by connecting those roles to religious beliefs.

…

From this, we see that the study of myth can help us to understand the social roles of women in history.

Outline 3

In history, women were held in high esteem, but they also were kept in subordinate social roles.

...

This is a paradox that is hard to understand.

...

Perhaps one way to understand it is to look at the function of myth in creating and preserving those roles.

...

Myths mold the attitudes of successive generations.

...

They do this by giving examples of people that one is supposed to admire.

...

The heroes of Greek legends, for instance, illustrate the virtues of brave and noble behavior.

...

Myths also preserve social order.

...

They do this not only by defining roles according to the attitudes they create about virtuous behavior but also by suggesting that these roles in civil society fit into a divine plan.

...

Myths about the gods show them to be very human in their actions, and they not only control but also model how human mortals should behave in society.

...

How do these observations about myths help us to understand the social roles of women in history? Let's look at some myths about women in these terms.

...

Myths that molded attitudes toward women include the myth of Atalanta and the myths of Homeric goddesses.

...

These suggest the attitudes that women are inferior to men and that they control men's actions.

...

Myths that preserve social order include the worship of Athena in Greek society.

...

This myth suggests that attitudes toward women in society are in accord with divine order and cannot change.

...

Therefore, we can see that the study of myths can help us to understand the social roles of women in history and why those roles have been hard to change.

...

Perhaps by understanding how myth functions to create and perpetuate women's roles in history we can begin to see how those roles can change in the future.

The basic reasoning in the enthymeme has been used to generate each of these structural outlines, and others could be generated from that same reasoning. None of these outlines is complete, of course. Each of the ideas that will make up parts of the essay must themselves be developed further, as the ellipses indicate. But each of these outlines might form the basis of a well-structured essay, one in which the structure develops out of the reasoning.

If the basic reasoning is the same in each case, then how do these three structures differ? Outline 1 starts out with the thesis itself. Next, it asserts and illustrates the first part of the because clause and then the second part, using each example to explain the implications of the because clause. When the explanation of the reasoning is complete, so is the essay, because the conclusion was already asserted at the outset.

Outline 2, however, does not assert the conclusion until the end of the essay. It begins, instead, with the examples, as if teasing the reader with these interesting details but not saying what their significance is until the reader is well into the essay. After the examples have gotten the reader's interest, the essay asks a question about them that is designed to lead into the reasoning of the because clause. The question at issue is then posed, and the reasoning that was developed is used to answer it in the form of a concluding assertion.

Outline 3 begins with statements intended to show why the question at issue is important, to raise the issue in such a way that the problem being solved is immediately clear. The essay then explains each part of the because clause, and only after that does it go into examples. The examples are used to further explain the because clause, and the conclusion is asserted. A further consequence of the reasoning (one that was not necessarily explicit in the enthymeme) is then asserted, as a way of ending the essay on a strong note.

My choice of which structure to use, or whether to think of another, depends on which parts of the reasoning need the most emphasis, on the kinds of information I want to include, on what I imagine to be my reader's needs and interests in this issue, and on the kind of effect I want to create for the reader. Any essay structured in each of the above ways would differ slightly in emphasis, in detail, and in both its initial impact and its final effect on the reader.

In each of the structures, the enthymeme also led me into further reasoning. Often, new reasons had to be developed to support the explicit parts of the enthymeme. In this case, some of those reasons were inductive (the actual myths that enabled conclusions to be drawn about the function of myth in general). As in any inductive argument, the number of examples was limited somewhat arbitrarily. Any of these structures could have contained further examples. The adequacy of the examples, the amount of development each one needs, and the range of my knowledge or research could affect the decision to use more or fewer examples. The idea outline generated by the enthymeme is like an accordion file: It expands to fit what needs to go into it at any point. If details or examples need to be added, the writer knows where they belong.

As the reasoning of the enthymeme expands to become a structure, further needs may arise. In the example, the reasoning depended on assertions that themselves required support. An essay contains more complex lines of reasoning than can be contained in the initial enthymeme. One reason becomes a minithesis that requires support in the form of another enthymeme. This is why I call the thesis statement a structural enthymeme, to distinguish it from all the other enthymemes that any essay might contain as parts of its reasoning. The structural enthymeme contains the whole argument and consequently generates the needs for subarguments, minitheses, and other local enthymemes. The result is an embroidery of reasons, stitched to form the overall design only sketched by the thesis statement and outline of ideas.

Among the needs that may arise as an enthymeme is expanded into a structure may be the need for examples, the need for definitions, the need for qualifications, the need for factual evidence, the need for explanations (perhaps by way of analogy or anecdote), the need for authoritative testimony, or the need to acknowledge or to refute potential counterarguments. It is impossible to say in advance whether an essay must respond to any of these needs, because they arise as the essay unfolds in relation to the nature of the case being made and the audience.

Here I illustrate how another enthymeme may generate different structures, this time showing how such needs might be addressed in different places. Suppose I draft this enthymeme to represent the argument I wish to make:

Education about date rape would reduce the incidence of rapes on college campuses

because

informing students that all forced sex is rape would make them less likely to force an acquaintance or date to have sex against her will.

I based my reasoning on an assumption something like this:

Anything that would make students less likely to force an acquaintance or date to have sex against her will would reduce the incidence of rapes on college campuses.

That assumption is one that I may or may not be able to take for granted, depending on my audience.

Here is one way I might develop this reasoning into a structure:

Outline 1

What is rape?

...

The law defines it as "the forcing of sexual intercourse upon a person against that person's will or without that person's permission."

...

The law does not say that it's a rape only if there is a gun or knife, or a threat of physical violence. It does not limit rape to the case of a deranged pervert breaking into a stranger's apartment.

...

The law does not say that it isn't rape if the man is the woman's husband or if he has bought her dinner or if he has been to bed with her in the past.

...

In fact, as many as 80 percent of the rapes reported to police have been committed by someone the woman knows, often someone whom she knows very well. Experts call this "date rape" or "acquaintance rape."

...

But many women do not report such rapes because they do not believe that what their friend or lover has done is the same as rape. They suffer in silence and do not get help.

...

And many men say they do not believe that the use of some force with a woman who says no, or sex with a woman who has had so much to drink that she cannot resist, is rape.

...

This ignorance—of the law and of what women and men should expect from each other as equal partners in sexual decisions—is the cause of many rapes.

...

These are rapes that could be avoided if education informed people of the law and changed people's way of thinking about sexual relationships.

Here is a structure that begins with a question of definition that is part of the overall attempt to answer a question of policy. The definition is needed because it is what the term *education* in the thesis refers to. The essay need not have started with that definition, but it is an effective way to work into the development of the because clause. The structure also incorporates several other parts that were not part of the enthymeme but turn out to be needed as the reasoning develops. Facts, of course, are introduced to support and to clarify the premise asserted in the because clause. Authorities are cited to add credibility to the facts. When the essay turns toward showing that women and men are ignorant of those facts, further opportunities arise. To show that the assertions are true, the writer could add the authority of surveys or more experts. Or, to give the reader a sense of the immediacy of the assertions and to illustrate just how often women or men mis-understand what rape is, the writer could add anecdotes or examples of events that illustrate rapes of these kinds.

A writer's structural choices may depend on the audience. In a differ-ent argumentative situation (as perceived by the writer), the same enthymeme could generate a very different structure and a very different kind of essay.

Outline 2

We have a serious problem on this campus.

...

Here are some documented cases of rape on this campus in the previous two months, told to me by the head counselor.

...

Tell about Bud expecting to have sex with Miriam because he bought her an expensive dinner. She said no, but he convinced her that she owed it to him. She blames herself.

...

Tell about Jesse getting drunk and passing out at the party, when house members then had sex with her. She is about to sue the fraternity and the university.

...

Tell about Edna who has finally sought counseling to get out of an abusive marriage. Her husband frequently threatens her with more violence if she does not have sex, but she says she doesn't think this is rape.

...

Tell about Teri who resisted when her date got a little rough and who was then raped. She didn't seek help for three weeks because her friends told her it happens all the time and she should toughen up. But she was too distressed about it to study.

...

These are just four of ten similar instances.

...

Here are statistics showing that for every rape reported to anyone, ten go unreported.

...

That means that there were probably twenty such rapes on this campus in the last two months.

...

So, as college deans, you must begin the date rape education campaign now or you will not be acting responsibly toward our women students.

Here is a situation (an exhortation to the college deans) in which all that needs to be done in the essay is to demonstrate the scope of the problem and its seriousness. Most of the actual reasoning, which is implicit, is undeveloped in relation to the citation of case histories and expert testimony. The deans do not have to be told that these are cases of rape according to the law's definition. They are presumed to know that. They do not need to be told that education is needed to overcome the ignorance of those who commit such rapes or fall victim to them. But they do need to be exhorted to act, and the structure is designed to have that effect.

A third possible structure based on the reasoning of this enthymeme follows.

Outline 3

In a recent case reported in the news, a jury acquitted a man of rape on the grounds that the woman was dressed provocatively and was therefore asking for it.

...

Such a case illustrates that attitudes toward rape are slow to change. Some people still think that a woman can be blamed when a man forces her to have sex.

...

Even the widespread success of the feminist movement has not changed many people's minds.

...

This is clear from the fact that most rapes are committed by acquaintances and even dates. Contrary to public opinion, rapes are most likely to be committed by the nice young man next door and not the armed stranger in the night. Altitudes in society, not deranged individuals, seem to be the cause.

...

One reason seems to be that young men and women practice courtship in ways that enforce the attitude that rape is an accepted form of sex.

...

Men are traditionally the aggressors in courtship situations, whereas women are passive.

...

Men spend their money, whereas women are supposed to be grateful.

...

Men believe that women who say they do not want sex don't really mean it.

...

Of course, it is true that not all men believe such things. But enough do to make the problem widespread, and even those who don't often find that peer pressure to score is too strong to resist.

...

Such beliefs result in some men forcing women to have sex because the men think it is consistent with male/female roles.

...

Beliefs are not inevitable. They can be changed.

...

College is one place where young men and women can be asked to confront their attitudes and change them.

...

Therefore, our campus is an appropriate place to conduct an educational campaign to reduce the number of rapes committed by men who do not believe that forced sex in some circumstances is rape.

...

Maybe then some of society's attitudes will change more quickly than they seem to have done.

This structure may be more suited to an audience of peers who may not consider acquaintance rape to be rape. Because this essay plan develops the idea of attitudes (or the "belief" term of the because clause), it can begin with a more indirect anecdote and it need not offer as many examples. Other ways of raising the issue of people's attitudes are possible. The essay will also contain one section that qualifies its statements about the beliefs of men, in order to answer a potential reader's objection that the generalizations are too large and sweeping. The essay later raises the issue of education (and college) to offer a positive solution to the problem for this audience.

The purpose of these examples is to show how an enthymeme can guide the writer in developing a structure for an essay. But the enthymeme does not predetermine one structure. As the essay must somehow fulfill the basic reasoning of the enthymeme, it must have certain parts. But the order they come in and anything else included to develop the reasoning are still up to the writer, based on the perceived needs of the audience. Such decisions will differ from argument to argument. No model can tell you in advance what parts your essay must have and what order they must go in. Because the enthymeme stands for the specific argument you wish to make, you can use it to guide your thinking about the specific decisions you face when structuring the parts of an essay. A structure generated by the conditions of a well-reasoned enthymeme is more likely to move the reader from beginning to end than one based on a prefabricated form or one that develops aimlessly.

Questions for Thought, Discussion, and Writing

1. If you have written a structural enthymeme to use as the basis for your next essay, use the criteria on pages 77 and 102 to revise it, if necessary.

2. Having done so, list some of the things for which an essay written for this enthymeme makes you responsible. Then write an outline of ideas that develops the reasoning contained in the enthymeme. The sentences in this outline should represent the stages in the reasoning suggested by your enthymeme, covering the terms and the relationships you asserted among them.

3. Where in the developing reasoning might your argument require, or be improved by, any of the following?
   a. further reasons
   b. dialectical distinctions
   c. examples/illustrations
   d. data
   e. qualifications
   f. acknowledgments of counterarguments
   g. analogies

    h. descriptions
    i. anything else

4. Based on this planning, draft your essay. Don't be afraid to change any part of the plan if you discover a better way while you are composing. Don't be afraid to try out anything that seems right; you can delete, tear up, rewrite, or move anything you want to.

5. After reading an argumentative essay, try to reconstruct the structural enthymeme that represents the main line of reasoning developed in the argument: the conclusion and the major reason (or reasons) offered to support it. How does the structure of the writing correspond to parts of that enthymeme? What accounts for the order in which the parts of the essay are arranged? Are there unnecessary parts? Are necessary parts missing? Try to analyze the author's choices in terms of the needs of the audience.

8

Revising and Editing

Revision as Rethinking

All writers revise. If writing is a process of discovering ideas, then we change what we have written for the same reasons we sometimes change our minds: New ideas alter our way of thinking about old ideas. But even if a draft of an essay does not lead to different ways of viewing the subject, revision is still necessary because, after honest reflection, the way in which our writing emerges is not necessarily the way we would like it to appear. In this sense, revision occurs throughout the process of writing; even rewriting one's enthymeme to make it work better is revision, and so is rethinking what one wants to argue. Revision takes place as soon as one has an idea and begins to think about it.

Even though I have waited to emphasize revision until Chapter 8 it is misleading to think of revision as the last stage of the writing process, because writers revise continuously. Revision takes place whenever a writer replaces one phrase or sentence with another, adds a word or phrase or sentence or paragraph, cuts out some part of a composition, or moves writing from one part of an essay to another. These actions can take place at any time during composing, or as a separate activity after a draft is completed. Revision is recomposing, and as such it is simply a matter of changing one's mind about any aspect of the writing. There is no right time for changing one's mind; it can happen at any time one discovers a better way.

Rethinking your choices may lead to the discovery of new ones. If writing is an act of taking responsibility for ideas, then revising acknowledges that responsibility as an ongoing obligation. Once a word or sentence or whole essay is committed to paper, you assume the responsibility of reassessing— and changing, if necessary—what is written. Where does this responsibility come from? In the terms of the discussion in Chapter 1, the need for revision is linked to one's membership in a discourse community. The need to advance understanding within such a community brings with it the responsibility to earn one's conclusions, and this is possible only if those conclusions, and the reasons that support them, are communicated to other members of that community with as much clarity and effectiveness as the writer can create. Clarity and effectiveness require accommodating one's sentences to the reader's needs, just as reasoning requires accommodating one's argument to the reader's assumptions. Both careful reasoning and careful revising are an attempt to base understanding on the common ground between a writer and the community of inquirers to which the writer feels responsible.

If revision is always possible, it's fair to ask: When is a piece of writing ever finished? A time must come, of course, when a deadline is reached, an assignment is due, or a piece of writing is simply abandoned in favor of something else. In that sense, writing is finished when it is submitted to its intended audience. Often, someone has imposed a deadline or a due date. Of course, the final product ought to be as good as you can make it, given the time available, but this does not mean that the final product is finished in the sense of no longer having room for improvement. Writing may never reach that mythical point of perfection simply because it is always subject to change. Thus, the decision to stop revising may be somewhat arbitrary, based on your sense that further change would not substantially improve the writing. There comes a time when it is more important to get the writing into the hands of its audience than to continue to tinker with it.

As I said earlier, writing itself encourages discoveries. This means that revision is necessary to be sure that all parts of a composition continue to work together, to satisfy your purpose, as that purpose refines itself during writing. Writers frequently discover that after they have finished a draft of a composition, they must return to the beginning to change aspects of the writing to fit a new sense of purpose that has evolved. This does not necessarily mean that the thesis itself has changed but rather that the writer's attitude, or even degree of conviction, may have changed the writer's approach to that thesis. Revision enables you to consider whether the whole essay, as written, consistently satisfies the needs of its thesis.

Obstacles to Revision

Revision is difficult without *critical distance*, the perspective required to see writing *as writing* and separate from one's self. Revising may sometimes seem harder than writing because we cannot separate ourselves from our thoughts enough to know whether they would be clear to someone who encounters them only through the words we have written. Our own words seem clear to us because they are intimately related to the thoughts we had while composing them. We may miss many opportunities to improve our own writing simply because as we reread it we are engaged in the same mental process we went through as we wrote it. Yet a reader lacks this intimacy with the mental process that led to those words. Therefore, it is necessary to achieve distance from the writing, somehow, to see it as if for the first time. Of course, our own words can never be entirely new to us as we reread them. What, then, can you do to achieve as much distance as possible?

The best source of distance is time. If it is possible to return to a piece of writing after a long period, its faults become more obvious. Allowing yourself the leisure to forget how the sentences sound, to let the words slip out of the mental grooves they have forged in the short-term memory, enables you to read them more critically. There is no better source of critical distance than a desk drawer, where a draft can be put away and returned to after enough time has gone by. But no one has enough time, of course, to make this practical. There is a lesson in this, however, that all writers can apply, even when the time available for composing is short: Don't procrastinate. No matter how much time is available, you should take advantage of all of it, and this means a certain amount of time between drafts to let the distance between you and your words increase. Returning to a draft of an essay after having done something else for a day or two—or a week or two, if possible—can provide just enough critical distance to make revision effective.

In acoustics, *critical distance* means the distance between the microphone and the sound source at which the level of reverberation is balanced. That's where the recording level is optimum. Critical distance in philosophy means objectivity, ridding oneself of presuppositions in order to see a thing as it really is. That's said to be thinking at its optimum. In reading and revising, critical distance is metaphorical: reading another's or one's own writing in such a way that it looks *like writing* and not a transparent window on meaning. The optimum for writing is to have the writing *as such* disappear so the idea stands forth clearly for the reader—but this happens *after* the writer has treated the writing *as writing* in order to make it as clear as possible.

I can suggest two effective ways to gain critical distance. First, *read your writing out loud to yourself.* Just the sound of the words is often enough to reveal flaws you might otherwise miss. The rhythm and balance of your sentences can often be improved after you have heard them. Second, *have someone else read your writing out loud while you listen.* This not only allows you to hear what you have written but also reveals trouble spots wherever the reader stumbles or gets the intonation of your meaning wrong.

A second obstacle to revision is an unwillingness to allow anyone to see our writing until it is finished. Perhaps we fear the possibility of negative judgments. Perhaps we want others to read what we have written only so that they will praise us. But such attitudes are not helpful to a writer. It is especially important to develop a positive

Lacking time, you can arbitrarily create other sources of distance. Writers are known to do some wacky things just to alienate themselves from their own prose so they can revise it from a new point of view. I heard about one writer who tapes his manuscript to a distant wall and revises while reading it through binoculars. A friend of mine revises by turning her manuscript upside-down to read it. Another reads her writing in a mirror. I don't advise any of these tactics; these writers obviously worked them out to suit their own needs.

attitude toward the honest criticism of others. By seeking this criticism, we learn new things about our writing and thereby learn how to make it better.

Most writers rely on a circle of trusted readers who comment on their drafts. These test readers can often ask questions or make observations the writer had not thought about. To have the benefit of a critical reader's response is enormously helpful to writers who wish to revise thoughtfully. Choose your readers carefully, therefore. Friends who only flatter you or readers who do not know how to read critically are of no help. This raises a third potential obstacle to effective revision.

To revise well, try to take criticism without offense and to be willing to make critical judgments about your own writing without damage to your ego. Yes, writing does come from the depths of our minds and hearts, but it is also separate from ourselves once it is on the page, and we can approach it *as writing*, as words on paper or on a screen that can be changed and played with freely. Thus, to revise well, you must be able to separate the personality in your writing from your own personality. This is especially important in college, and in a writing class in particular, because teachers and other members of the class must be able to talk about your writing without making judgments about you as a person.

In reading others' writing, and in accepting the comments of others about your own, the Golden Rule should apply: Comment about others' writing as you would have them comment about your own; accept the comments of others as you would have them accept yours. If we could accept all advice about our own writing as if it were given solely for the purpose of helping us to write better, we would be fortunate. But advice, like other aspects of human relations, can come with hidden intentions and can be defended against by rationalization—sometimes beyond our conscious control. It is necessary, therefore, to make a real effort to accept criticism gladly and to respond to it thoughtfully.

Responding to Your Teacher's Comments

It's one thing to revise in response to the criticisms of a friend, classmate, or peer, but responding to the criticism of your teacher is more difficult. Your teacher is indeed a member of your intended audience and should therefore function as a critical reader, responding to your ideas just as she or he might respond to the ideas in others' writing. But, let's face it, your teacher is also the person who judges your performance and who you would like to please. More importantly, as the person whose responsibility it is to help you become a better writer, your teacher comments on your writing with that end in view.

The way in which you should respond to comments will differ depending on whether the teacher expects the essay to be revised or not. Direct responses to comments in revision, because they are guided by the teacher's observations, can also be the most perfunctory kind—for the student who is content to do the minimum a teacher asks for. It is always tempting to respond to a teacher's specific comments without understanding fully why those comments are there or what difference the revisions actually make to the quality of the essay. It is too easy, in other words, to make changes just to satisfy the teacher. A teacher's comments are meant to guide you in rethinking what you have done, and if you respond by automatically doing whatever the teacher asks for, you do not take the opportunity to use those comments to your best advantage. A teacher's comment is not a commandment; it is a suggestion. Only you can decide whether the comment will lead to a better way of writing, and only the thoughtful application of that suggestion can produce a change that will benefit you in the future.

If a teacher's comments are expressed in ways you do not understand, it is your responsibility to consult with the teacher, to be sure that you and the teacher are reading your essay in the same way. I'm not talking about arguing with the teacher over your grade but rather about seeking to understand the intention and the source of whatever troublesome comments the teacher may have made. Most teachers respond positively to this kind of inquiry, even if they may not, understandably, respond favorably to complaints about grades. Make it clear that what you want is a genuine understanding of your own writing. A good deal of the learning that takes place in a writing course can happen in the teacher's office during such conferences.

In revising an essay, your attention should be on the nature of the case you are trying to make and the structure of the argument first, letting matters of lesser significance have your attention only when the first-order issues are under control. You should determine which of the teacher's comments address the most basic aspects of the essay—its reasoning and structure—so you can respond to those comments before editing the essay.

It may be that a teacher's comments suggest problems with the thesis itself or with the general approach you took in arguing it. In that case, an appropriate response is to reconsider the thesis and the logic, which might result in a revised essay with a different argument and structure. If what is most in need of revision is the thesis of your essay, your revision may well turn out to be a wholly new composition based on a revised intention.

It isn't necessary to revise each essay in order to get the benefit of a teacher's evaluation. But a somewhat different strategy for applying comments is necessary if you aren't going to revise because you have to apply concepts you derive from the comments to new writing situations. Although comments that refer to particular aspects of one essay may not apply to another essay, *principles* derived from those comments can still be applied to any new composition. It is necessary for you to derive those principles yourself.

One specific practice may help you to do this most effectively. When you read a teacher's comments, keep a record of the kinds of problems your teacher has found in your writing. Say, for instance, that your teacher has marked sentence fragments or suggested that in several places in your essay you have not supplied a clear transition. On a separate page, in a note intended only for yourself, you might write "Watch for fragments," or "Concentrate on clear transitions." (It would be best to have separate pages for different kinds of problems—one for misspelled words, another for grammar, another for more general concepts—tailored to your own needs.) These notes, no matter what kinds of advice they contain, will be invaluable to you as you revise your next essay by providing a guide for focusing on problems you especially need to work on. You can add new features to the list as you receive comments on each essay you hand in, and over the course of time you will find yourself gaining more control of most of the writing problems your teacher has pointed out to you. If you simply read comments once and make no such attempt to remember and apply them, you will probably not learn what your teacher is trying to teach you.

Style and Attitudes

Up to this point, we have discussed revision in general as applying to any aspect of the writing at any stage. One aspect of writing we haven't discussed is style. Anything you write has some kind of style, and paying too much attention to it as you compose may result in distracting you from your ideas. But paying attention to style during revision is very important.

Style is the texture of the writing, the way it sounds and the kinds of words and sentences it uses to communicate to the reader. Qualities of style contribute to the *tone* of a piece of writing, which refers to the mood or attitude the reader *hears* in the words. Behind the silent words on a page, we are able to hear a voice—not necessarily the real voice of the flesh-and-blood writer, whom we may not know, but that of a possible or apparent speaker of the words. If we judge a writer to be condescending or patronizing, angry or deeply moved, open-minded or intolerant, sincere or hypocritical, we do so in part because the writer *sounds* that way.

If style communicates the writer's attitude to the reader, then a consideration of attitude might be a useful place to begin thinking about stylistic choices. Attitude is a combination of the writer's feelings toward the subject, toward the intended audience, and toward the writer's self. These feelings change from situation to situation and even from time to time as the writer works on a composition. The purpose of this discussion is to give you some basis for thinking about how the stylistic choices you make reflect your attitudes.

The first consideration is that the self reflected in your writing is not necessarily the same self you reflect in other situations. Even in different pieces of writing, depending on their purpose, you construct an image of yourself that may be different. The aspects of our personalities we present to others at different times reflect the circumstances within which we act and the purposes behind our actions. There are times when it is appropriate for us to emphasize one aspect of ourselves while making certain to deemphasize other aspects. We do this not because we are dishonest but because we are adaptable. In writing, this means that we choose how we wish to appear to our reader, based on who the reader is and what we wish our writing to accomplish. I may come across as an entirely different sort of person when I write a letter to my parents, to my former professor, or to my senator. I may seem like an angry person if I am writing to complain about something, a tolerant person if I am writing to defend someone, a serious-minded person if I am writing to express my concern over an injustice, or a clown if I am writing to get people to see something in a comical light. All of these are aspects of my true self, but I may choose from them to fit my purpose and my reader.

How well you are able to find the right self for your writing depends on how well you judge the situation, how clearly you understand your own purposes, how you view the subject, and how you wish the reader to view it. As you think about the ideas you wish to present to the reader and the reasons you wish to offer in support of those ideas, you are engaged in defining all of those attitudes at once, and you have already done most of the work of adapting the right style. It is not necessary to do all the thinking first and *then* to make all of the decisions about how to present yourself, because by doing the thinking you are already working on this presentation. You are adjusting your attitude to fit the subject simply by giving it your best thinking in the first place.

All of us have probably encountered writing we thought was somehow flawed in its tone and have judged it accordingly. Whether we accepted the ideas in spite of this or not, we could characterize our response to the writer's way of presenting himself or herself to us by using adjectives that otherwise would apply to personality: This writer is childish, we might say, or self-indulgent or selfish or dishonest or conceited or petty or condescending or closed-minded. All such adjectives, when applied to writing, reflect our judgment of the writer's attitude toward the subject, toward us, or toward himself or herself. Thus, the writer's tone is determined by how well those attitudes are shaped in the writing and kept in harmony with one another. Let's take a closer look at those attitudes and see how they may work for or against a writer's purpose.

When we are led to characterize a writer's style by using adjectives such as *pedantic, lifeless, monotonous,* or even *trivial,* we are probably responding to our feeling that the writer has taken the subject more seriously than it deserves by neglecting to consider the needs of the reader who must be helped to understand it.

Here, for instance, is an example of writing that is serious about its subject but contains inappropriate stylistic choices:

> It is often contended that the citizens who protested this nation's involvement in the conflict in Vietnam during the anti-Vietnam demonstrations of the 1960s did so out of an abiding sense of patriotism for the country. Indeed, it is so often said by those who have not thoroughly analyzed the

conflict that to suggest otherwise is to make one vulnerable to the charge that one believes in the slogan "My Country Right or Wrong." It is the case, however, that one can come to the inevitable conclusion that the protesters acted out of treasonous motives, in sufficient numbers of cases to warrant a skeptical attitude toward the protest movement in general, without becoming guilty oneself of any rashly suspect form of blind patriotic fervor. . . .

What about this writing gives us the impression that the writer has neglected to consider the needs of the reader? It is enough, perhaps, to hear the writer's sneering tone and to conclude that he had no respect for the opinions of any reader who does not already agree with his stance. This blindness to other points of view emerges as disrespect; any reader who might entertain another opinion is labeled as someone who has "not thoroughly analyzed the conflict." His attitude of superiority makes the prose sound pompous. His contempt for the audience is evident also in the kind of appeal he makes in his reasoning; he asserts his own invulnerability to emotional stereotyping while engaging in the same tactic himself. He calls others names while attempting to defend himself against name-calling used against his own position.

The style of the paragraph contributes to this impression. Notice that the writer tries to stay aloof from the discussion by making the prose impersonal. The paragraph contains three long sentences, each of which starts with the vague "it is" construction. The structures of these sentences make them unnecessarily difficult to read. The first one contains wordy repetitions ("who protested this nation's involvement in the conflict in Vietnam during the anti-Vietnam demonstrations of the 1960s," "patriotism for the country"). The second one has an awkward word order, forcing the reader to reconstruct its meaning after reaching the conclusion. The third is interrupted by a distracting subordinate clause, one that makes a new point worth a sentence of its own. Notice, too, that the writer's diction is inflated. He uses *citizens* because it seems to sound more high-toned than *people*, and it may seem to the writer that he is being scornfully ironic to call them *citizens* rather than *protesters*. Likewise, the words *involvement* and *conflict* are chosen to make the role of the United States sound innocent; they are euphemisms. Some of the language is loaded; the writer uses *inevitable* and *treasonous* in ways that implicitly threaten the reader who might not accept them. The phrase *rashly suspect* is simply a clumsy oratorical flourish that makes no sense, and *blind patriotic fervor* is a bumbled cliché.

The subject matter of this paragraph is not so unfamiliar or complex that it can't be communicated plainly and inoffensively. There are subjects, however, that may seem to call for writing the reader will find difficult simply because they are complex or unfamiliar. If you have a specialized knowledge your reader is assumed to lack, your writing may contain concepts or vocabulary that make the reader's task difficult. If the ideas you are trying to communicate are especially complicated, it won't help to translate them into baby talk just to satisfy the reader's need for simplicity. You must use your best judgment about the appropriateness of stylistic choices; it is as easy to insult the reader's intelligence by condescending as it is by obfuscating simple concepts.

Style, in this sense, is like logic: Its clarity and effectiveness depend not only on what is said but also on what assumptions about the reader are appealed to in the saying. Stylistic choices, like logical connections, are often neither good nor bad in an absolute sense but only in their appropriateness to the knowledge shared by the reader and the writer. What appears obscure to one reader is clear to another. It is your task to adjust the style, as well as the reasoning, to the audience. The writer who tries to sound intelligent or educated by adding stylistic flourishes—complex sentences and inflated diction—does not fool the careful reader. But the writer whose style makes appropriate assumptions about the reader's knowledge and reflects a shared understanding and respect for the subject earns the reader's goodwill.

Writers who believe they can improve their image by inflating their diction sometimes turn to a thesaurus in search of synonyms. This misuse of an otherwise useful resource generally results in stylistic problems. The writer who tries to substitute a high-falutin' word for a simple one, consulting the thesaurus for a better-sounding word, risks two undesirable effects. The first is the possibility of misusing a word that sounds better but doesn't quite mean what the writer wishes to say. If a word is not part of a writer's working vocabulary, if he or she never would have thought of it without looking in a thesaurus, then chances are the writer doesn't really understand what it means. It is better to let the meaning choose the word for you than to let some unfamiliar word alter your meaning. The second potential effect is that the writer's tone will become pompous as a result of putting long or fancy words in place of simple, direct ones. When Mark Twain said, "I never use *metropolis* when I can get the same price for *city*," he was exaggerating. *Metropolis* has appropriate uses, or it wouldn't be in the language. But *city* will do in most situations where *metropolis* would be phony.

Writers may pay too much attention to the reader and too little to the subject, producing styles that are inappropriate because they suggest an attitude of someone who would rather conform to the reader's tastes than tell the truth. If a writer's tone sounds condescending or patronizing, it is because the style is out of control somehow; the balance between respect for the subject, respect for the reader, and respect for the self has somehow been lost. Here is an extreme example of this sort of imbalance:

> In this essay, I will try to persuade you that college athletic programs benefit all students. As a fellow student at this college, you are aware of this controversy, so I need not explain to you why it is important. You have heard that the college pays too much attention to sports, and perhaps you agree that the college could pay more attention to your education if sports programs were eliminated or cut back. As I discuss this issue, I will begin by describing the sports programs and their relation to academics, and

then I will list the benefits that you receive as a student from the existence of these programs. I will also attempt to refute whatever objections you may have to my reasoning, as I argue that athletics is indeed a benefit to you, whether you realize it or not.

All this talk addressed to the reader is unnecessary. It implies, although inadvertently, that the writer thinks the reader is unable to understand the writer's purpose without hand-holding. The writer also makes assumptions about the reader's beliefs that may or may not be shared with actual readers, and the essay further insults the reader's intelligence, therefore, by pretending that the writing is addressed only to those readers who need the writer's superior guidance. Even though there is nothing wrong with refuting potential objections in a persuasive essay, this writer gives the reader no credit for having any objections that are valid.

The paragraph actually says very little. It announces its stance and refers to a controversy. The first three sentences contain information that could be communicated quite efficiently in a single sentence introducing the issue. Then the last two sentences explain what the essay will proceed to do. These are also unnecessary; if the essay is well organized, there is no reason to provide the reader with these clues to what will come later. Sentences of this sort often find their way into writing, unnecessarily.

I am now going to take up the second part of my topic. . . .

At this point, let us look at the related question of . . .

I will now begin the discussion of my reasons. . . .

Such road signs are seldom necessary, but writers often include them out of a sense that the reader needs help. Such overt transitional markers bring unnecessary attention to the structure and distract the reader's attention form the content. If you construct a clear transition from a given discussion to a related question, showing what the relation is, there should be no need to say, "At this point, let us look at the related question of. . . ." It goes without saying. Too many such phrases, meant to help the reader through the structure, can seem like condescension. They should be used sparingly. (Sparingly does not mean never. Do you think I have overused such phrases in this book?)

You may have encountered a writer who seems to care more about pleasing the reader than about telling the truth. A writer's failure to write from a point of view that does justice to the writer's thoughts on an issue can result in a desire to entertain that overwhelms any desire to find good reasons. Thus, the writing can take the form of an elaborate bluff. This is likely to be the case if we detect in the writer's style some attempt to use language to draw attention away from the subject and to the style itself. Here's an example from an essay on evolution:

What's all the trouble about anyway? If our grand-daddies and grand-mommies got created in one big bang (no pun intended), or if they crawled out of the water, shook off their feathers and said, "Where's the exit of this zoo?" it really can't make much difference to us. We all have to get born, whether the chicken came first or the egg. But, you know, some people are never satisfied with not knowing something, so they feel like they have to invent an answer or bust. So the scientists, who could be trying to cure cancer, put their big brains to work theorizing about "evil-lution," while the glory brigade sing hallelujah to a creator who didn't have to make cancer in the first place.

This clever style has some interesting and original turns of phrase, and even some sophisticated uses of sentence structure (such as the parallel clauses about cancer in the last sentence). But are we amused, as the writer clearly intends that we should be? Maybe, but also puzzled. What's the point of this glib talk? We would like to see a spark of wit in the things we read rather than an unremitting glumness. But wit can be purposeful, or it can be a way of thumbing one's nose at ideas in order to avoid having to think about them. That's the impression I get from this writer, who clowns at the expense of confronting the questions the writing raises.

The issue of whether or not to use humor, like other stylistic questions, cannot be answered with a rule. The only rule is this: It depends. It is as mistaken to take everything more seriously than it deserves as it is to take nothing seriously enough. A balance, some kind of golden mean, is the best answer, and it is found when the writer is conscious of having a choice. How do I want to sound in this essay? What attitude do I want to reflect, given my stance and my readers' attitudes? What kind of style do my subject and my audience deserve? These considerations do not guarantee that the style is appropriate in every case, but without them a writer may fall back on convenient habit, sheer clumsiness, or bluff.

Style and Clear Thinking

It is important to pay attention to style in order to be sure that your writing conveys an attitude appropriate to the reasoning. There is another reason that paying attention to style is important. We not only write in words and sentences, but think in them as well. The thoughts we think can be affected by any habits we may have in the use of words. This is not a reason to use any particular style in a particular piece of writing; it is a reason to remain conscious of the possibility of being controlled by stylistic habits.

The potential effect of stylistic habits on mental habits is discussed in a famous essay by George Orwell, the British author whose novels include *Animal Farm* and *Nineteen Eighty-Four*. As you know if you have read these novels, Orwell was keenly interested in *groupthink*, or the control by totalitarian regimes of how and what people think. He showed how language can be a powerful tool to suppress freedom of thought, open-mindedness, and independent judgment. The control of language by the state, he believed, was the same as the power to control thinking. Similarly, he believed that control of language by the individual was the same as freedom of thought, and that consciousness of style could, therefore, help the individual remain free of the unwarranted power of others' uncritical ideas.

Orwell's argument, in his essay "Politics and the English Language" (found online at http://eserver.org/langs/politics-english-language.txt), goes something like this: It is easy for people to imitate stylistic habits that become conventional in the language they hear all around them. Some of these habits have their origins in uses of language that are deceptive, such as the euphemisms, half-truths, or misleading expressions that may be found in political writing, advertising, or journalism. Some may be caused by simple neglect; sloppy and inaccurate thinking has given rise to sloppy and inaccurate expressions. Whatever the origin of such habits, they can, in turn, become the cause of poor thinking. The English language, Orwell wrote, "becomes ugly and inaccurate because our thoughts are foolish, but the slovenliness of our language makes it easier for us to have foolish thoughts." Thus, failure to pay attention to style can produce unclear thinking, without our being aware of it. But, Orwell believed, "if one gets rid of these habits one can think more clearly."

Thus, although Orwell believed that language can have an insidious effect on our thinking, we can prevent this effect by taking the trouble to choose our manner of expression carefully. In what is to me the most powerful part of his essay, Orwell put it this way:

> A scrupulous writer, in every sentence that he writes, will ask himself at least four questions, thus: What am I trying to say? What words will express it? What image or idiom will make it clearer? Is the image fresh enough to have an effect? And he will probably ask himself two more: Can I put it more shortly? Have I said anything that is avoidably ugly? But you are not obliged to go to all this trouble. You can shirk it by simply throwing your mind open and letting the ready-made phrases come crowding in. They will construct your sentences for you—even think your thoughts for you, to a certain extent—and at need they will perform the important service of partially concealing your meaning even from yourself.

It is that closing irony that makes this passage most effective, I think. Orwell reminds us that life would be simpler if we did not have to think for ourselves, and we are often ready to give up freedom of thought for the comfort of conformity. But the price we pay for this comfort is self-deception.

Orwell supported his argument with many examples drawn from contemporary writing. It is amazing how many of his examples continue to be found in popular language habits of today. Language, like other fashions, has fads and trends, some of which last longer than others. If you read Orwell's essay, you will be able to think of many expressions in fashion today that could be added to his list of examples. Based on his examples, Orwell devised six general rules of style that he said could be relied on "when instinct fails." His rules are:

1. Never use a metaphor, simile or other figure of speech which you are used to seeing in print.
2. Never use a long word when a short one will do.
3. If it is possible to cut a word out, always cut it out.
4. Never use the passive when you can use the active.
5. Never use a foreign phrase, a scientific word or a jargon word if you can think of an everyday English equivalent.
6. Break any of these rules sooner than say anything outright barbarous.

Orwell's rule number 6 is another reminder that when it comes to style there are no real rules, in the sense of laws that cannot be broken. Style serves a purpose. The purpose must determine the validity of the rule. It depends.

As a writer, you could probably not keep these rules in mind all of the time while you are composing. Worrying too much about rules can distract you from your ideas. The point at which you ought to think about such rules consciously is during revision. Rules, as Orwell said, are at our service when instinct fails. Applying them thoughtfully, as a means of revising, can help to make them instinctive.

Editing as Rethinking

Editing a rough draft is a process of looking at the words and sentences with the intention of making them express just what you mean and do just what you want them to do. Deliberately editing according to certain principles can also provide you with a source of critical distance. By looking for particular features, perhaps those that someone has made you aware of by offering you criticism, you can separate yourself somewhat from the flow of your thoughts and look at the writing *as writing*. But because the question of whether or not any specific editing change actually improves the essay depends on the purpose of the writing and the context of the whole argument, editing in this way leads to rethinking the ideas.

Before we consider editing techniques that may help you to improve your writing, I want to say something about the difference between editing on paper and editing with a word processing program on a computer. On the next page I reproduced a piece of rough draft from an earlier section of this book, written by Brad Hawley and then edited and retyped by me. It's not the particular editing decisions I made that I am illustrating by reproducing this page but rather the messiness of the process. When I retyped the page and entered it into my computer, this messiness disappeared, of course. Then I edited again, and on the computer screen it continued to look neat and clean, even though what I was doing was the same kind of editing I had done with a pen on paper. Computers remove from our sight the actual editing changes we make. As we insert and delete on a computer, no record is left behind such as there is when we edit on paper.

This is a great advantage of computers, but consider that it may also have hidden risks. For one thing, when the computer erases the deleted words or phrases, we no longer have them in front of us to compare, and it may be harder to change our minds and return to the original phrasing (even though we can use the Undelete command to bring back some deleted text). But more importantly, the very neatness of the writing we produce on a computer screen can sometimes delude us into thinking that we do not have to change anything: It looks like a typeset page. Parts of this book were delivered to the printer looking a bit like this illustration; what I submitted as editing changes to the

For this course, you will
∧Most often, ~~you will~~ read nonfiction argumentative essays and develop
                response to
questions at issue in ~~terms of~~∧ those essays. ~~in preparation for writing~~
~~your own academic paper.~~ But how do we come up with questions at issue
when reading a different kind of text? How do we understand an
author's argument when it is presented through a fictional text?
Asking this question assumes that fictional works—short stories,
        poems
novels, plays,∧and ~~even~~ films—actually do convey arguments. Remember
that even though you are writing academic essays to make your
            is an act   ed
arguments, all writing ~~all acts~~∧ of communication, ~~or rhetoric~~ intend∧
to have an effect on an audience. This ~~intentional aspect of rhetoric~~
            a kind of
means that all writing, even fiction, conveys ~~an~~∧ argument.

 The best way to understand the arguments made in fiction is to consider
one of the main differences between essays and stories: ~~The use of~~
          a
~~characters.~~ While∧non-fiction essay~~s~~ present~~s~~ ~~a thesis that dictates~~
~~the structure of~~ an argument that is given *directly* to the audience,
            plots with
fictional stories present∧characters to whom we respond and through
whom a complex argument is made *indirectly*. This indirection ~~is one of~~
~~the reasons many people prefer to read fiction rather than nonfiction,~~
~~but this indirection also~~ makes the arguments presented in fiction
harder for us to respond to because we usually can't locate a directly
            We respond sympathetically or unsympathetically to
stated thesis. ~~Another difference is the way these authors use the~~   characters
~~three appeals. Though all writers of argument use ethos, pathos, and~~ rather than
~~logos, authors of nonfiction essays often focus more on logos than~~   to reasons.
~~pathos, while fiction writers place an emphasis in pathos.~~

text of the third edition was in the form of handwritten additions and dele-tions. So the neatness that you see on the page now is not the result of my edit-ing but of the typesetter's cleaning up of my editing. The computer does not write and edit; it sets type. Don't be fooled by the neat appearance on the page; edit anyway and reread the result carefully.

This advice may sound strange to you because a word processor actually makes editing easier. Cutting and pasting, moving text, inserting words—all of these are easier on the computer. But the experience of many teachers sug-gests that most students do *less* editing when they edit on computers than when they edit on paper. And despite the ease of editing on a computer, many teachers find that students who edit on computers make more mistakes than those who edit on paper. Because of the finished appearance of words on a computer screen, perhaps we simply feel less responsibility to reread our writ-ing or to look carefully for mistakes. Do we think the computer is doing this for us? It can't.

Be cautious of giving away your responsibilities as a writer to the computer. If you use a spell-check program, for instance, remember that it won't guarantee that you use words correctly. Spell-checks do not know the difference between words like *their*, *they're*, and *there*, for example, and if you use the wrong one, the computer will not fix the mistake for you. A spell-check or even a grammar-check can't tell you whether a word you have used is the *right* word in the *right* place. You know more about grammar than your computer's grammar-check does, and if you don't read your writing carefully, as if simply putting it through such a program is enough, strange mistakes may enter your writing.

In learning to apply the editing techniques in this chapter, perhaps it would be a good idea to start out doing most of your editing on paper and then enter-ing those changes into the text on the computer. This will make it easier to learn to edit well, and when you have become a proficient editor of your own prose, you will be able to use the computer's advantages more purposefully.

Now, let's take a closer look at each of Orwell's editing principles.

Using Figurative Language

Orwell's first rule refers to the use of figurative language: *Never use a metaphor, simile or other figure of speech that you are used to seeing in print.* Notice that Orwell is not telling us to avoid figurative language but rather cautioning us against using it thoughtlessly. When certain figures of speech become overused, they lose their power to communicate and become clichés. Because such phrases are overused, they often cease to convey a precise idea and reflect instead the writer's disregard for precision.

A figure of speech is simply a means by which words are able to say one thing while communicating something else. From this fact comes the power of figurative language—its novelty and ability to suggest unique connections—but this is also the source of its potential imprecision. For example, the philoso-pher Aristotle took advantage of the suggestive power of language when he wrote, "Poverty is the parent of revolution." He assumed his readers would know that he did not mean "parent" literally. He assumed they would associate the relation between poverty and revolution with the relation between parent and child. If he could not assume these things, he would have risked being misunderstood. Because figurative language works by suggestion, one must control it to get just the right effect.

When writers use figures of speech that have become clichés, this control is surrendered. Consider this passage:

> The administration is grasping at straws in its policy toward Albania. We hear harsh words being spoken about ethnic cleansing on the one hand, and on the other we hear glowing praise of the Albanian government. Our waffling Congress should get its act together and tell the White House to get off its horse. The bottom line is whether we are going to support any government that condones the moral bloodbath taking place in the name of economic necessity.

The only clear idea being communicated here is that the writer wishes the Congress to impel the administration to condemn ethnic cleansing practices. The overuse of figures of speech makes the meaning harder to find than necessary. *Straws* and *waffles* clash in meaning, *house* and *horse* in sound. Some of the phrases are simply not clear. This writer blurts out commonplace sentiments without giving them much thought—an impression that does not depend on whether or not the reader agrees with the stance.

Figures of speech and clichés are not always easy to find because some dead metaphors seem to have become literal. You probably identified the following as clichés:

grasping at straws

waffling Congress

get its act together

get off its horse

moral bloodbath

But other figurative phrases are more subtle:

harsh words

glowing praise

on the one hand . . . on the other hand

White House

bottom line

in the name of

These phrases are so common that we can easily forget they are metaphors. Whether a metaphor communicates the writer's meaning precisely is a question that must be asked of all such phrases, no matter how literal they may sound. This is why a careful assessment of one's own metaphors, as Orwell prescribed, is important.

Forgetting that figurative language draws on one aspect of experience in order to describe another can lead to losing control of its use. There must be an appropriate connection between the kinds of experiences being associated. Examples of experiences inappropriately connected may be found today in the popular application of metaphors deriving from computers. For instance, consider these phrases:

> I will provide my input to our discussion of Plato's concept of beauty.

> Abusive parents have difficulty interfacing with their children.

The metaphors here seem inappropriate to the subject matter because there is no reason to compare the experiences under discussion to associations we have with computers. *Input* was originally technical jargon for entering data into machines, but it has now become a common metaphor for thoughts, opinions, or ideas. Similarly, *interface* is jargon for the capacity of computers to combine functions, but it is often used to refer to human relations as well— such as *talking* or *understanding*. As these terms lose their metaphoric power through overuse, it becomes easier to apply them to experiences for which they are inappropriate. The popular overuse of this kind of language to refer to human actions or problems (as well as other metaphors taken from business or military or education jargon, such as *bottom line, target of opportunity,* or *gifted*) can change the way we think about people or issues, if we do not remember that they are metaphors.

It is not possible, and certainly not necessary, to write without ever using commonplace expressions. Avoiding all such phrases could produce a style that is sterile and officious, lacking a human voice. Figurative expressions give our speech color and liveliness, they suggest the personality of the writer, and they communicate special meanings. Orwell's rule cautions us against using worn-out and commonplace figures of speech, but it does not prevent us from using occasional figures that contribute to the effectiveness of our writing.

Inflated Diction

Orwell's second rule, *Never use a long word when a short one will do,* returns us to the caution against inflated diction. It is worth going into further. Don't assume that long words make you sound more intelligent or that short ones make you sound simple-minded. Let the meaning choose the right word, and length will take care of itself. What Orwell is getting at is the habit common to many writers of substituting polysyllabic monstrosities (!) for the simple, direct terms of everyday English. As an editing technique, Orwell's rule leads us to examine the long words we use, to see whether we have chosen them because they are right or simply because they are long.

The way some writers try to imitate a learned style, editing for precision can seem like translating from one variety of English to another. Here's an extreme case:

> Utilizing civil disobedience methodologies pursuant to the conceptual-izations of Thoreau facilitated the efficacious attainment of the primary objective of civil rights activists, namely the modification of statutory pro-hibitions deleterious toward racial minorities.

Translated into plain English, this means:

> Using civil disobedience according to the ideas of Thoreau made it easier for civil rights activists to reach their goal of changing laws harmful to racial minorities.

Although the meaning is much the same, the effect on the reader is much different.

Notice that the goal of the editor of this sentence was not to get rid of all words over two syllables long. That would be silly. Rather, the goal was to get rid of long words for which perfectly good short ones exist. Thus, the phrase *civil disobedience* remained, because no shorter phrase could be substituted for it without changing the meaning. The same is true for *activists* and *minorities*. But because all of the other monstrosities found in the sentence have simple equivalents, they are easily replaced.

utilizing	=	using
pursuant to	=	according to
conceptualization	=	idea
facilitate	=	make easy
efficacious attainment	=	reaching
objective	=	goal
modification	=	change
statutory prohibitions	=	laws
deleterious	=	harmful

Some long words are perfectly appropriate in some contexts, but they are misused by writers who habitually prefer the puffed-up to the plain. Orwell blames politicians for overusing such words, which are parroted by others— those who can be fooled into thinking that *selective disinformation* means some-thing other than *lying*. Many long words cannot and should not be avoided. But the English vocabulary is so vast that many words have become popular whose only function is to bedevil those who wish to express themselves clearly. Remember that you aren't trying to achieve the fewest possible number of syl-lables; you are trying to avoid the ponderous effect of wordiness. This brings us to Orwell's next rule.

Cutting

If it is possible to cut a word out, always cut it out. Clumsy writers not only use longer words than necessary, they also crowd their writing with empty words and roundabout phrases. Empty words contribute no meaning to the sentence in which they occur. Roundabout phrases are those that substitute several words for one.

Almost any word can be an empty word if it contributes no additional meaning to a sentence. Here are some examples:

Her decision was painful in nature.

I am majoring in the field of accounting.

Despite various minor flaws, the essay shows a good reasoning process.

Each of these sentences could be made more economical by cutting words that have no function, thus:

Her decision was painful.

I am majoring in accounting.

Despite minor flaws, the essay shows good reasoning.

No reader would respond to these sentences by wondering, "Do you mean painful in *nature*?" or "Do you mean the *field* of accounting?" or "Do you mean a good reasoning *process*?" or "Are the flaws *various*?" These words contribute nothing essential. Yet they are all words that in other contexts might have a specific function:

By nature, people question authority.

You have to choose one field for your major.

Writing is a process, leading to a product.

The same end can be reached by various means.

The words that did not contribute meaning before are doing so here. Thus it isn't the word itself that is empty; it depends on the role it plays. The context of a sentence within the whole composition determines if any words are superfluous. Editing for economy thus requires a writer to reexamine the meaning carefully and to ask what each word contributes to it.

Here's a passage in which the writer would face many such considerations as he or she edited for economy. I exaggerated the wordiness on purpose to illustrate several ways that language can be inflated.

The question to pose now is whether or not the acceptance of the basic concept of renewable energy resource production is justified at this time. Each and every kind of nonfossil fuel energy source, such as hydroelectric, nuclear, solar, and wind, etc., has recognized advantages over fossil fuels, but due to the fact that each also has unsolved problems attendant with its use, there is no consensus of opinion up to this point in time that the various benefits tend to outweigh the actual costs. Hydroelectric power resources make use of abundantly available supplies of water, but nevertheless there is opposition against their use from many who view the protection of lakes and streams from negative effects as a higher priority than meeting the energy needs of this nation. The reason why nuclear power is a controversial issue is that the extent to which nuclear waste materials will have lasting effects on the surrounding environment cannot be determined at the present time. Notwithstanding the fact that wind power is a feasible approach technologically, it is not practical from the stand point of cost-effectiveness. Solar power is dependent on the climate situation to a large degree, and in consequence its maximum possible potential may be viewed as restricted to certain regions of the country. But yet it is the one other alternative that does not have drawbacks sufficient enough to prevent us from directing our efforts toward its further development on a widespread scale.

Get out the blue pencil. Let's start cutting words. (In the following discussion, be prepared to refer to this passage, because I make lists of words from it, out of context.) This gassy writer has used more than twice the number of words necessary. Does anybody really write this badly? Maybe not, but many writers slip into one or another kind of wordiness. Some of the gas results from the kind of empty words I have already discussed. These phrases add no meaning to the passage in context:

to pose (What other kinds of questions are there?)

basic (The word is just noise.)

the concept of (More noise.)

attendant (Can problems ever not be attendant?)

various (Sheer humbug.)

situation (More noise.)

Getting rid of those is a start, but the writing still overflows with other kinds of waste. It is polluted by many other phrases that are simply redundant.

now . . . at this time

whether or not

each and every

such as . . . . etc.

unsolved problems

consensus of opinion

this point in time

but nevertheless

opposition against

reason why

controversial issue

surrounding environment

possible potential

but yet

other alternative

sufficient enough

further development

Eliminate half the words, and the meaning is the same.

Another kind of redundancy persists in the passage (not *continues to persist*). It results from including words that refer to concepts already clear from the context, as in these cases:

resource production (*Production* is understood in context.)

energy source (In context, *source* is redundant.)

problems . . . with its use (More empty words.)

up to this point (Implied by the use of the present tense.)

tend to outweigh (Either they do or they don't.)

available (How could they be abundant but not available?)

protection . . . from negative effects (Who protects anything from positive effects?)

the energy needs of this nation (We weren't thinking of any other nation.)

nuclear waste materials (What else could the wastes be if not materials?)

at the present time (We weren't thinking of any other time.)

feasible . . . approach (Just wind.)

practical . . . cost-effectiveness (Cost is practical by definition.)

maximum . . . potential (A useless modifier.)

regions of the country (Could it be regions of anything else?)

Practice the art of not saying the obvious by eliminating such repetitions. The paragraph is shrinking before our eyes.

The passage contains yet another kind of wordiness. Many of its phrases consist of strings of words that can be replaced by one word that means the same thing. These stringy, roundabout expressions should be translated into their economical equivalents:

due to the fact that	=	because *or* since
not withstanding the fact that	=	although
from the standpoint of	=	in
to a large degree	=	largely

in consequence	=	so
may be viewed as	=	may be (or is)
directing our efforts toward	=	trying
on a widespread scale	=	widely

With these changes, the passage is really shaping up. It may even be starting to sound human.

But before we finish with it, we still have to attack one last source of wordiness, the extended noun phrases that hide verbs. One way in which writers unknowingly add extra words is to transform verbs into nouns by attaching suffixes and auxiliary words to them, as in these examples from the paragraph:

the acceptance of	=	accept
make use of	=	use
there is opposition to	=	(someone) opposes
the protection of	=	protect
is dependent on	=	depends on
directing our attention toward its development	=	trying to develop

When you edit your writing for economy, then, look for verbs hidden inside noun phrases. The offending nouns often contain these suffixes:

-ive	(*is indicative of* instead of *indicates*)
-sion	(*made a decision* instead of *decided*)
-tion	(*gave consideration to* instead of *considered*)
-ment	(*made an improvement* instead of *improved*)
-ance	(*has the appearance of* instead of *appears*)
-al	(*made an arrival* instead of *arrived*)

Sometimes no suffix is needed to turn a verb into a noun, although it does require adding words, as in

do harm to	*instead of*	harm
is in need of	*instead of*	needs
effect a change in	*instead of*	change

None of these phrases by itself will make your writing clumsy, and there may be times when any such phrase is more appropriate than its shorter equivalent. But the habit of substituting noun phrases for verbs results in wordiness if it is not kept under control.

It may seem that editing for economy is fairly mechanical: Remove empty words, cut redundancy, transform hidden verbs. These are good principles, but they do not automatically result in a neat, economically worded product without further editing. Applying the blue pencil to our long passage of overwritten prose might result in some sentences that are still in need of polishing.

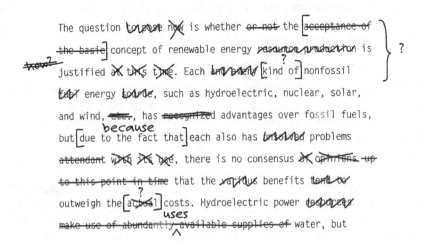

Editing like this is not intended for your readers' eyes. A rough draft is like a sketchbook, a record of your thoughts in process.

Having edited the passage for each kind of wordiness, we may still have to touch up the prose. When you cut words from a sentence, you must often rephrase some parts of the sentence to make it sound right. Now that we have cut out the verbal fat and put the sentences back together, here is the result:

> The question is whether using renewable energy resources is justified. Each alternative to fossil fuels has advantages, but since each also has problems there is no consensus that the benefits outweigh the costs. Hydroelectric power uses abundant supplies of water, but many oppose it who view protecting lakes and streams as a higher priority than more energy. Nuclear power is controversial because the lasting effects on the environment from nuclear waste cannot be determined. Although wind power is feasible technologically, it is not cost-effective. Solar power depends largely on climate, so its potential is restricted regionally. Yet it is the one alternative that does not have drawbacks sufficient to prevent us from developing it further.

The edited version of the paragraph could probably be reduced still further, although not much would be accomplished by cutting alone at this point. It now has 117 words, compared with the 243 of the original version. That's a "flab factor" of 52 percent.

The Passive Voice

Orwell's next rule is *never use the passive when you can use the active.* Some writers overuse the passive voice out of habit, and the result is confusion. The passive voice can result in unclear statements or in deceptive ones. A simple example shows how it works. Here's a sentence in the active voice:

> The chicken crossed the road.

In this sentence, the *agent* of the action is the chicken; that's what's doing what ever the verb indicates is happening. The *object* of the action is the road. In the passive voice, the agent and the object change places, thus:

The road was crossed by the chicken.

These two sentences describe the same action, but the change from active to passive changes the emphasis, from the chicken to the road. Both sentences are clear, although the second one is wordier. What makes the passive voice potentially unclear is that it permits a writer to ignore the agent, as in:

The road was crossed.

This is a grammatical sentence, whereas if we tried to get rid of the agent while keeping the verb in the active voice we would not have a complete sentence: ". . . crossed the road." This is what makes the passive risky, or convenient, depending on how you look at it: It permits you to get rid of the chicken! Actions take place in the passive, but nobody *does* them.

The need for higher standards is established.

It is believed that the strike should be canceled.

The new theory is regarded as practical, but it has not yet been tried.

Because they eliminate the agent, these sentences also hide information. The reader is left to wonder what that information is: "Is established" by whom? "Is believed" by whom? "Should be canceled" by whom? "Is regarded" by whom? "Hasn't been tried" by whom? When writers habitually use the passive voice, they seem to be hiding something. In fact, the passive voice has gotten its bad reputation because it is often used when people *do* have something to hide: "A decision was made to cut your budget," an administrator might say, so he or she can avoid having to admit that he or she decided it. The deliberate use of the passive to deceive is probably rare, but unintended deceptions happen frequently when writers habitually use passive verbs and fail to ask whether or not the excluded information is relevant. In editing, you should first identify the passive verbs and then ask whether they exclude necessary information.

Jargon

A long discussion of Orwell's next rule would repeat much of what I covered earlier. It too concerns diction: *Never use a foreign phrase, a scientific word, or a jargon word if you can think of an everyday English equivalent.* Jargon words and scientific words belong to the specialized vocabulary shared by a specific group. If you are writing for an audience that cannot be expected to share such terms, avoid them. If a jargon term or a scientific term is more convenient because it is precise and eliminates the need to repeat a string of plainer, explanatory words, use it, but not without being sure that your audience will understand it. If your motive for using jargon or scientific language is to impress the reader with your knowledge or to make your ideas sound more important than they really are, forget it.

The same might be said for foreign expressions, if their meaning would be obscure to the intended audience, unless there is some particular reason for using another language. If you were writing an essay about the way in which American tourists use foreign idioms, for instance, you could hardly do the subject justice without giving examples in foreign languages. Or, if you were arguing that a translation of a poem sacrificed emotional intensity for literal meaning, you would want to use examples to clarify and support your thesis. In such cases, you would have to depend on your knowledge of the audience to decide what examples to use and whether to provide translations. Reasons to include foreign expressions depend on the writer's purpose. If you are unreasonable in your expectation that a reader will know the meaning of a foreign expression, or need that expression to understand your point, then that expression may be functioning, like some jargon, to bluff rather than to communicate.

Rules Are Not Laws

Orwell's final rule is the least specific and the most interesting. *Break any of these rules sooner than say anything outright barbarous.* What Orwell is saying, perhaps, is that rules can take you only so far, and if you rely on them slavishly, they might result in making your writing worse instead of better. Rules are for convenience but they cannot replace good judgment. Applying editing rules can help you to gain control over your writing. To be in control of your writing means that *you* decide how to phrase what *you* have to say; it is not control to let rules decide for you. But you earn the right to break rules when you know your options and have good reasons for choosing one way instead of another.

What does Orwell mean by *barbarous*? I'm not sure I know. I think he chose the word to make us think about what it means to be educated and civil, or whatever we think of as the dialectical opposite of *barbarous.* Although the word is usually applied to behavior in general, it has special connotations when it is applied to language. To write barbarously is to write without care, without respect for the reader or the subject. It is to mimic the prevailing style of others without thinking. But, ironically, to write in an educated way can often mean the same thing, when the writer uses big words or padding or passive verbs to bluff and bluster and impress rather than to speak honestly and clearly. The educated writer may be the most barbarous of all, if he or she has learned how to imitate official-sounding prose without at the same time learning to think more responsibly. Once again, ideas come first. The educated writer is one for whom reasoning well is the most important goal. Editing well is a responsibility that follows from this goal and that helps the writer to achieve it.

Proofreading

Revision generally occurs in the rough draft stage, when a piece of writing is meant to be recopied or reprinted. The final draft is the actual manuscript that a writer submits. The reader of this version assumes that the writer intends no further changes. Proofreading refers to the limited kind of revising that a writer does to a final printed or typed draft. Proofreading appears to the reader as last-minute changes the writer made, usually to correct typographical or spelling or grammatical errors, or to make minor stylistic changes overlooked in earlier drafts.

Careful proofreading is a sign that the writer has said exactly what he or she intended to say. If it matters to a writer that his or her ideas are communicated, the burden of making all parts of the writing work—from the reasoning and structure to the style and finally to the correctness of mechanics and grammar—is assumed by the writer. Proofreading is the final check that what the reader actually sees is what the writer intends.

It is during the proofreading stage that writers must think about aspects of grammar that may not have occurred to them earlier. Most of the time, grammatical errors are caught and corrected during revision, so the following advice applies to revision and to proofreading. If there is any aspect of grammar you are uncertain about, take the trouble to look it up or ask someone who knows the answer, like your teacher. You may make some mistakes in English usage that you do not know are mistakes—and you shouldn't be afraid to make them because you should hope to learn from having them pointed out to you. But at this point in your education, you probably know those areas of grammar that give you trouble. When in doubt, find out. Not knowing when to use *who* and *whom*, for instance, is not a sign of stupidity or of moral negligence but rather a mistake that may distract your reader from your ideas. You can avoid such errors and learn the grammatical principle involved by consulting a good handbook. The conscientious writer keeps such a reference handy to consult when any question of grammar arises.

Proofreading consists of neat, legible corrections added to the final draft. Your reader should not be distracted by such corrections. Too many of them might mean that you should consider recopying, but it is better to include all necessary corrections than to give the reader the impression that you did not see errors or did not care whether they existed. The example on the next page shows part of a manuscript that has been carefully proofread and corrected. Notice that most of the changes are minor. A stylistic change here and there does not detract from the writer's credibility; it suggests that the writer is still thinking. Notice that some of the errors corrected on the illustration would be caught by a computer program, but others would not.

Be sure that you understand the proofreading marks your teacher may prefer or require, because there are many ways of indicating such changes. A good handbook describes specific proofreading conventions. The main objective of careful proofreading is to make sure that the final manuscript says exactly what you want it to say.

Teachers appreciate careful proofreading because it tells them exactly what the student understands about his or her own writing. A writing teacher is justified in thinking that any error you leave in your writing is the result of your ignorance of some aspect of English usage, and the teacher will therefore mark your errors for you in order to teach you. If you allow errors to go uncorrected in your writing when you do understand the correct way, you are not getting credit for what you know, and you may be putting an unnecessary obstacle between your reader and your meaning.

```
The film attempmted to explore the question of what is "normal"

behavior in our society by having the main characters reverse

roles and putting them in situations where their otherwise

"abnormal" attributes make them more able to cope. Tom, the
                                            i
radical dropʘout, does not suffer the anxietes of his fellow
                            not
workers because he does take the business world all that
                                            her
seriously. And Sarah, who is equally fanatic in desire to be

upwardly mobile, is never persuaded that the revolution is just,

but she makes it more efficient with her businesslike approach to

organizing people. As light farce, the film leaves too many issues
                                I
unexplored, however and this reviewer missed the depth of

questioning found in films like One Flew Over the Cuckoo's Nest or

King of Hearts. Compared to these, this film suffers from myopia.
```

Questions for Thought, Discussion, and Writing

1. Analyze the style of a piece of argumentative writing you think is effectively written. What stylistic choices make the sentences more readable? What choices make the writer sound more reasonable, credible, honest, sincere? What choices hinder the writer's credibility?

2. Analyze a piece of your own writing in this same way.

3. After looking carefully for features that characterize the texture of your prose, make a list of any stylistic *habits* you find in it.

4. A literary critic once said, "Every change in style is a change in meaning." Do you agree with this claim? Why or why not?

5. In your outside reading, locate several examples of figurative language used effectively and ineffectively. What reasons do you have for judging the examples in these ways?

6. Find examples of metaphors common in speech and writing that have the power to affect how people perceive reality. What gives them this power?

7. Find a piece of writing you completed some time ago for a different class. Then:
   a. Locate and list all the metaphors. Do they work? Would you want to eliminate them? Why?
   b. Edit the writing by looking carefully at the diction, cutting unnecessary words, changing passive verbs to active ones in appropriate cases, changing the length and shape of your sentences, and trying to find effective, honest transitional phrases where they might be needed.

8. Once you have completed a rough draft of an essay for class, revise it according to principles discussed in this chapter. Try first to get someone to read it to you aloud. Listen carefully. By hearing it read, what do you learn?

9. After you receive an essay back from your teacher, analyze the comments according to the advice in this chapter. Reread your essay. What do the comments teach you as you think about applying them?

Implications for Research

Research as Inquiry

College writing often requires some kind of research. Because some students sometimes produce writing that looks like research but really isn't, we should consider for a moment what the term means in a college setting. Research is inquiry into the unknown. It is the pursuit of answers to questions that are yet unanswered. Research takes different forms, of course, but all research derives from a basic desire: to find out what is true.

Given these definitions, you can see why I said that the writing of college students sometimes resembles research but is, in fact, something else. The standard term paper—sometimes called a research paper—might not involve any genuine research at all, if, for instance, the writer only repeats information found in sources to confirm a conclusion that was never in doubt. Merely going to the library or using the Internet to compile information is not research; it is more like reporting on the research of others.

A long essay, with correctly documented footnotes from many bibliographic sources, is a research paper only if it results from the writer's having sought and found an answer to a question. Research writing is the process of arguing that answer in such a way that the knowledge the writer has discovered can be shared with others. Research is like learning: It proceeds from not knowing to knowing. Research writing is argumentation: It shows why answers should be accepted.

Research is not a process that begins with complete uncertainty and ends with complete certainty; it is, therefore, not possible to become fully informed first and then to decide what to believe. There are always gaps in one's knowledge—even if one reaches the point, after years of research and study, of becoming an expert. One learns by doing research that there is always something more to know before absolute certainty is possible. Thus, the research writer must always argue for his or her discoveries on the basis of the best information available. The research writer, in other words, must know how to argue well and responsibly without having all the answers. The researcher, as a writer of argumentation, must seek clarification and belief within the limits of what it is possible to know. As a writer of argumentative essays, you must learn to measure conclusions against the quality, not the quantity, of the available reasons. This is exactly what a good researcher also must know how to do.

In the sections that follow, I develop some of the implications for research, as I have just defined it, of some of the key concepts of this book.

Critical Reading and Research

As a student—and as a voter, a consumer, a person who must decide things—you often need to find out more than you already know about some subject before committing yourself to a conclusion or a course of action. Critical reading is necessary in order to know what to make of the knowledge you discover when you look into some subject, but it also helps you to decide what needs looking into. When, in your reading, you try to judge the conclusions you find against the adequacy of the reasons given for them, you can isolate the areas in which your knowledge needs to be increased. By reading critically, you may find that you need not read further in one area, such as anesthesia, but do need to know more about some other, such as sodium pentothal.

In formal research, you are responsible for finding information to explain a phenomenon and evidence for arguing a reasonable conclusion about it. In informal research—the kind we do whenever we have unanswered questions, even if no writing will result from it—you want to assure yourself that your ideas or actions are founded on reasons you understand and trust. The goal of either kind of research is confidence in what you know. Critical reading guides you in gaining that confidence, even though, as we saw in Chapter 2, confidence is not easy to come by.

Because of its convenience, the Internet has increasingly become a place to start when one is looking for information as part of a research project. One can access a wealth of information on the Internet from the comfort of one's own room or nearly anywhere. However, if you look for information on the Internet exclusively, without adding to what you know the ideas and information potentially available in a research library, you are probably limiting your inquiry too narrowly. And, given the nature of the Internet, you need to consider its limitations as well as its strengths.

As in the case of using any limited research source, you must be aware that simply reporting information or repeating arguments you find on the Internet is not genuine research but merely gathering the ideas and information of others. *Research*, as I defined it above, is "inquiry into the unknown." To answer questions by repeating the obvious or downloading some source, isn't inquiry in this sense. When you perform research on the Internet, despite the air of authority computers impart to information because of their speed of access and the sometimes seductive forms in which that information is graphically displayed, you are still responsible for being a critical reader, an independent evaluator of ideas and information. You will find that the questions for critical reading from Chapter 2 will help you to evaluate Internet sites and visual information in the same way they are meant to help you to evaluate the printed texts you encounter in books, newspapers, or magazines.

There is, though, a significant difference between information presented on most Internet sites and certain kinds of printed information. Printed texts, before they are published and located in libraries or bookstores, especially if they are written by experts in their field and published as scholarly research, go through a rigorous process of evaluation by other experts in the field. This process cannot guard against all errors of unsound reasoning and may require much time before the information is available in print. Yet because of that peer review process, printed texts generally are reviewed for accuracy and soundness in a way that most Internet sites are not.

The nature of the Internet is to enable anyone with a little knowledge of website design and an Internet connection to set up a website and put anything on it that that person wishes. In most cases, there is no peer review of that process at all. So information found there is more likely to be dated, incomplete, prejudicially opinionated (as opposed to reasoned), or just plain wrong. Because it is so easy to put up a website, what is found there may not have the thoroughness or carefully researched quality likely to be found, say, in a good scholarly book or reference guide on the subject. Also, Internet websites often emphasize graphic design over content, and many sites that are constructed thoughtlessly let the graphic design determine the nature and quality of the information rather than the other way around.

Therefore, as a responsible researcher, you must be cautious when researching on the Internet, and if you are seriously investigating a subject, follow up with some time in a research library, such as the one at your college. The following questions can help you to becoming a more critical Internet reader: Who is the author? Is he or she taking responsibility for the information? Is he or she connected with an organization that can be trusted to be unbiased in its reporting of information? Does the author provide a bibliography or other resource materials that allow you to check on the accuracy of the information cited? Is the argument developed as thoroughly as it would be in a printed medium? Is the information developed for that site or simply downloaded from another? Is it timely? Are there political or commercial motives that might make you suspicious of the site's rigor or thoroughness? How has the graphic design of the site been used—as an aid to understanding the information or as a substitute for or mask for information?

Of course, the Internet is a wonderful resource for many kinds of visual or reference texts, and it can link us to others in ways nothing else can. It provides, for instance, the ability to put us in direct, almost instantaneous touch with researchers or experts. Taking advantage of these wonders is an important part of your education. But if you experience these benefits of the Internet without knowing about the many wonders of the library as well, your research will be incomplete. Further, you deprive yourself of the kinds and quality of resources and research texts found in libraries but not on the Web.

If you are interested in looking further into the issue of critical evaluation of Internet sites, you might want to take a look at a World Wide Web site called Evaluating Internet Information at http://www.library.jhu.edu/research help/general evaluating. Now, does it seem ironic to you that in my cautioning you to be critical of Internet research, I would direct you to the Internet for more information? Indeed. So, be sure to evaluate this site using the same criteria.

Asking Questions for Research

It may have seemed from Chapter 5 that coming up with a reasonable thesis is a matter of thinking only about what you already know, that it does not require you to become well informed before jumping off into speculation. Not so. Coming up with a reasonable thesis is *primarily* a matter of thinking hard about what you know. You will not find your own thesis by going to the library or surfing the Net in search of what to think. But in the process of thinking about potential theses, you will encounter gaps in your knowledge of a subject, and if these gaps prevent you from thinking about that subject further because you do not know something that is vital to your understanding, then you should attempt to fill those gaps. There is a difference between rash speculation and honest speculation. If you are unsure of something that is crucial to your position, or if you are assuming that some part of your idea is true because you "heard it somewhere" or because "my sister told me," then you are being rash. An honest commitment to an idea is based on your confidence that the knowledge that idea seems to assert is real knowledge.

The lesson here is simple. You must think hard about your ideas; there's no way around that, except to be irresponsible. But you might, by thinking hard, discover that you need to look something up, to find out or to verify the knowledge you want to claim. If that is the case, then finding out becomes your further responsibility.

Formulating a research question can be an aid to conducting such an inquiry. It enables you to define the unknowns, to determine the boundaries of the inquiry, and to keep the inquiry focused as you seek to become better informed. Of course, the question starts out as a tentative formulation, subject to change. The more you discover and the more thought you give to the possible answers, the clearer you may become about the kind of question you wish to answer. Research is seldom so straightforward that no side trips, dead ends, detours, or unexpected changes of plan happen along the road to answers. The process of becoming informed seldom follows a predictable route.

Having formulated a research question, you might ask yourself something like "What do I need to know to answer this question?" At this point you might sketch out a plan and list some of the specific areas you need to know more about. Any question can be broken down into constituent parts, even if the categories are temporary or turn out later to be irrelevant. You may not yet know what all of the categories are—research is, after all, exploring the unknown. Yet you never start out without *some* knowledge because you had to understand something already in order to perceive the significance of the question you decided to explore. Trust that knowledge and sketch out some possibilities based on the question you have formulated.

If you have not become familiar with the resources of a research library, you can ask the reference staff for their advice. All good libraries have educational material available to students who wish to acquaint themselves with the basic functions of the library. Often, the best way to discover what kinds of resources the library has available in your own areas of interest is to get in there with your questions and begin to follow leads wherever they take you. It is often adventurous and fun to explore as a means of becoming familiar with the library at the same time you seek to inform yourself about your subject. A researcher, like a detective, has to be watchful for unexpected clues. The library is full of these, and you should be prepared to investigate any that might take you into important discoveries.

Research is often classified as either secondary or primary research. Secondary research consists of locating and using the research that other people have already conducted and written about. One way of going about answering research questions is to read the writing of other researchers who have investigated the same or related questions. Primary research consists of investigating any phenomenon on one's own by working directly with the phenomenon rather than reading about other people's work with it. Secondary research is ordinarily conducted in the library, because that is where one usually goes to find out what others have written. Primary research is ordinarily conducted outside the library.

The distinction between primary and secondary research applies to all fields of inquiry. Science provides the most obvious examples. A biologist, for instance, may be interested in discovering how a particular species of plant reacts to changes in light. There are many things about this question that she might learn in the library. To answer it, she would have to know as much about the plant as possible and about how other species of plants react to similar changes, information that can be found in the published research of other biologists. She would also want to know whether anyone has already discovered the answer to her question or to questions that bear on it. But having informed herself in this way, the researcher must move from the library to the laboratory to complete the study by conducting experiments with plants and light sources. The secondary research provides preparation for the primary research. Depending on the kind of question under investigation, primary research takes place in the laboratory or in the field or simply in the privacy of one's thoughts. An anthropologist investigating what kinds of traditions accompany marriage in urban subcultures may learn a lot by reading, but at some point he must go out and collect primary information by talking to people and observing the phenomena first-hand. A sociologist studying the attitudes of teenagers toward alcohol abuse can learn much by reading in the library, but she must also question teenagers to find her answers. A scholar studying the possible influence of impressionist painting on the literary style of Gertrude Stein would learn much by finding sources in the library, but her primary research must consist of careful observations about the paintings and the writing. The way in which primary research is conducted varies from discipline to discipline, depending on the kinds of questions being asked, but all research moves from the secondary collection and assessment of others' ideas to the primary study of the phenomenon under study. Primary research *extends* secondary research. Without both, no research would be complete.

Finally, remember that the researcher enters the process of becoming informed without knowing where that process may lead. The research question like the thesis of an argumentative essay, may change as the researcher discovers more information or complexities and continues to think about them. Further questions may arise. Answers may have to remain tentative. But just as the writer of an argumentative essay has to decide when a line of reasoning is adequate, a researcher must decide when a question can be answered reasonably. In either case, there is nothing wrong with admitting that the answer is only as good as the quality of the evidence that supports it, so the possibility of further inquiry remains open.

Research and Reasons

Reasons, like conclusions, are assertions and therefore subject to verification if they rely on information the writer is not absolutely confident about. In that case, everything I just said about the possible need to inform yourself before making rash statements in your thesis applies to the claims you decide to use as reasons. Your reasoning does not depend solely on the validity of your logic, it depends equally on the dependability of your information. But you know by now that simply looking up information is not sufficient. How do you know whether to trust what you find? Let's look at how some of the considerations in Chapter 6 might help to answer this question. As you read, for instance, consider the *kind of appeal* the writer is making. Does this give you more or less confidence in the source? As you read, isolate the enthymemes and reconstruct the assumptions you are expected to accept as self-evident. What does this say about the writer's view of his or her reader? How does this affect your understanding of the subject?

Rather than try to offer a dependable procedure for knowing when a source is right or wrong, let me describe the worst kind of uncritical research and see what it tells us about our responsibilities as evaluators of reasoning. I have seen student term papers in which many sources were cited to support the writer's idea, but in each case those sources consisted exclusively of the conclusions of studies that agree with the writer. In other words, the writer's thesis is argued by constructing a list of authorities all saying the same thing, as if such a list alone proved the point. This catalog of authorities does not constitute an argument, however, because the *reasons* these sources give for their conclusions are not explored. Such a writer has located many sources and found their conclusions, but he or she has not tried to assess those conclusions according to the process by which they were derived. The resulting "research paper" does not discriminate between conclusions derived by adequate means and conclusions derived by inadequate ones. As an argument, it is weak. As research, it is useless.

Clearly, then, anyone conducting serious research has the responsibility of doing more than skimming through sources to find conclusions. Once you find a source that seems relevant, you must know not only what its conclusions are but also how those conclusions were derived. In other words, you must consider the arguments presented in support of those conclusions and assess the conclusions accordingly.

What does it claim?

By what process have the conclusions been derived? What reasons are presented? What qualifiers?

On what assumptions do the reasons depend?

How adequate is the logic?

Your answers to these questions are just as important to your research as the conclusions themselves. Your own presentation of the results of your research must demonstrate that your inquiry has included such questions. Your reader, after all, can be assumed capable of asking them about your own conclusions.

It is also the researcher's responsibility to locate and consider studies that do *not* support whatever potential conclusion he or she intends to reach. Research questions are open-ended, but researchers often work from a hypothesis, whether it is defined early in the study or late. Whenever answers begin to emerge, it is essential to know which reasons may contradict those answers as well as which reasons support them. This way of looking at arguments, whether others' or one's own, is called *falsification*.

The process of falsifying ideas is an important mental exercise, involving seriously trying to answer questions like:

What if this idea is wrong?

What kinds of reasons could be used to argue against it?

What would have to be true for those reasons to be valid?

What assumptions are available to support those reasons?

To be able to consider such questions seriously, a researcher must have the mental agility to shift points of view. (We all probably increase our mental agility simply by trying to answer such questions.) It helps to see the weakness in a given line of reasoning to know how a different conclusion might be argued. To learn this requires that we be able to imagine how someone who holds a different view might defend it. No harm is done if by this means we come to question our ideas, or even to change our minds.

Structuring Research

The researcher, in the process of gathering information and discovering reasons to support a hypothesis, amasses much information and tests its relevance and validity. Not everything the inquiry turned up is necessarily relevant, and the writer may eventually use only a portion of the actual information he or she discovered. The writer should include whatever is necessary and sufficient to lead to a conclusion, as well as whatever may need to be said to refute the arguments of others or suggest limitations on one's own. To do this requires planning along the lines discussed in Chapter 7. The writer can perceive the necessary structure of the essay by analyzing the parts of the whole argument, which can be summarized in an enthymeme. It is important to remember here that the order in which the research findings appear in the essay is not necessarily the same as the order in which the researcher discovered them. The structure of the final essay is not, usually, a narrative of what happened to the researcher during the inquiry. The structure of the final argument is made up of ideas discovered during research, in whatever logical order binds those ideas into a whole, developing argument.

The structure of research writing in some disciplines is determined, in part, by conventional formats. It may or may not be necessary for you to follow them in writing for college courses, because the formats generally derive from the conventions of publication in different fields. Thus, an academic journal of research in psychology may specify that papers submitted for publication have a certain form. Articles in the social sciences often follow the conventional divisions of scientific reports, with all the material organized under headings such as:

Problem and hypothesis

Review of relevant literature

Experiment design

Results

Analysis

Conclusion and discussion

The specific headings differ from discipline to discipline, and even from publication to publication, so you should not try to reproduce a standard format of this kind unless you are fulfilling an assignment that specifically calls for one or writing for a publication that does. If your audience expects to find your research organized in such a way, then your use of a conventional format will make their reading easier. If not, you should be guided only by the ideas you present. Do not confuse structure with format. You are no less responsible for structuring your ideas *within* each of these conventional sections, if you use them.

As a research writer, you have a special obligation to provide whatever the reader needs to know to assess the validity of your findings. Remember that you are interested in finding the best possible reasons for drawing a conclusion, not in bullying the reader into believing some idea you haven't adequately supported. This means that you should consider including a description of the methods you used in your study and any limitations imposed by those methods. In some cases, this may mean a description of an experiment, a survey, or some other form of primary research, together with a description of the sorts of conclusions that such methods are not able to support. Or it may mean that you should inform the reader about prior assumptions or perspectives that guided your inquiry. If you have doubts about any of your sources, you can say so. If you think there are weaknesses in your conclusions, qualify them accordingly. If you have discovered reasons against your case (by reading sources that disagree or by falsifying your conclusions), present them fairly and let the reader assess them as you have done. Be sure that your reason for leaving anything out is that it isn't relevant or necessary, not that you wish to hide it.

Ethical research, like ethical argumentative writing, is intended to put the whole case forward, as you see it, so the reader's understanding and agreement are *earned*.

Questions for Thought, Discussion, and Writing

1. What have been your experiences as a researcher before this point in your education? Did the research you conducted fit the definition of genuine research I presented at the beginning of this chapter? Under what circumstances did it fit that definition or not fit it? If you have a copy of a research paper you wrote for another class, consider these questions in regard to that paper:
   a. Did you begin with an open mind, or was your conclusion already established before you began to look for sources?
   b. Did you read your sources critically or just look for conclusions in them that supported your own ideas?
   c. Did you evaluate the credibility of your sources?

     d. Did you look for sources of opinion that were different from your con-
clusions, and did you incorporate them into your argument?

     e. Did you engage in primary as well as secondary research?

     f. Independent of the grade you got for the paper, how do your answers
to these questions affect your assessment of the quality of that writing
now?

2. As you decide on a question to investigate, formulate a research plan that
will result in giving you the information you need. As you look up the
information, consider these questions:

     a. What *kind* of resource best provides the *kind* of information I need?

     b. How much information is enough for my purposes?

     c. How is my understanding of the issue improved by this information?

     d. What further questions does the information raise?

3. As you do the preceding exercise, or as you look up information for
another purpose, deliberately seek the same information in several library
and Internet sources. Compare the results by asking these questions:

     a. Which resource is more likely to provide accurate, thorough, or suffi-
cient information?

     b. How do different kinds of library and Internet resources differ in
terms of their potential usefulness for research?

     c. How do the library and Internet resources differ in the way informa-
tion is presented?

4. As you formulate a thesis in the form of an enthymeme for an argumentative essay, construct a series of research questions that need to be
answered before you can make the argument responsibly. Create a research
strategy that will begin your search for answers. As you conduct that
research, consider how what you discover may change the argument you
drafted. Deliberately search for credible arguments that come to different
conclusions from your own, and consider how your own argument must
be written in order to acknowledge or to do justice to those opposing arguments you have found.

5. In response to the principles discussed in Chapter 4, can you describe the
difference between research that is ethical and research that is unethical?
Are additional principles needed to make this distinction?

Appendix

Essays by Student Writers

Mindy Dodge, "Revising Our College Education: Participation Is the Key"

Todd Pittman "Nonviolent Resistance: A More Courageous Show of Power"

Matthew Stewart, "A Beefed-up Industry"

Katie Fidler, "The Self-Imprisonment of American Society"

FORUM ON ZOOS
Zach Blume, "The Reality of Zoos"

Leah Brandt, "Zoos: The Evil Empires"

Devlin Timony-Balyeat, "The Education Experience of the American Zoo"

FORUM ON ART AND CULTURE
Katie Wright, "Funding for the Future"

Rosei Rocha-Judd, "The Seduction of Hyperrealism and Overblown Images"

The following essays were written by students enrolled in College Composition I or II at the University of Oregon. They were chosen from essays submitted by instructors for possible inclusion in this book—not necessarily because they are the best essays but because they illustrate ways in which students have used the principles of this book. Whether they have used these principles successfully or unsuccessfully is for you to decide. They are offered here as examples for critical analysis. The strong voices and struggle to find and structure good reasons evident in these essays also show how an attempt to join a larger conversation about issues can make significant contributions to the world of ideas.

These essays are works in progress. As such, their authors have already revised them by considering responses to earlier drafts from teachers and peers. A good way for you to think about revising your own writing might be for you to consider how you would advise these authors to revise these essays. How could they improve the reasoning, the structure, or the style to make their arguments more likely to encourage inquiry?

Revising Our Education: Participation Is the Key

Mindy Dodge

In the following essay, Mindy Dodge responds to Mark Edmundson's "On the Uses of a Liberal Education," which details his concern about the changing learning environment at American universities. Dodge considers why the changes mentioned by Edmundson might have arisen and contemplates how both students and educators should react to those changes.

In the essay, "On the Uses of a Liberal Education," Mark Edmundson argues that American universities are no longer places where students look for a challenging and enriching education. According to Edmundson, university culture has been overtaken by consumerism and now the entertainment value of instructors and their courses is what reigns supreme. Although this image of an entire population seems rather harsh (especially to those of us who are currently students), there can be no doubt that over the years the profile of American college students has changed. Change of course is inevitable. Edmundson, however, describes the majority of today's students as either being apathetic or entirely missing the point of the material he teaches. He complains that there is no intellectual discourse among classmates and that these days they have to be spoonfed answers to the questions he asks. Although I would like to argue that this is a false representation of today's college population, I have witnessed (and sometimes displayed) this behavior in most of my own classes during the past four years. Does this point to some inherent flaw in the current student population, or does it signal that today's teachers are missing the mark? Edmundson would argue that the fault lies with those who perpetuate popular consumer culture by following the crowd and not acting out as individuals, in any capacity. I agree with his conclusion that the responsibility for change rests with both parties. In order for college classrooms to once again become places for intellectual discourse and sounding boards for novel ideas, active and constructive participation by both students and professors is necessary.

What does this entail for students? Active participation inside the classroom is a start. Why do students, myself included, try at all costs to avoid being called upon when a teacher asks a question of the class? We refuse to make eye contact, look suddenly enthralled with the notes that we've just written, or (and this is my favorite diversion tactic) rifle through papers like we are searching for the answer. What are we so afraid of? Is it that we will give the wrong answer and be contradicted by the teacher and embarrassed in front of other students, or that we are just nervous about how our answers will be perceived and how others will judge us? Speaking from my own experience, I would say that often it is a combination of both. Obviously, no one likes to appear ignorant in front of others. However, the drive to fit in and be accepted by our peers is an incredibly strong one, one that I believe governs the majority of students' classroom behavior. In my own classes I notice that if I am interested in a particular topic, and I am the only one doing much talking, I will tend to modulate my behavior so that I will not appear overeager to others. Although this type of self-monitoring to avoid the negative judgment of peers is comfortable, hiding within the status quo is a complete waste of an education. By not presenting your view or asking intelligent questions during your classes, not only might you be missing out on valuable information that you never thought of before, you might be missing out on the opinions and viewpoints of others that arise from such discourse. Arming ourselves with the power to approach and analyze issues from all sides, learning how to make informed decisions, and thereby growing intellectually, is the purpose of college. None of this will occur, however, if we are satisfied just to sit through our classes witlessly accepting information as it is "spoon-fed" to us.

Students are not the only ones to blame for the climate in today's classrooms. Professors and teaching assistants set the tone for the way a class is run. Although this goes against Edmundson and his dislike for popular consumer culture, presentation is everything. Just as students must take an active role in processing and analyzing the information given them, teachers must first present the material in an interesting and effective way. By effective I mean that teachers need to demonstrate genuine interest in what they are teaching. Students are not going to be interested in or care about subject material that a professor cannot even find the will to muster excitement about, especially considering that it is supposed to be his or her area of expertise. In some of the classes I have taken, there have been professors who have acted like they would much rather be concentrating on their own research projects than be anywhere near the classroom. This kind of indifference toward the subject matter and teaching in general is almost always transmitted to the students. As a result, students show little concern for delving deeper into the subject material.

Presenting material in a way that is "enjoyable" for students and catches their attention does not have to mean selling out to consumerism as Edmundson suggests. Professors can present information in novel ways, that relate it to present-day issues. These are techniques that usually help me remember material because it makes it more *accessible*. After all, isn't this really the teacher's job? Also, what is wrong with instructors asking themselves the same questions before they teach that we do before we begin writing? "Who is the audience and is this an issue?" To me, a consumer culture (the one described by Edmundson) suggests one in which students, and my generation in general, are looking for the quick fix or the easy out. With this view, we are looking for information that is heavy on the entertainment but light on content. There is a distinction, however. Entertaining does not have to equal devoid-of-challenge. When I am presented with material in one of my classes that is challenging, yet also interesting and applicable, I actually do get excited. These experiences reinforce my joy of learning and make me remember why I am pursuing a higher education. I do not believe that I am alone in my opinion either. There are too many students out there who do incredibly well in their classes for me to believe that they do not derive some enjoyment from what they are learning.

In some ways this societal shift toward consumerism does not seem altogether terrible. Students are now allowed to take a more active role in what their education consists of (through course evaluations), and why shouldn't they? With the skyrocketing costs of tuition and fees leaving many of us with thousands of dollars of debt as soon as we are handed our diplomas, haven't we earned the right to be picky? I think it only fair that we be able to exercise some control over the money we spend.

Edmundson is correct when he asserts that consumerism has overtaken colleges and universities. These days universities are businesses aimed at attracting potential customers. Although this is a sad commentary on our society, it does not have to follow that the quality of our education is also for sale. It is the responsibility of both students and teachers to ensure that the classroom is a place conducive to intellectual discourse. The first step toward achieving this kind of challenging and motivational atmosphere is through participation by both students and teachers.

Work Cited

Edmundson, Mark. "On the Uses of a Liberal Education: As Lite Entertainment for Bored College Students." *Harper's* (Sept. 1997): 39–49.

Nonviolent Resistance:
A More Courageous Show of Power

Todd Pittman

This essay grew out of readings and class discussions that addressed the question of whether nonviolent tactics are a reasonable alternative to war. Students read excerpts from Gandhi's writings, Martin Luther King, Jr.'s "Letter from Birmingham Jail," and several recent essays on nonviolence. Most students in the class argued that nonviolence simply could not work, especially on an international scale. This essay responds to their position.

The prevailing opinion in our Writing 122 class seems to be that nonviolent resistance is an impractical, utopian idea. But in my view, nonviolent resistance can be more effective than the alternative of taking up arms and fighting back, which only facilitates more fighting. One need only look to Northern Ireland of the 1980s and 1990s, or to the ongoing Israeli/Palestinian crisis to realize that answering violence with violence leads only to more violence. It becomes an endless game of one-upmanship, with no clear winners—just ever more body bags. Great leaders, such as Mahatma Gandhi and Martin Luther King, Jr., realized this. The most effective weapon at their disposal was to push the atrocities into the light of day—or, to use King's analogy (from his letter written in the Birmingham, Alabama jail as a response to fellow clergymen who had been urging him to take it slower and not to be a "rabble-rouser" [480]): injustice is "like a boil that can never be cured as long as it is covered up but must be opened up with all its pus-flowing ugliness to the natural medicines of air and light . . ." (479). Nonviolent resistance is not the same thing as doing nothing. Indeed, it is much more courageous and difficult to challenge violence with peace than to resort to the temptation of physical violence. It was not that Gandhi and King were weaklings or afraid to fight, but, rather, that they were pragmatists.

In Gandhi's case, he knew that even millions of Indians were no match for the military might of their British oppressors—if they were to fight them. The 100,000 British soldiers, armed with the best weapons of the day, would summarily slaughter millions of unarmed Indians before control of the country would be wrested from the British. But, as Gandhi knew, the great strength of his people could prevail through nonviolent resistance. As he made clear to the British commander in the film clip we saw from the movie, *Gandhi,* "One hundred thousand British soldiers cannot make three hundred million Indians cooperate, if those Indians do not choose to do so." Gandhi also understood that the British would find few allies in the court of world opinion if the British were seen as violently oppressing a peaceful, non-warring people. We saw evidence of this in the same film clip when the American reporter wiring his news story back home talks about the Indians "offering up their bodies, one after the other, well into the night."

During the Civil Rights Movement in the United States, Martin Luther King, Jr. showed great interest in Gandhi's methods. He saw parallels between the struggles of his people and the struggles of Gandhi's a few decades earlier. King knew what it was like to be under the thumb of an unjust oppressor. His people knew the great indignity of what it was like to be considered somehow less human than those who kept them down. But King also understood that violence could not raise his people to the level of those oppressing them, let alone above them and their evil ways. His deep faith in God convinced him that violence was not the answer. "I'm grateful to God," King wrote in his letter from Birmingham Jail, "that . . . the dimension of nonviolence entered our struggle. If this philosophy had not emerged, I am convinced that by now many streets of the South would be flowing with floods of blood" (480). King, like Gandhi, knew that it would be morally wrong to answer violence with violence. But, perhaps more important, his sense of pragmatism told him that his people stood no chance of winning if they chose to use violent force to resist the entrenched racism of the American South. For, although his people had shown great fortitude in just surviving as a race beneath the weight of hundreds of years of slavery and racism, they would be no match for the horrific violence that would be wreaked upon them by an oppressor equipped with the best weapons and military of the day—and the license to use both to quell "an out-of-control mob of lawbreakers."

Violence by the oppressed is exactly what an oppressor is hoping for, because, as the British understood in India, violence would be seen as having been justified if used to "resist" violence. Susanne Kappeler speaks to this in "Resistance and the Will to Resistance" when she says that "the concept of 'resistance' becomes part of the ideologizing structure of justifying one's own action, where the other's action preceding ours is said to be the cause of—or to have given us cause for—violent action on our part" (506). In other words, violence somehow seems less violent, indeed even noble, when used to resist another's violence. This is like the concept of "doublespeak" (to borrow from George Orwell's *1984*) which is exploited everywhere there is war, by the very people who are perpetrating the war, to make themselves out to be the "good guys." Birmingham Alabama Mayor Bull Connor ordering his policemen to turn their fire hoses on peaceful Civil Rights protestors was, I believe, not so much an attempt to break up a peaceful protest as it was an attempt to rile the protestors into responding violently—which would free Connor to use an even more violent means of squelching the protest. (Some people credit the image of people being blown down the street with fire hoses, shown on televisions and in the press worldwide, with turning the tide against segregation in this country.)

Violence, it seems, has long been the default mode of oppressors worldwide, but in this age when news travels the world instantly, oppressors can only get away with the use of violence if *both* sides choose to use it. It is not just the fact that nonviolent resistors are trying to appeal to the humanity of those who are oppressing them that makes nonviolent resistance successful, but also the fact that cruelty can no longer be so easily hidden—either by remoteness or by intention. Now when atrocities are discovered they are aired across the planet within hours, if not minutes. Oppressive governments are exposed immediately to the judgment and ridicule of the world community. Images like that of a lone pedestrian facing down a tank in Tiananmen Square still burn in our collective conscience, as does the image of a naked Vietnamese child with great fear and anguish on her face, fleeing from her American soldier pursuer.

The image of an oppressor using violent force against a peaceful protestor, or of an innocent child being victim to violence, reaches in and awakens our conscience. It impels even the docile among us to cry foul. This is what makes the bringing of atrocities into the light of day so powerful. And therein lies one of the most powerful aspects of nonviolence—its appeal to our sense of what is right or wrong. As Petra Kelly put it in "Nonviolent Social Defense," "Nonviolence is a spiritual weapon that can succeed where guns and armies never could" (503). Or as Gandhi put it, "Nonviolence is the greatest force mankind has ever been endowed with. Love has more force than a besieging army" (qtd. in Kelly 503). Nonviolent resistance may sound utopian, but it appeals to a part of the human animal that is the antithesis of violence. It awakens in us a sense of decency and morality that not even the harshest violence can stand up to. Granted, violence will never be removed from our psychological makeup—and even Gandhi acknowledges that it has its place. But choosing violence as our first option when reacting to being wronged is the same thing as submitting to violence. We resort to violence because we do not have the strength to be nonviolent. Nonviolence has its place in our psychological makeup, too; we just do not seem to want to acknowledge its strength.

Those searching for evidence that nonviolent resistance can work have the aforementioned evidence from Gandhi and King, just to name two high profile cases. But there are also many cases of its successful use that don't make world headlines. In "Nonviolence and Peacemaking Today," Michael Nagler said that there are some 40 nongovernmental "peace armies" in the world today, operating in many countries and intervening in conflicts such as those in Bosnia and Nicaragua (512). And by all accounts they work. Conversely, violence has been tried in many more situations, and there is little evidence that it *has* been successful—indeed, it always seems to breed more violence, if not at the time then in later generations. For whatever reason, nonviolence seems to take a back seat to violence. Or, as Theodore Roszak put it, "People try nonviolence for a week, and when it 'doesn't work,' they go back to violence, which hasn't worked for centuries" (qtd. in Kelly 497).

Works Cited

Dilks, Stephen, et al., eds. *Cultural Conversations: The Presence of the Past.* New York: Bedford/St. Martin's, 2001.

Gandhi. Dir. Richard Attenborough. Perf. Ben Kingsley, Candace Bergen, Edward Fox, John Gielgud, Trevor Howard, John Mills, Martin Sheen. Videocassette. Columbia, 1986.

Kappeler, Susanne. "Resistance and the Will to Resistance." Dilks et al. 505–10.

Kelly, Petra. "Nonviolent Social Defense." Dilks et al. 497–504.

King, Martin Luther. "Letter from Birmingham Jail." Dilks et al. 472–86.

Nagler, Michael. "Nonviolence and Peacemaking Today." Dilks et al. 512–22.

A Beefed-up Industry

Matthew Stewart

Matthew Stewart's class discussed animal rights in the context of the United States meat industry, asking questions such as: When do moral concerns about the treatment of animals outweigh the economic concern with efficiency? Who is more responsible for the success of humanely operated farms: the consumer or the producer? Is there an ethical way to consume animals?

The stage is set in a crowded grocery store. People saunter down the aisles in a daze under the glow of fluorescent lights. New products line the shelves with shiny packaging and proposed health benefits. In the back of the store, a crowd gathers around a glowing white light. A customer pushes her cart to the back to get a better look at what is happening. She sees other customers calling out orders to the hurried attendants working in the butcher block. The One Day Meat Sale has caused a swell of activity that can be witnessed the first Friday of every month. The people are drawn by the allure of New York steaks selling for $1.99 per pound, extra-lean hamburger for $1.49 per pound, pre-cooked frozen shrimp for $3.99 per pound, and pork ribs for $2.99 per pound. The woman asks for her hamburger in ten separate one-pound packages, for freezing purposes, and leaves the butcher block counter pleased with herself for being a good customer.

At the same time, in small holding pens all over the country, millions of cows are well fed, hormone treated, and waiting for Execution Day. Hundreds of millions of chickens have their beaks seared off by heated blades. Their legs break underneath the strain of top-heavy bodies created by sedentary, shoe-box cell living. The supply and demand process with meat rarely makes itself evident when the end result is placed upon a rack for people to pick and choose through the remnants of an animal's life. Because most of the meat seen on supermarket shelves comes from large factory farms, the demand for beef affects the small farmer.

According to a spokesperson for Farm-Aid, a small farm is lost every fifteen minutes ("Farm-Aid"). The families who own these small farms are left with no land-holdings and a great amount of debt. Supporters of Farm-Aid value the life of the small farmer as well as the local environment in which he or she lives. The threat of industrial farms worries small farmers; they think of large-scale agriculture as lacking in natural balance and inhumane to the animals that they "harvest."

There's no doubt that the threat of large factory farms is present, and the cruel treatment of the animals we eat is visible to anyone who wishes to look into the situation. The problem lies in our society's demand for meat products. If champions for the rights of animals and farmers achieve their full agenda, we can assume that cattle and poultry would become free range animals. Factory farms would diminish, creating a space for government subsidies for small farmers. That sounds good, right? Stronger than this, however, are the statistics available regarding our society's intake of beef. The ideals of animals' and farmers' rights are in paradoxical relationship for the American consumer because many concede that cruelty to animals exists, yet people aren't willing to pay higher prices for meat and higher taxes for farm subsidies.

The beef and chicken industries remain large pillars of our nation's economy even in the shadow of a recession. Channel News Asia reported that last year the U. S. beef industry employed 1.4 million people and had sales of forty billion dollars, and that ninety percent of beef it produced stayed within the United States ("United States Beef"). The United States Department of Agriculture (USDA) estimated the retail equivalent of the U. S. beef industry at seventy billion dollars in 2003, with 26.03 billion pounds produced. In 2002, 35.7 million head of cattle were slaughtered in the United States ("Beef Industry"). The poultry industry also posted some formidable figures. In 2001, 8.56 billion chickens were slaughtered. The simple value of chicken production was 16.7 billion dollars in 2001 (*USDA Annual Report*). According to Channel News Asia, the average American consumed 68 pounds of beef in 2003, running second only to chicken, of which the USDA says the average American ate 94 pounds in 2003 ("United States Beef," *USDA Annual Report*). In the future, the value of beef will be even greater due to protein-based diet phenomena such as the Atkins diet. If the demand for beef continues to increase, how can small farmers ever stay afloat?

In a recent Country Music Television special entitled "Farm-Aid: The Fight Goes On," music legends such as Willie Nelson and Neil Young joined with farmers to voice the need for government subsidies for small farmers to continue to own their land. An activist group claimed that large factory farms were causing undue damage to the surrounding environment by exploiting large tracts of land for the same crop each year. Film footage of cows clustered together and chickens placed in cages put a tortured face on the burger or fried chicken that most Americans consume. Furthermore, the group worried about the continued outsourcing of farms to places with cheaper labor costs, such as Mexico, where the use of harmful pesticides was not regulated. Their points were valid, and their cause aimed for small town people to become concerned about the future of their communities. But while their points are strong and passionate, it's hard to overlook the present attitude of the taxpayer. Whether or not people agree with George W. Bush, his tax cut plan did not deviate from the desires of most Americans. The last two referendum ballots concerning temporary income tax increases failed miserably in the state of Oregon, as similar measures have all over the country. I say this because the programs that subsidize small farmers cost a lot of money in a multi-billion dollar industry which already subsidizes large agri-business.

Perhaps these farmers' inability to diversify their product should bear some of the blame for their plight. In any economy, a large business will enter the picture in a small community and threaten the well-being of a small business. What can the local paint shop with three employees possibly do to compete with the low prices of a Home Depot or Wal-Mart? They can offer more personalized service and values based upon the human capital that large businesses lack, perhaps by catering to interior decorators and making sure to add special services that come from years of experience dealing with people. Similarly, perhaps small farms would survive if they altered their cattle growing practices to embrace larger, franchise beef labels, such as Angus or Laura's Lean Beef. For example, raising certified Angus Beef allows the producer to raise free-range cattle and sell at higher prices. Laura's Lean Beef claims that the beef they produce has no hormone-growth treatment. These types of beef are available to smaller farmers who do, however, have to trust that some consumers are willing to pay higher prices for beef and chicken.

United States beef prices reached an all-time high in 2003, averaging $4.32 per pound in November (USDA "Background"). Even though the statistics I cited showed the vastness of the beef industry, the high prices reveal a low beef supply while demand for the product remains high. If more farms went the way of free-range beef, wouldn't the supply of beef become even less, raising prices even higher? A sales executive and economic analyst for Albertsons Inc. stated that implementing local farms and animal rights, while a noble cause, would inevitably raise the price of beef and put a strain upon the businesses that sell the products. The One Day Meat Sale, mentioned earlier, generates sales of about ten thousand dollars for one Albertsons store in one day. The high sales of beef create jobs for people who work in the marketplace, as well as the 1.4 million workers in the beef industry as a whole. Are the large businesses heartless for not thinking of the rights of the animals, or are they giving the customers what they want? It is not a question of economic efficiency or morals. Simply put, the blame lies on us as consumers, because we create the demand for the beef, we elect the government who implements the laws governing commerce, and we are the consumers driving the wheels of big business. People who treat themselves as separate from government or big business missed important information in high-school civics class.

We are a nation of meat eaters, and while the conditions of commercialized livestock persist, it is hard to imagine making large-scale changes to the current way of living. Nicols Fox wishes for drastic changes to be made in the way of society's thinking. In "The Case Against Efficiency," Fox argues, "My own preference would be simply for banning super-efficient technologies" (B1). He argues that rising demand for efficiency possesses serious consequences that people overlook, such as feeding cow parts to cattle, the cause of mad cow disease. While his case against efficiency makes light of the negative consequences for things like factory farms, he calls for large scale non-incremental changes which may be just as dangerous in a short amount of time as the long-term effects of efficiency.

Perhaps the animal rights movement should focus more on its small victories and attempt to change the minds of consumers rather than advocate drastic, short term changes to the industry. Jeremy Rifkin writes, "Researchers are finding . . . that many of our fellow creatures are more like us than we had ever imagined." His column raises awareness that these animals display what we thought of as human characteristics, such as mourning of the dead among elephants, playful activity among pigs, and the use of tools by ravens. The struggle for animal rights continues, and has won some victories. People for the Ethical Treatment of Animals (PETA) just won a class action lawsuit against Kentucky Fried Chicken for lying about the treatment and conditions of their chickens (PETA "KFC's Lies"). PETA is also starting a new campaign to show elementary school students the harvesting process of the chicken nuggets from school lunches as well as the health risks which are evident from hormone-treated meat (PETA "New Trading"). It may seem possible that these small victories will lead to beef temperance. Similar to what happened in the 1820s with alcohol consumption, the idea that decreasing meat consumption means fewer animal deaths could become common. Decreasing beef consumption by even a quarter pound per week amounts to over twelve pounds a year, and if this spreads out across the entire nation, then millions of cows will live to see another day.

It's difficult to ask a business to take a ten-thousand-dollar hit in sales for the purpose of protecting the well-being of animals. Perhaps big businesses are concerned, in part, because raising prices would be detrimental when so much is demanded and sold at lower prices. It may be easier for someone to pass up a quarter-pounder each week in exchange for pasta or a salad than to pay more in beef prices and taxes out of empathy for farmers and animals. Organizations such as PETA and Farm-Aid have truly honorable and noble ventures, yet there's little one can do to halt the consumer's desire for satisfaction.

Works Cited

"Farm-Aid: The Fight Goes On." CMT. 6 Mar. 2004.

Fox, Nicols. "The Case Against Efficiency." *Washington Post* 15 Feb. 2004: B1.

PETA. "KFC's Lies Stopped: Campaign Full Speed Ahead!" *Kentucky Fried Cruelty.com.* 8 Mar. 2004 < http://www.kfccruelty.com/victory1.asp > .

———. "New Trading Cards for Kids Show Ugly Side of Chicken 'Nuggets.'" *People for the Ethical Treatment of Animals.* 8 Mar. 2004 < http://www.peta.org/Automation/NewsItem.asp?id = 4004 > .

Rifkin, Jeremy. "A Change of Heart About Animals." *Los Angeles Times* 1 Sept. 2003.

USDA. "Beef Industry Statistics." *ERS/USDA Publications.* 8 Mar. 2004 < http://www.ers.usda.gov/news/BSECoverage.htm > .

———. *United States Department of Agriculture Annual Report 2003.* Ch. 8. *USDA. gov.* 8 Mar. 2004 < http://www.usdagov/nass/pubs/agr03/03 ch8.pdf > .

"United States Beef Market Statistics." *Channelnewsasia.com.* 8 Mar. 2004 < http://www.channelnewsasia.com/stories/afp_world_business/view/633551.html > .

The Self-Imprisonment of American Society

Katie Fidler

Katie Fidler's class was pursuing lines of inquiry about surveillance and privacy in a consumerist society. They read Michel Foucault's discussion of panopticism, selections from Thorstein Veblen's Theory of the Leisure Class, *and recent articles about advancements in surveillance technology, which helped them think about surveillance and privacy issues in a free society as well as how marketing and consumerism make use of surveillance techniques.*

People are constantly striving to better themselves. This does not seem like an adverse notion; most improvement should be amiably accepted and respected. But when applied to the whole of American society and when the underlying causes are examined, it is clear that much of what we call improvement is done to satisfy the faceless opinions of other people. In a nation that is divided by class and other social distinctions, there is a desire to be perceived as one step ahead of the sordid and squalid. Previous societies had the fear of death, but we have overcome this in many ways with technology and advanced medicine that has eradicated small pox and decreased the seriousness of diseases such as influenza. Today's American society suffers from the fear of criticism, which it seems unable to surmount. This concern over negative criticism has seeped into the hearts of most Americans, causing them to become conspicuous consumers. The people of American society regulate themselves in a panopticon-like fashion because they are part of a society based on anxiety over other people's opinions.

In a Panopticon, which is a prison system that was originally designed in the nineteenth century, inmates are always visible, but they themselves cannot verify if they are being monitored at any time. At the center of a Panopticon is a tower housing a supervisor who watches the periphery through large windows.

The periphery is separated into cells that have two parallel windows, one looking toward the inner tower and one that allows light to enter from the outside. These windows create backlighting and thus ultimate visibility for the supervisor and complete isolation for the inmates. The genius of this system lies in the fact that the actual surveillance of the detainees can be irregular while the effects remain unceasing. A prisoner is thus contained in "a state of conscious and permanent visibility that assures the automatic functioning of power" (Foucault 230).

The people of American society are simultaneously supervisors and prisoners in their own panopticon. While they devise what is currently popular or in fashion, they also must strictly adhere to their own concepts of popularity "on pain of losing caste" (Veblen 88). For the most part, they do not know if another member of society is judging them at any given moment, but the anxiety over being "in fashion" is always there.

Many people shop at Abercrombie & Fitch, Saks Fifth Avenue, and The Pottery Barn, not for the durability of the goods, but for the logos and status affiliated with these companies. The majority of products that come from companies like these exist merely for style, not for function. This is because "apparel is always in evidence and affords an indication of pecuniary standing to all observers at the first glance" (Veblen 167). Expensive apparel or merchandise is automatically agreeable to society, and by the same token Veblen argues that most in society feel that what is inexpensive is inferior and unworthy, thus rendering the buyer inferior and unworthy also (169). Most members of society would rather buy a twenty-dollar whisk from Pottery Barn than a five-dollar one from the local supermarket, despite the fact that both serve the same practical purpose. In American society "people will undergo a very considerable degree of privation in the comforts of the necessaries of life in order to afford what is considered a decent amount of wasteful consumption" (Veblen 168). Few people have the audacity not to appear as if they are living up to the standards of luxury and reputability because most want to avoid the embarrassment that comes with unflattering comments or attention when they do not live up to these standards. In turn, they are often required to depreciate other areas of their life so they are able to buy symbols of status. Even though personal income has risen seventy-two percent in the last decade, the average credit card holder has an outstanding balance of $4,400 (Lim). At this point, society no longer owns material goods, but is being owned by them. American society is formed by this conspicuous consumption, with material possessions being amassed at high costs.

Moreover, this system of standards lends itself to the formation of a class structure that is rigidly monitored. Most Americans would like to believe that there is a bell curve to the class structure of their society, with a fraction of its members either impoverished or exceedingly affluent and most resting comfortably in the middle class. As wealth becomes necessary to have any reputable standing within American society, the bell curve begins to shift upward toward the more affluent end while also creating another curve at the end of the poor.

In "Wiping Out the Middle Class," Bob Djurjevic says that in Washington State the level of income required to "achieve a 'middle class' standard of living—e.g., a single family home in a decent neighborhood, enough money to raise at least two children responsibly, etc.—is about eighty thousand dollars annually." This is hardly a "middle class" wage when government statistics are defining a middle class family income as thirty-four thousand dollars a year.

Despite the mass of shoppers bearing the logos of Abercrombie & Fitch and the BMW Corporation, not everyone chooses to be a brand-name, high price shopper. Finding ways to reuse the products already in their possession instead of buying new materials, recycling paper, plastics, cardboard, and glass, and reducing the amount of energy and water used are all daily activities for a counter-culture within American society. Their food is organic or grown locally, not shipped in from South American countries, encased in pesticides, or grown with hormones, and they bring their own bags to take their groceries home in. Their clothing is often handmade using natural fibers and has durability so it does not need to be thrown away within a year. The products they buy impact a separate part of the economy than products from Abercrombie & Fitch; counter-culture shoppers influence small businesses and local farmers instead of major corporations. This portion of the economy is on a personal, face-to-face level. In some parts of America this lifestyle is well-established, while in others it is merely beginning to be influential as more people learn about the pesticides and hormones found in most foods and the economic benefits of recycling.

This counter-culture does not result in the type of disposability found in the rest of the economy, but it does result in consumption that is a manifestation of social discipline. This counter-culture requires people to adapt themselves to keep reputability within a "sphere of personal acquaintance and neighborhood gossip" (Veblen 16). Many individuals only eat organic or pesticide- and hormone-free food, so to accommodate them, businesses must possess these types of food as well. A good example of this is with Free Trade Coffee. Many universities have switched to offering only Free Trade Coffee because students have sparked protests over coffee that is cultivated by workers who are paid slave labor wages. Starbucks Corporation, the largest coffee chain in the United States, has been subject to heavy petitioning to change to more socially accountable practices. In these cases, it is not the Abercrombie & Fitch label across a t-shirt that people are looking for, it is a little sticker that says organically or locally grown. When it comes to other items, they are bought with the knowledge that they can be used for a considerable amount of time or recycled. This is a portion of the population that is more fervent about reusing and recycling than the rest of the population is about trends and wearing what is up to the standards of society so as not to lose caste. Within this counter-culture there is an effort "to hold the consumer up to a standard of expensiveness and wastefulness in his consumption of goods and in his employment of time" (Veblen 116). Because this counter-culture does not buy from major corporations who mass-produce their products, there is a level of expensiveness in the products they do buy that can only be achieved by the middle and upper classes. Thus, a kind of class system is perpetuated even by this counter-culture. Even though this standard is in direct opposition to the standard set by the rest of society, the manifestation of the discipline is the same.

Therefore, American society has incarcerated itself in a prison system originally designed to separate individuals, and that is exactly what has transpired. Members of this society are relentlessly under examination by one another and are aware of it too. Hence they are accountable for the power that is confining them. Sense of self and social placement dictates where they will shop and with whom they will associate. The portion of the economy to which the counter-culture contributes is subject to a very high level of social discipline as well. If the wrong logo is endorsed, it is not only looked down upon but might lead to protest and boycotting. Though this social discipline auspiciously dictates social responsibility and accountability, the rest of society is not that fortunate.

Works Cited

Djurdjevic, Bob. "Wiping Out the Middle Class." *Chronicles: A Magazine of American Culture* 22.5 (1998). *Truth in Media.* 4 Feb. 2003 < http://www. truthinmedia.org/truthinmedia/index.html > . Path: Djurdjevic's Columns; Wiping Out the Middle Class.

Foucault, Michel. "Panopticism." *Ways of Reading: An Anthology for Writers.* 6th ed. Ed. David Bartholomae and Anthony Petrosky. Boston: Bedford/St. Martin's, 2002. 223–57.

Lim, Paul J., et al. "News You Can Use: Digging Your Way Out of Debt." *U. S. News and World Report.* 19 Mar. 2001: 52 + . *USNews.com.* 4 Feb. 2003 < http:// www.usnews.com/usnews/nycu/money/articles/010319/debt.htm > .

Veblen, Thorstein. *The Theory of the Leisure Class.* New York: Penguin, 1979.

Forum on Zoos

The next three essays arose from readings and discussions about animal rights and zoos. Though the essays the students read shared a concern for the well-being of zoo animals, the authors differed widely in their opinions about zoos; for example, Melissa Greene argues in "No Rms, Jungle Vu" that zoos help protect endangered species and raise awareness about habitat loss, while John Berger contends that zoos are symptomatic of our inability to see animals as autonomous others in "Why Look at Animals?" Together with their classmates, the student writers whose essays follow considered questions such as: Are zoos necessary? Can zoos be operated ethically in a capitalistic society, or will desire for profit outweigh concerns about animal welfare? Can zoos' educational functions be untangled from the entertainment they provide for zoo-goers?

The Reality of Zoos

Zach Blume

In a capitalist society, all is centered on maximizing profit. In the entertainment industry specifically (an industry that is especially prominent in the United States), the focus is clear and singular: creating a product that will be undeniably appealing to the masses, exploiting the consumers' wants and desires in order to make the most money possible.

In this industry of entertainment there are endless possible activities, ranging from a trip to the movies to entertainment parks to restaurants. Among these activities, zoos rank as one of the most prominent. In America alone, 115 million people go to zoos every year, a staggering number considering that it exceeds even the number attending sporting events (Greene 234). With much money to be made, zoos are an industry that fits perfectly into the capitalist framework. Thus it is unreasonable to believe that zoos can be a prominent source for promoting education and awareness about animals because the number one priority of zoos, as with all other entertainment industries, is to maximize capital. The room for zoos to promote education under the capitalistic formula is therefore essentially limited.

What differentiates zoos from other theme parks, such as water slides or roller coasters, is that their primary source of entertainment is live animals kept in captivity. Therefore, there are certain responsibilities zoos must face that other theme parks do not, such as maintaining a certain quality of life for the animals and educating the zoo-goers. While some zoos seem to focus on this aspect more than others, by no means is that where the money lies. The money lies in the unique form of entertainment the zoo provides. The sense of wonder, the excitement, and the exhilaration in experiencing "exotic" and "untamed" wild animals only feet away is what continues to pull people into the zoos of America.

At the San Diego Zoo, a world renowned zoo, one trip costs 32 dollars. Exhibits include "Tiger River," "Polar Bear Plunge," "Absolutely Apes," and "Panda Central." The emphasis on entertainment is obvious in this teaser for the panda exhibit: "Visit our panda cub! Little Wi Sheng is growing fast, so come see him while he's still a cub. He and his mother, Bai Yun, are on exhibit each day from 10:30 a.m. to 3:45 p.m. You'll either find him romping, exploring, or sleeping—he's fun to watch no matter what he's doing!" (San Diego Zoo).

In addition to its array of exhibits, the zoo features five different restaurants, seven gift shops, and four ATM machines. It is open 365 days a year and offers a theme park pass value price, in conjunction with Disneyland, Seaworld, and Knott's theme park (San Diego Zoo). All this information is placed prominently on the zoo's comprehensive website.

At the other end of the spectrum, the zoo does include a few educational programs designed to further children's understanding of the animals and their habitats. The zoo maintains a mission of international conservation, in which they state: "The Zoological Society of San Diego is a conservation, education and recreation organization dedicated to the reproduction, protection and exhibition of animals, plants and habitats" (Zoological Society). In addition, the zoo offers children's programs and summer camps, such as "kindernights at the zoo" ($25), "Joe Nyiri art classes" ($42–220), and "preschool safaris at the zoo" ($30) (San Diego Zoo). While these aspects of the zoo seem to be almost required in order for the zoo to maintain a sense of integrity and an appeal for the kids, by no means is this where the focus lies. Education is simply not as exciting and intriguing as the animals themselves. For example, out of every four zoo-goers, it is likely that only one will read the informational signs (Greene 235).

While the increased attention on educational programs and the conservation mission statement of the zoo are steps in the right direction, the clear concentration, as stated earlier, remains providing visitors with an unparalleled animal adventure experience. This experience leads to more entrance tickets bought and more meals and souvenirs purchased.

Although it is a positive sign that zoos are improving the quality of life for their animals and incorporating more educational programs, it is unrealistic to envision a zoo whose primary focus lies in education over entertainment (as mentioned before, it is the entertainment aspect of a zoo that leads to profit, not the education). Even in the area of education, the zoo is still expanding its money-making potential with prices of up to $220 for a class. It is highly unreasonable, therefore, to rely on zoos as prominent factors in the improvement of animal awareness. Furthermore, if we choose to hope that in the future zoos will change from money-making enterprises into institutions committed to animal rights and protection, we will be disappointed. This may need to come from another area of business, most likely a non-profit. While zoos have the potential to have a positive effect on their consumers, and that potential is increasingly being realized, the potential is fundamentally limited because the focus will always remain the money to be made from entertainment, not education.

In "No Rms, Jungle Vu," Melissa Greene introduces a current revolution (the "landscape revolution" as she calls it) in the zoo business. These new zoos, as exemplified in the Woodland Park Zoo in Seattle, are designed to create a much more realistic wilderness setting, and according to Greene, this will lead to a more positive future in the evolution of zoos. According to leading zoo designer Jon Coe, these new zoos "create a situation that transcends the range of stimulation people are used to and enhances the visitor's perception of the animal" (Greene 227). The goal of these increasingly realistic zoos is that the zoo-goer will feel more immersed and involved in the habitat of the animal. Because zoo designers such as Coe are finally starting to realize that "they are, in part, responsible for the American public's unfamiliarity with ecology and lack of awareness" (Greene 234), they are hoping that by providing an even more thrilling first-hand experience, the zoo-goer will become more interested in increasing his or her knowledge of the animal kingdom. In addition, he or she will be able to see the animals in their natural state, and will therefore have an improved appreciation and more correct understanding of the animals.

While the link Coe and Greene make between a better and more realistic zoo experience and a subsequent increase in animal awareness can be understood to a certain degree, the awareness created by these zoos is not strong enough to truly bring animal understanding to the necessary level. Animal education must lead to a realistic desire to make a difference. The situation of animals on this planet is increasingly dire, as we are losing more than one species a day globally and most megavertabrates will be endangered within the next twenty years (232). These mind-blowing facts cannot be learned by seeing a gorilla in its natural habitat but instead by reading a book or by taking a class. While first-hand experience is valuable, education and actual action in the protection of animals outweighs these entertainment experiences drastically. No matter how realistic zoo designers such as Coe can make their zoos, education will unfailingly be left behind because of the overall culture of a zoo. In this increasingly important issue of animal awareness, I do not believe that we can place our complete trust in zoos, even these new zoos that Greene introduces, because their focus will be limited to entertainment, not education. While entertainment and education can be linked and can work together, as Coe would like to have it, the link is not nearly strong enough to consider zoos as a major source in realistically improving the situation of animals in the years to come. We must look elsewhere.

Ideally, zoos would be in a completely different category than other theme parks. They would exist outside the capitalist framework and would be able to focus their energy on teaching our youth the reality of the animal situation. They would motivate people to learn more and make a difference. However, this is unrealistic. As long as zoos remain a profit-making industry where spectacular tours and landscapes to exhilarate the viewers remain the primary way to maximize capital, education and awareness will forever remain a distant second to the glitz and glamour of zoo entertainment.

Works Cited

Greene, Melissa. "No Rms, Jungle Vu." *A Forest of Voices: Conversations in Ecology.* 2nd ed. Ed. Chris Anderson and Lex Runciman. Mountain View: Mayfield, 2000. 223–37.

San Diego Zoo. "Welcome to SanDiegoZoo.org!" *SanDiegoZoo.org.* 12 Mar. 2004 < http://www.sandiegozoo.org > .

Zoological Society of San Diego. "International Conservation of the Zoological Society of San Diego." *SanDiegoZoo.org.* 12 Mar. 2004 < www.sandiegozoo.org/conservation/homepage.php3 > .

Zoos: The Evil Empires

Leah Brandt

Is there a reason that many humans are drawn to zoos, despite their false representations of real wildlife settings? Many species of animals continue to go extinct each week. Shouldn't our efforts be concentrated on preserving natural environments for these animals to exist in instead of creating false ones that distract us from the real problems at hand? It is time we set aside our personal desire to use zoos for entertainment and invest in the preservation of wildlife areas for these animals to inhabit. Through education about conservation needs and animal rights we can decrease the amount of land and resources we consume and hopefully avoid further extinctions of species still living in the wild.

Many people argue that zoos do serve important purposes. Many hardworking U.S. citizens like to take their kids to see the animals for entertainment. It gives them the opportunity to see animals that they may never be able to see otherwise, and it provides an opportunity for a nice family outing. In his article about the Tucson Zoo, Lewis Thomas argues that we, as human beings, have a need to be transfixed by certain animals, to connect with something wild and beautiful: "There was only one sensation in my head: pure elation mixed with amazement at such perfection.. All I asked for was the full hairy complexity, then in front of my eyes, of whole, intact beavers and otters in motion" (239). Still others argue that the public will be educated about conservation issues through zoos and become more concerned with preserving the natural habitats of animals. This may result from their compassion for the poor, caged creatures, or simply through reading educational information posted within zoos. This new awareness could help to prevent the extinction of more species in the future. Another argument in favor of zoos is the profit value of the entertainment business that they support.

Three out of five of these reasons in favor of zoos are anthropocentric, or centered on human desires and so-called "needs." Few of the reasons derive from concern for the benefit of the animals living in the zoos. As we discussed in class, the idea that zoos will create greater awareness for conservation and preservation issues is a myth. In order to educate the public about animal rights and conservation needs, we can utilize public school systems to teach children and implement more community educational programs. The myth continues because more species continue to go extinct each week. For example, "The deaths of 540 animals at the National Zoo in Malaysia over the last two years have been blamed on 'poor management' and lack of experience in veterinary care" (Morse). This is just one of many cases where human ignorance produced fatal results for animals in zoos. Even though some zoos respect strict animal rights laws and have high standards for creating as healthy and natural an environment as possible for the animals, they cannot deny that this trapped existence is an unhealthy solution for animals who might as well take their chances in the wild. It is better to live free and die early than face a life of restriction.

Zoos create a false sense of reality. By not seeing animals in their natural environment, people's images of them are distorted. People are easily distracted from the real problem of the rapid rate of extinction. Taking animals out of their natural habitats and placing them in cages for us to gawk at is demeaning. It places animals at our disposal, creating a hierarchy between us in which humans control the final decision, the fate of the animals. By supporting zoos we perpetuate this unbalanced vision of the relationship between animals and humans, which has consequences for humans' relationship with the natural environment. By unbalanced vision, I mean one that places humans in complete control, using the land and wildlife at our discretion and lacking a basic respect for the earth that provides us with homes and resources to live. I agree with Thomas that our need to make a connection with animals or be transfixed by them is important. But this need can be satisfied in a natural environment as well. You don't have to search for exotic animals in a distant jungle to satisfy this human desire; rather, you can look in your own backyard at the chipmunk in the tree or the bird flying above you.

The zoo 'industry' is facing a lull in consumer support, discrediting the capitalist argument. Consumers are looking for other places to spend their money, as in the case of the Fresno Zoo where "attendance has been flat for nearly 30 years" (Davis). Despite efforts to make the zoo more natural looking, attendance rates have still decreased. The future of this zoo is uncertain.

Despite the difference in intelligence levels between animals and humans, animals still show signs of comprehension and varied learning abilities. For example, one of the gorillas at the Gorilla Foundation in Northern California, Koko, knows over 1,000 signs and has an extensive English vocabulary (Rifkin 2). Research indicates that "learning is passed on from parent to offspring far more often than not and that most animals engage in all kinds of learned experience brought on by continued experimentation" (Rifkin 2). However, the question is not about animals' intelligence or ability levels but rather their right not to *suffer* from human-inflicted torture. Despite Michael Pollan's assertion that the concept of morality is a human invention, this is a question of morality. It is precisely the reason we cannot deny animals the freedom to live in their natural habitats. I disagree with him that "just as we recognize that nature doesn't provide an adequate guide for human social conduct, isn't it anthropocentric to assume that our moral system offers an adequate guide for nature?" (Pollan). This may be applicable to an idealist focusing on individualism versus animal collectivity or group identities (the individual animal versus an entire species), but our ability to use ethical reasoning is what makes us unique as humans. We have to utilize this for the benefit of animals and take responsibility for our chosen interactions with them.

For the benefit and well-being of animals, zoos are unnecessary. We don't really need them for entertainment because we have other ways of entertaining ourselves that aren't detrimental to the livelihood of innocent animals. Our inability to communicate with animals is not an excuse to mistreat them. Alice Walker argues that, as humans, we judge others as being ignorant (animals or humans) if we cannot communicate with them using language. According to Walker, these judgments are "only our own reflections" (45). Her article is about a horse that lived near her house as she grew up. Eventually she came to understand that horse's need for affection and its ability to feel emotion. Her connection with this animal helped Walker to further understand human behavior and psychology. We can learn so much from animals. They are all amazing creatures that are too often underestimated. It is our responsibility to respect and protect them so that we can continue learning from each other and co-existing peacefully, putting an end to exploitation altogether.

Works Cited

Davis, Jim. "Fresno Zoo Stands at Crossroads: Retiring Director Says Resource Must Be Found to Save It." *Fresno Bee.* 16 Nov. 2003: A1. *Animal Concerns* 26 Nov. 2003 < http://www.animalconcerns.org > .

Morse, Sherry. "540 Zoo Animals Die Because of 'Poor Management.'" *Animal News Center* 26 Nov. 2003. < http://www.anc.org/wildlife/wildlife_article. cfm?identifier = 2003_1_126_zoo > .

Pollan, Michael. "An Animal's Place." *New York Times* 2 Dec. 2003, late ed., 58.

Rifkin, Jeremy. "A Change of Heart About Animals." *Los Angeles Times* 1 Sept. 2003: B15.

Thomas, Lewis. "The Tucson Zoo." *A Forest of Voices: Conversations in Ecology.* 2nd ed. Ed. Chris Anderson and Lex Runciman. Mountain View Mayfield, 2000. 239–41.

Walker, Alice. "Am I Blue?" *A Forest of Voices: Conversations in Ecology.* 2nd ed. Ed. Chris Anderson and Lex Runciman. Mountain View Mayfield, 2000. 242–45.

The Education Experience of the American Zoo

Devlin Timony-Balyeat

The average person is not aware of how many animal species exist in the world. This ignorance is due to the fact that it is nearly impossible for many Americans to travel to the natural habitats of these animals. As the natural world is increasingly threatened, it has become necessary to learn about the natural world around us. By bringing wild animals to America, zoos are providing opportunities for people to experience the jungles of Africa or the forests of South America. Visitors are transported to these distant locations without disrupting their normal lives. Lewis Thomas, author of "The Tucson Zoo," describes a pleasurable experience of being transported to the natural habitats of otters and beavers. Although learning about animals in their natural habitats would be ideal, the zoo presents an alternative that is much more practical.

While zoos are educational, they are also entertaining for their visitors. Zoo creators understand that people will tend to come more often and learn more if they enjoy themselves. In order to be successful and attract a large number of guests, zoo creators must find a balance between the goals of education and entertainment. Zoos set out to bring the human world and the animal world closer together for the sake of education; they should not be criticized simply because they are entertaining since entertainment is a necessary aspect of the educational process.

In "No Rms, Jungle Vu," Melissa Greene describes Woodland Park in Seattle as an example of a zoo that is succeeding in being educational and awe-inspiring at the same time. The carefully designed exhibits at Woodland Park allow the visitor to see the same wild animals as in other zoos and at the same time be thrilled by the sense of proximity to the animal in its natural-looking habitat. Changes in exhibit design, which lead to a change in the way the animals are viewed, enable a zoo like Woodland Park to be successful at educating people about conservation. By providing a less anthropocentric view of the lives of the wildlife, the zoo in Seattle is able to address conservation issues of habitat loss and endangered species.

Critics argue that zoos give their visitors the wrong impression about wild animals. In "Why Look at Animals?" John Berger is intransigent in his argument that the way zoos are designed means that they cannot possibly succeed at displaying wild animals so that viewers see wild creatures as they really are (26). Berger argues that "The public purpose of zoos is to offer visitors the opportunity of looking at animals. Yet nowhere in a zoo can a stranger encounter the look of an animal" (26). Zoos are nothing more than a place for the public to go and admire the "beautiful" or "interesting" animals (Greene 236). Melissa Greene argues that "the subliminal message here is that animals are like gentle pets and thrive nicely in captivity" (Greene 236). Simply stated, the zoo will inevitably fail at its mission of bringing humans and animals close together, and the visitor will come to view wild animals simply as the creatures behind the glass. The extreme argument is that zoos should be abolished because they simply display caged animals as spectacles to amuse humans and do not serve a true educational purpose.

In response to this criticism, American zoo designers have worked to alter the layouts of zoo habitats so that they might be more realistic and educational. Zoo directors struggle to display the animals in a way that both holds the attention of the audience and portrays the animal accurately. At the zoo in Seattle, using a technique called "landscape immersion," exhibit designers are striving to duplicate the wilderness as accurately as possible (Greene 229). Unique in its progress, Woodland Park aspires to strengthen the connection between the world of humans and the world of animals. According to Melissa Greene, zoos are supposed to take humans back to their origins as a species and thus strengthen a perceived connection with animals (223). The designers of the gorilla exhibit, Jon Coe and Grant Jones, were particularly successful at creating a naturalistic habitat that gives the impression of being carried to a far away place: "Coe measured and calculated the sight lines to ensure that the view was an uncorrupted one into the heart of the rain forest" (Greene 225). Throughout the design process, field scientists and gorilla experts were consulted in order to discover how gorillas live in the wild (227). In this way, the gorillas do not appear to be caged animals held in captivity. The gorilla habitat in Seattle successfully exhibits for the guests what gorillas are like in the wild. The innovative architecture designed by Jon Coe and Grant Jones allowed the gorillas to remain wild jungle animals, even though they are captive.

In addition to his efforts to create a natural looking gorilla habitat, Jon Coe offers suggestions for ways to improve the zoo as a whole. In order to educate guests about the animal world, all aspects of the zoo must be natural. These aspects include the way the zoo staff treats the animals. In the wild, cheetahs and elephants are not given names and they do not celebrate their birthdays. Therefore, the elephants and cheetahs in American zoos should not be given pet names and their birthdays need not be celebrated (Greene 226). Giving the wild animals pet names leads visitors to see the animals as domestic and no longer as the wild creatures that they really are. Zoo-goers will not learn about conservation issues if they are unable to differentiate between wildlife and domesticated animals.

Though zoos should not be abolished, many of them need to be revised. American zoos have a job to perform and they must uphold certain standards in the process. The American Zoo and Aquarium Association has developed an accreditation system of standards in order to assure high standards of animal care and husbandry. Woodland Park is one of the zoos that has met such standards. Sadly, of the thousands of zoos in America, Seattle's is one of only 213 that are accredited. Those remaining must make changes and strive for accreditation in order to better meet the needs of both the animals and the visitors. These unaccredited zoos are not yet in a position to focus on conservation issues.

When Lewis Thomas visited the Tucson Zoo, he had an experience with wild animals that was both pleasurable and educational. In the zoo, a family of otters is exhibited a few feet away from a family of beavers. Thomas details his feelings of joy from the closeness of such beautiful creatures: "Within just a few feet from your face, on either side, beavers and otters are at play, underwater and on the surface, swimming toward your face and then away, more filled with life than any creatures I had ever seen before, in all my days" (239). Without having gone to the zoo, Thomas would not have experienced the amazement and pleasure that comes from watching wild animals in their natural surroundings. At the Tucson Zoo, he was both educated by observing the behaviors of wild animals and entertained by the playfulness of the creatures.

As an increasing number of species are disappearing from the earth, zoos are becoming vital places of species conservation. Directors face the reality that the wilderness across the planet is being destroyed at an alarming rate and that animals are being lost as well (Greene 232). Zoos are now striving to ebb the tide by employing a variety of tactics: "The front-line strategy is conservation biology and captive propagation, employing all the recent discoveries in human fertility, such as in vitro fertilization, embryo transplantation, and surrogate motherhood" (Greene 233). Using technology, zoos are even able to mate animals from different zoos. Melissa Greene discusses another tactic employed by zoo personnel: "The second-line strategy is to attempt to save the wilderness itself through educating the public" (233). Directors remain hopeful about their chances. If ten percent of the 115 million Americans who visit zoos annually decided to take action by joining conservation organizations, boycotting goods from endangered species, or helping developing countries to preserve their forest, they could have a strong voice (Greene 234).

It is true that many zoos, in the process of balancing entertainment and education, are guilty of presenting a domesticated view of the wild animals to the zoo guests. Yet, it is not entirely accurate to say that zoos are strictly made up of caged animals as they were in the past (Greene 232). Today, the process of designing a successful zoo is more complicated. Zoo directors now find themselves to be competing with the amusement park industry. As such, directors are faced with many new questions: "Are our visitors having a good time? Will they come back soon? Would they rather be at Disney World? What will really excite them?" (Greene 231). It is no longer sufficient for zoos to be places where visitors can go and admire the animals if zoos are to thrive as businesses. Visitors have other needs that must be addressed and met so that they enjoy themselves and want to return.

It is true that thousands of zoos are struggling to find a balance between education and entertainment. Many zoos are failing at their mission of educating the public. The reason lies in the layout and design of such institutions. Simple changes that can be made include the list of ideas Jon Coe has presented to the zoos where he worked. American zoos should not be altered simply because they are entertaining since visitors can learn about and enjoy the animals at the same time. The truth is that a majority of American zoos do not uphold strong standards for animal care. To be able to better address issues of conservation, zoos must make changes in how they treat and exhibit wildlife. Only when every zoo in America has received accreditation can the needs of both humans and zoo animals be met. Only then will the zoo truly succeed in its mission of bringing the two worlds closer together.

Works Cited

American Zoo and Aquarium Association. "About Accreditation and Certification." *American Zoo and Aquarium Association.* 13 Mar. 2004 < http://www. aza.org/Accreditation > .

Berger, John. "Why Look at Animals?" *About Looking.* New York: Pantheon, 1980. 1–26.

Greene, Melissa. "No Rms, Jungle Vu." *A Forest of Voices: Conversations in Ecology.* 2nd ed. Ed. Chris Anderson and Lex Runciman. Mountain View Mayfield, 2000. 223–37.

Thomas, Lewis. "The Tucson Zoo." *A Forest of Voices: Conversations in Ecology.* 2nd ed. Ed. Chris Anderson and Lex Runciman. Mountain View Mayfield, 2000. 239–41.

Forum on Art and Culture

The next two essays were written in response to class inquiry into African American identity and the arts, though each essay engages with a different aspect of the conversation that resulted. Katie Wright's essay replies to a discussion of Glenn Loury's "Free at Last? A Personal Perspective on Race and Identity in America." Near the end, Loury reflects critically on his discomfort at the thought of his son wanting to play hockey and his desire to see his son interested in "black" activities, a passage that generated much comment in class. Rosei Rocha-Judd's essay takes up the question of how we should interpret the violent and sexist content of hip-hop music, a question at issue that arose after the class read an essay by Joan Morgan, who argues that African American women should "recognize hip-hop's ability to articulate the pain our community is in and use that knowledge to create a redemptive, healing space" (203).

Funding for the Future

Katie Wright

America is a country whose history lies mostly in the stories of immigrants. It has long been known as, and continues to be known as, the land in which dreams can come true for those who have come from hardship and economic turbulence in other countries. In fact, the Statue of Liberty, which greets new arrivals, boasts the message, "Give me your tired, your poor, your huddled masses yearning to breathe free." This landmark is seen as a symbol of America, a country which is considered to be a melting pot by many. I disagree with the theory of the "melting pot" and subscribe to a newer, more realistic theory which compares America to a salad bowl. This analogy means that when all of these different races and cultures come together in one land, they do not form one cohesive culture which finds parts of them all within it, but rather keep their own cultures solid and separate, coming together to make a salad of distinctive shapes and cultures.

When we look at this "salad bowl" of cultures, the problem of domination is still present. Wherever one looks, there is always a dominant race or culture surrounded by minorities. This is not an issue of contention; it is simply the make-up of the population. But what can be helped is the role that these minorities get to play. In order to keep these different cultures alive, they need to be identified as unique and special, and work not only to preserve their histories, but also to share them with those who might not otherwise be exposed to that knowledge. People must be willing to teach these subjects, but in order to do this, they must also have financial support. This is why I believe that the government should give more funds to culturally centered programs, because teaching cultural histories and values promotes community pride, especially in the midst of a dominant culture.

Preserving cultural heritage needs the support of people who are willing to teach it, as well as financial backing so that those who give of their time are rewarded for it. Even though many government grants are available, there is not enough specific focus on the cultural arts of minorities in America. All too often, an activity that is specific to a group has to be incorporated into the mainstream culture in order to get any notice. It is only through its popularity in the dominant culture that the activity is able to gain funding and therefore survive. When a culture faces the challenge of proving its worth to outsiders, it runs the risk of losing its focus by catering to how others view it. This has happened in many places around the world when outsiders, like settlers or tourists, came into the area and changed the make-up of the existing culture. Any cultural group that has contact with others faces the possibility of extinction through assimilation. I believe that we need to give more funding to minority groups so that they will not have to sell themselves out to the majority in order to keep their cultural activities to pass on to the community, as well as to those from outside the community who are interested in learning about them.

In Newport, Oregon, the Siletz tribe is on its way to opening a new charter school with a curriculum based on Native traditions. This school will not only teach Native cultural aspects and values, but will also use the tribal language in its classrooms (Ryan). This type of school is exactly what is needed for communities that feel that the dominant culture does not encompass their own story. As much as we could say that the American school system simply needs to be more diverse in what it chooses to teach, I don't believe that it would ever be possible to incorporate the histories, values, and cultures of all the different groups in America into a curriculum used in all schools. It is simply unrealistic to think that this is a possibility, especially when funding for public schools is at such a low that they can barely keep up with the basics. I propose that the government provide more funding so that more schools like this one can be accessible for students of different cultures. When children are taught using the values and the ideas that are already present in their households and communities, they will have a better understanding of the material they are learning. This is why, when planning the national tests, it is so difficult to find shared terms and experiences to which all children can relate. If community-based schools with specialized programs were the norm, then perhaps nationally-based tests would become a thing of the past, allowing kids to succeed on their own terms.

Certain activities are viewed as belonging exclusively to the people of a particular culture. During one of our class discussions, we talked about Glenn Loury's essay, "Free at Last? A Personal Perspective on Race and Identity in America," pausing to consider the idea that a sport or an activity can be associated with one racial group or another. Most people seemed to think that this was sad and wondered if this was a realistic picture of America or simply one man's racial assumption. Just by looking at portrayals of race within the media, it is obvious that this is not only Loury's point of view, but an actual issue that affects the choices that people make about what types of careers or interests to pursue. One person in class said that she did not feel as if there was anything that she could not participate in based on her color, but then again, she was white. When a person is a part of the dominant culture, it is true that there are very few sports, careers, or activities which would not include them, but that is not the reality for those who are not part of the majority culture. Yet I wonder if what this person said is really true when seen from a different angle. There are many activities which are culturally or racially specific and when a person from outside of that group tries to participate, it either makes the group uncomfortable or the person who is now considered the minority.

As an example of culturally specific activities, we can look at gospel singing. Gospel songs have their roots in African-American culture, specifically slavery and Sorrow Songs, as W.E.B. Du Bois discusses. Gospel music is a cultural activity that has become well known throughout the world; its melodies are even found as the background to many famous rock songs. It has been able to survive dark times and weave its way into the fabric of American history. In fact, gospel music is generally considered an integral part of American culture. Yet it is specific to a group of people, more notably, a minority group. There are no rules surrounding gospel choir, nothing that says who may join or who may not, given that one can sing properly. But if the dominant culture starts to creep in to this activity, will it not eventually lose a great deal of its meaning for those who have their roots in gospel music? Of course, a white person can become involved in gospel singing, and I'm sure that there are, in fact, quite a number of white people who do enjoy singing in gospel choirs, but I worry that if an activity specific to a certain racial group is integrated into the dominant culture, it might lose the ability to convey the history and values of a people to their next generation. With government funding in place, it could be the choir groups' decision as to how they share their art, choosing whether or not to perform concerts, sell CDs, or participate in other money making activities. Other cultural groups could join gospel choirs without as much concern that their joining would take away from the value of the art for those who cherish its historical roots.

It could be argued that promoting the different cultural values of all of the unique groups in America could take away from the culture at large. If different communities are learning different things, then what is to stop them from discriminating against people of other races based on their lack of information? But I believe that when somebody is taught about their people and their history, they are embued with a greater sense of self-confidence than they would be if they were taught about someone else's history and values. As it stands today, in most American schools, the majority of readings are about white men changing the world, inventing things, and generally dominating society. This leads to a lack of self-confidence, thinking that your forefathers and foremothers did not have any impact on the world. But when students are taught about the history, the literature and arts, and in some circumstances, the language of their people, they will have a greater sense of self-worth and be able to share that with the world.

Our American society in general would greatly benefit from the promotion of cultural values within specific communities. People proud of their heritage are often willing to share it, and a culture based on sharing diversity could get a brand new start. The media speaks of a mounting tension between races in America, and when the citizens of a country cannot get along, then the future of the country is unstable. This lack of toleration between races is spurred by fear of the unknown. With the government's help through funding, a bridge of understanding can be built and cultural tensions can be eased. By putting more money into grants for minority arts, including them more in the educational system, and generally accepting that America should be proud of its diverse heritage, the entire feeling of America could change.

Works Cited

Du Bois, W.E.B. "The Sorrow Songs." *Cultural Conversations: The Presence of the Past.* Ed. Stephen Dilks et al. Boston: Bedford/St. Martin's, 2001. 136–45.

Loury, Glenn. "Free at Last? A Personal Perspective on Race and Identity in America." *Cultural Conversations: The Presence of the Past.* Ed. Stephen Dilks et al. Boston: Bedford/St. Martin's, 2001. 173–80.

Ryan, Sue. "Siletz Tribe Envisions Native Culture for Charter School." *News-Times* [Newport, OR] 7 Feb. 2003: A4.

The Seduction of Hyperrealism and Overblown Images

Rosei Rocha-Judd

There is a constant, grumbling debate in this country concerning censorship of many things, from ridiculously sexualized "reality" television to violent video games to MTV music videos. Popular music is a particularly virulent area in this debate—people have been arguing about songs whose lyrics contain swear words, slurs, sex and violence for about as far back as pop music has existed. When Elvis Presley first performed on television, for example, producers refused to show his hip gyrations as he sang. Of course, Elvis would be considered extremely tame by today's standards, considering he was not dressed sexily, or surrounded by nearly-naked dancers, or even singing objectionable lyrics. As our society's standards have relaxed, however, new acts have emerged that continue to push the limits. Nowadays there are music videos that are so violent, sexual or offensive that even MTV refuses to play them during certain hours, or to play them at all. Politicians and citizens alike run indignant campaigns to shut down this type of music, or at least slap a warning label on it. We may laugh at the stodginess of the Elvis example, but how will we feel about our own controversial music fifty years from now? We may feel that things have gotten to such an extreme that they must be stopped. But censoring this type of music isn't really the answer if we want to eliminate the types of messages it is spreading throughout our culture. Instead we should try to understand why this type of a product is being created, because this would help us to better understand our own culture and improve upon it.

It is human nature to seek the easiest route from point A to point B, but too often this leads us to whitewash problems rather than to address their roots. It is certainly easier to cover something up rather than trying to dig under the surface to find the essential causes. But quick fixes, whether for a leaky roof or a corrupt corporation, rarely hold for long. Neither does blanket censorship.

The people who have the strongest opinions on 'unsavory' hip-hop and rap music rarely seem to have listened to it enough to have an informed opinion about it, nor do they bother to think about why this type of music is coming out and why it is popular. My best friend's mom hated Eminem with a passion after hearing about him on the news, even though she had never listened to a single song of his. While it is true that many of Eminem's songs are outrageously violent (to the point of silliness, actually), many of his lyrics address important issues, and he even raps about the criticism he so frequently receives. When I finally convinced my friend's mom to listen to a few of his songs, her opinion shifted. She was still horrified by his slurs against women and gays, but she also had to respect what he was saying in some of the other songs. For example, in some of Eminem's newer songs he talks a lot about how his music affects adolescent listeners and how that has both positive and negative consequences. Overzealous censors may feel that he has no sense of responsibility or awareness about his actions, but this simply isn't true. It is important to at least listen carefully to an artist before advocating banning all of his or her music.

A better issue for these critics to tackle would be to wonder *why* so many of their kids embrace Eminem and other rap artists. Even Eminem comments on how interesting it is that rich white kids are some of the biggest consumers of 'black' culture when often the lifestyle and messages presented are completely foreign to these children's own lives. When 50 Cent raps about being shot, serving time, or living in the ghettos of New York, no suburban kid from LA really understands those types of hardships or negative experiences. However, the general emotion of feeling angry, fed up, and put out *is* shared. This is particularly potent for middle- and upper-class white children, who often lead sheltered lives and deal with family problems that, while just as troubling, are not as obvious as the types of problems an inner-city youth might face.

In the case of rap music, these troubles are often exaggerated to an extreme and then remedied with images of money, casual sex, and power. Just like any type of fantasy, this appeals to unhappy kids, particularly when more 'approved' musicians aren't offering a world which is so blatantly negative and yet exaggeratedly fantastic in the other extreme. Art that pushes the limits of acceptability to an extreme forces a feeling of hyperrealism, so that one's experience becomes exaggerated—more violent, more glamorous, and sexier than real life can ever feel. If children are obsessed with this type of art, attempting to force them to stop listening to it won't change the impulse, only the source of the satisfaction. Making an artist's music unavailable won't erase the desire to listen to it, but encouraging children to deal with their own negative emotions might. Although all children are rebellious to some extent, I never felt the same strength of desire in wanting to listen to typically 'offensive' music from my friends who were relatively happy as those who had a lot of emotional issues. It's hard to relate to an over-the-top song about killing your mom or dying early when you don't really share those feelings.

Likewise, the very fact that music is manifesting in this way is indicative of some underlying cultural problems, not some random occurrence that could just as easily be about sunshine and puppies as cocaine and handguns. Joan Morgan makes that point pretty clear when she points out that all this music about substance abuse and drugs is quite sad. Violence and pain can sound exciting in a song, but there are too many real-life examples of musicians destroyed by drugs and violence for the reality of this world to be ignored. As Morgan writes, "when brothers can talk so cavalierly about killing each other and then reveal that they have no expectation to see their twenty-first birthday, that is straight-up depression *masquerading* as machismo" (202). This country has a huge problem with substance abuse and depression, and it would be far better to address this than simply to ban music that says out loud what we wish were not true.

Completely rejecting censorship, however, provokes the worry that perhaps there are some artists who go too far and create products that are too horrible to ever be accepted into our society. This is an unrelenting dilemma, but ultimately censorship is never the answer because there will never be total agreement on who or what crosses the line. No one person or organization should have the power to decide that for everyone else. Furthermore, if a rap artist writes a song and manages to get it produced and sold to the public, that says something about both the artist and the public. Things that are popular on a widespread scale are indicative of our culture in general, and as such must be treated as a system-wide ailment rather than a small blip in paradise. If our children enjoy videos that depict nearly naked women prostrating themselves at the feet of famous rappers, we should probably ask ourselves why that image is accepted before trying to ban it because it is unpleasant. Because, in reality, if something is playing eight times a day on MTV it has long passed the point of being a marginal part of the greater culture and is most definitely deeply embedded in the national psyche.

Even more importantly, parents and citizens in general need to take a more proactive role in deciding what is appropriate viewing and listening material for themselves and their families. Having self-censorship is as important as *not* instituting nation-wide censorship. Parents need to take control of their children's media habits until they are mature enough to make their own decisions. There is nothing wrong with sheltering children from unpleasant images and ideas—this is a very important part of childhood. But children also need to be taught how to make smart decisions when they are old enough to choose for themselves. In this way we could raise a nation of true adults who could individually decide what types of media to consume.

Simply censoring the things that are unpleasant in this world will never succeed in ending them. In fact, we should examine the uncomfortable things more closely than anything else in our society, to better understand how they arise and how they can be stopped organically. This is a more difficult task than slapping a black label on a CD case but would ultimately prove much more useful to the healthiness of our society and its art forms. We should examine the art and music that we find objectionable and in this way learn more about our problems and their solutions.

Work Cited

Morgan, Joan. "From Fly-Girls to Bitches and Hos." *Cultural Conversations: The Presence of the Past.* Ed. Stephen Dilks et al. Boston: Bedford/St. Martin's: 2001. 201–05.

Text Credits

"America's Food Fight" from *Crossfire*, March 10, 2004. Copyright © 2004 Cable News Network, LP, LLLP.

Blume, Zach. "The Reality of Zoos." Reprinted by permission of the author.

Brandt, Leah. "Zoos: The Evil Empires." Reprinted by permission of the author.

Dodge, Mindy. "Revising Our College Education: Participation is the Key." Reprinted by permission of the author.

"Drinking to Excess" from *The New York Times*, July 22, 2004. Copyright © 2004 The New York Time Co. Reprinted by permission.

Fidler, Katie. "The Self-Imprisonment of American Society." Reprinted by permission of the author.

Kunhardt, Dorothy Meserve and Kunhardt, Jr., Phillip B. Excerpts from *Mathew Brady and His World*, copyright © 1977 by Time-Life Books, Ltd. Reprinted by permission.

Pittman, Todd. "Nonviolent Resistance: A More Courageous Show of Power." Reprinted by permission of the author.

Rocha-Judd, Rosei. "The Seduction of Hyperrealism and Overblown Images." Reprinted by permission of the author.

Stewart, Matthew A. "Untitled." Reprinted by permission of the author.

Timony-Balyeat, Devlin. "The Education Experience of the American Zoo." Reprinted by permission of the author.

White, Paul. Excerpts from senior seminar "War and Remembrance" on Mathew Brady, Fall 1998. Reprinted with permission.

Wilbur, Richard P. "What is the opposite of hat?", "The opposite of doughnut?" and "The opposite of spit" from *Opposites: Poems and Drawings*, copyright © 1973 by Richard Wilbur, reprinted by permission of Harcourt, Inc.

Wright, Katie. "Funding for the Future." Reprinted by permission of the author.

Photo Credits

13: *Stone Soup* © 2003 Jan Eliot. Reprinted with permission of UNIVERSAL PRESS SYNDICATE. All rights reserved

14: top, Courtesy of U.S. Environmental Protection Agency; bottom, Courtesy of The Pew Center on Global Climate Change

15: top, Courtesy of CEED

16: top, Anita Maric/News Team International

20: Alexander Gardner, Selected Civil War photographs, Library of Congress

21: Selected Civil War photographs, Library of Congress

65: © 2005 Mark Hess/Theispot.com

66: Courtesy of FDR Library

67: top, AUTH © 2001 *The Philadelphia Inquirer*. Reprinted with permission of UNIVERSAL PRESS SYNDICATE. All rights reserved; bottom, Courtesy of Bureau of Justice Statistics, U.S. Department of Justice, Washington, D.C.

69: Courtesy of PA Graphics, UK Press Association